SOLITO, SOLITA

Praise for *Solito, Solita*

"Intense testimonies that leave one shivering, astonished at the bravery of the human spirit. Mayers and Freedman have done a magnanimous job collecting these histories. America, are you listening?"
—**Sandra Cisneros**, author of *Puro Amor* and *The House on Mango Street*

"*Solito, Solita* gives readers the rare chance to hear directly from young migrants who have risked everything for a better life on our side of the border. With unflinching clarity, they detail the violence they left behind, the fear and difficulties they face after arrival, and the hope and resiliency that carries them through it all. They have courageously shared these experiences with the idea that people like us might read their stories and be moved to action, and we owe it to them to do so."
—**Francisco Cantú**, author of *The Line Becomes a River*

"This book fills a crucial missing piece in today's immigration debate. Everyone who cares about immigration—and about migrants—should read it. . . . The searing, heart-wrenching firsthand accounts in this book bring to life the experiences of Central Americans before they reach the United States: the tragic experiences of poverty, violence, and abuse that push individuals to flee their homes, the agonizing and perilous journeys across Mexico and Central America, and the baffling bureaucracy and abuse they find upon arriving in the United States." —**Aviva Chomsky**, professor at Salem State University and author of *Undocumented*

"Stories of war and exile, of migrations and survival—a most pertinent collection for our times, one that puts a human face on the greatest tragedy and humanitarian crisis of our generation. This collection is a must-read for politicians who demonize refugees and a call to action for everyone else." —**Alejandro Murguía**, San Francisco poet laureate emeritus and professor of Latina/Latino Studies at San Francisco State University

"Immigration narratives are too often reduced to tropes, to statistics and numbers, to binary politics and manipulative rhetoric, but not so in this volume of stories. *Solito, Solita* reaches beyond and beneath the headlines, clearing the mess and the noise so that we can hear the voices that matter most in contemporary migration: those of young migrants themselves." —**Lauren Markham**, author of *The Far Away Brothers: Two Young Migrants and the Making of an American Life*

"These raw voices pulse with heartbreak, resilience, hope, and even joy, shining a light on the forces that compel young people to flee their homes in the Northern Triangle in search of safety and solace in the United States. A must-read for today's immigration debate." —**Sara Campos**, codirector of the New American Story Project

"This is a thorough, compassionate, and necessary book that allows a unique set of voices—child refugees—to be heard. The framing of the narratives and the introduction offer important information about the US role in the proliferation of violence and corruption, but the work remains focused on the crucial individual voices." —**Ariana Vigil**, professor at University of North Carolina–Chapel Hill

Additional Interviewers
Oscar Garcia, Alberto Reyes Morgan

Transcribers and Translators
Anna Aleshire, Siuzanna Arutiunova, Ara Avedian, Mauro Javier Cardenas, Ruthie Cartwright, Katie Fiegenbaum, Jimmy Gonzalez, Lisa Hoffman, Gina Krawiec, Ana Claudia Lopes, Maria Maione, Cindie Meyer, Alberto Reyes Morgan, Marisela Musgrove, Kevin Ramirez, Laura Schroeder, Janey Skinner, Morena Urutia, Miguel Wise

Research Assistance
Maria Maione, Cindie Meyer, Miguel Wise

Fact-Checking
Reading List Editorial, readinglisteditorial.com

Copyeditor
Brian Baughan

SOLITO, SOLITA

*Crossing Borders with Youth Refugees
from Central America*

EDITED BY STEVEN MAYERS
AND JONATHAN FREEDMAN

WITH A FOREWORD BY JAVIER ZAMORA

Haymarket Books
Chicago, Illinois

Published in 2019 by
Haymarket Books
P.O. Box 180165
Chicago, IL 60618
773-583-7884
www.haymarketbooks.org
info@haymarketbooks.org

ISBN: 978-1-60846-618-4

Distributed to the trade in the US through Consortium Book Sales and
Distribution (www.cbsd.com) and internationally through Ingram Publisher Services International (www.ingramcontent.com).

This book was published with the generous support of Lannan Foundation
and Wallace Action Fund.

Special discounts are available for bulk purchases by organizations and
institutions. Please call 773-583-7884 or email info@haymarketbooks.org
for more information.

Cover design by Michel Vrana. Cover photograph by Dominic Bracco.
Narrator portrait illustrations by Christine Shields.

Printed in Canada by union labor.

Library of Congress Cataloging-in-Publication data is available.

10 9 8 7 6 5 4 3 2 1

CONTENTS

FOREWORD

Javier Zamora

I struggled many times to begin this essay. How do I speak before voices as strong and as necessary as the ones in the following pages? It was difficult reading these testimonies. It was difficult finding details and images too similar to those of the lives of my relatives, of my friends, of my very own life. I tried reading Edwidge Danticat's *Create Dangerously*, then Albert Camus's lecture by the same name, then Jose Antonio Vargas's memoir, *Dear America*. In them, I found bits I needed to hear, advice on how to stay truthful, advice on how to dictate how I want to be seen.

It is September 23, 2018, a Sunday. I'm working late in the library of Columbia University with my partner, a child of Irish immigrants and of Colombian immigrants. All around us, faces of all colors, but mostly of the darker shade, a shade that once populated this island of Mannahatta and the larger island that is the American continent—not "America" in the United States' self-important sense, but América with indigenous and Black roots. The current US president denies us this history, as well as our entire humanity. So have past presidents, and perhaps future presidents also will deny us our humanity; us, immigrants or children of immigrants. But not in the pages that follow. What follows are stories of young people who have suffered, who have struggled, and yet, they show the capacity to dream up a solution to the hardest problem of all: survival.

I was born in El Salvador and migrated unaccompanied to California when I was nine years old. My dad had left when I was one. My mom when I was four. Both of their migrations were initiated by the US-funded civil war. Their stories, the story of my family, are not unique; a fifth of my country's population fled between 1980 and 1992. Thousands continue to risk their lives every year. El Salvador is Guatemala is Honduras is the 258 million immigrants around the world. "For the migrant writer, far from home, memory becomes an even deeper abyss," writes Danticat.

Reading these pages, I was transported to my physical places of trauma: my childhood home, Tecún Umán, the Pacific Ocean, Oaxaca, Acapulco, Guadalajara, Tepic, Los Mochis, Hermosillo, the Sonoran Desert, the border patrol truck, the detention cell. Some of these stories are told when the trauma is fresh. Others, months or years later when the trauma is still fresh, but in the aftermath, that same trauma has learned how to hide, how to pretend to forget. It's this internalized evasion, evasion as by-product of survival, that is revealed here, uncovered, but for what purpose?

Albert Camus says, "The sea, rains, necessity, desire, the struggle against death—these are the things that unite us all. We resemble one another in what we see together, in what we suffer together." *What we suffer together*—I always return to that phrase. I believe I started writing because I wanted to expel the suffering inside me. Later, I wanted the reader to suffer with me—not the present-day me, but the nine-year-old that follows me like a shadow. I wanted others to feel what I had felt so that they could understand me, so that they could fully *see* me for who I am: a human being with all his complications.

Julio Zavala calls his shadow "his other self." All of these stories show the "other self." We share ourselves, our lives, I think, in the hopes that we can turn this other self into a physical thing—a recording, a story, a book, art—so that we can better control it, so we can see it, mold it, and hopefully understand that we can and should treat ourselves better. It is Julio who also states, "My name is Julio. This is my goal: to change, to move forward, have a new life." It wasn't until I began to see my own trauma as a creation myth that I could truthfully begin to heal. A myth is only a myth after all. It is not set in stone. It *was* truth, but shouldn't be truth forever. There is potential. The myth can change, as Julio states. After years in therapy, I've learned that the trauma will never go away. What I can do is learn to live with this nine-year-old shadow, learn to treat him with kindness.

All of the stories (and mine) share a similar creation myth, yet we are much more than refugees, than child migrants, than people who have experienced trauma. While reading, please do not forget that outside these testimonies there is also joy. There are moments of love, of laughter. Every time we retell a story, we fish into the abyss and pull them out. The fish is constantly changing, the water as well. Both the fish and water will never go away, but we can envision a better future for our trauma. That's what we're trying to do. We're trying to be seen in our entire humanity and not how the media paints us; we are not defined by our suffering.

As Jose Antonio told me in a conversation, "We know the who, the when, the where, and the how immigrants migrate to this country, but we haven't yet understood or fully explored the *why* of migration." I hope the narratives here can shed light onto those realities too. I hope once you read and suffer with each of these stories, you don't stop there, but act. Don't let these stories expose suffering in vain. Do something: read and reread the "Ten Things You Can Do" section at the end of the book. Let's build a better future together. Let's not let any more children risk their lives again.

Javier Zamora was born in El Salvador and immigrated to the United States at the age of nine. His book of poems, Unaccompanied, *was published in 2017.*

INTRODUCTION

El Coyote, La Bestia, y La Hielera

At this moment, thousands of children are trekking from Central America to *El Norte*, clinging to freight cars, fording rivers, fleeing cops and gangs. Some of the children's parents hire *coyotes*, human smugglers who can charge upwards of $10,000, to guide their children to the border.[1] Some kids take buses, vans, and trucks. Some have no choice but to jump onto the cargo trains migrants colloquially call *La Bestia*, "the Beast," to make the two-thousand-plus-mile trip.[2] Those who survive the journey either turn themselves over to the authorities in the hope of gaining asylum or make a run for it and pursue underground lives. Those who seek asylum at the border are often placed in detention in *la hielera*, "the freezer," where guards are known to crank up the air conditioning and toss frozen ham sandwiches to them once a day.[3]

Human migrations across this continent have taken place

---

1. A *coyote* is a person who smuggles immigrants into the United States.

2. See glossary and appendix essay on "La Bestia."

3. *La hielera* means "icebox" or "freezer." The Spanish root, *hielo*, means "ice." Migrants call detention facilities *hieleras*. There are numerous, documented reports that many US Customs and Border Patrol detention facilities are artificially cooled to a very low temperature that would preserve meat. Migrants describe shivering uncontrollably and being unable to rest or sleep. See glossary.

1

throughout history. The historical constructs of nations, laws, and inequality impel people to migrate to places of relative safety. While politicians, journalists, and "experts" portray young migrants in simplified, often charged, terms, each young person has a story to tell. What would make children flee their homes and families? What would make parents send their children on a dangerous and life-threatening journey through Mexico to a hostile foreign land?

A partial answer leads back to the Cold War when, in the name of fighting Communism, the United States intervened in Central America, overthrowing a democratic regime in Guatemala, and backing right-wing dictatorships in El Salvador, Honduras, and Nicaragua. In the 1980s, the United States covertly trained Central American militaries in counterinsurgency and torture. To pay for covert operations in Nicaragua, the CIA secretly shipped drugs to the United States, abetting the growth of drug cartels.[4] In El Salvador, death squads killed civilians and government troops committed massacres, killing men, women, and children. In Guatemala, US-backed military troops committed atrocities against the Maya people and campesinos.[5] More than a quarter-million people died in the civil wars, hundreds of thousands were displaced, and tens of thousands of refugees were resettled in Los Angeles, where war-traumatized kids joined street gangs known as *maras*.[6]

The United States deported gang leaders back to their war-torn homelands, where, funded by profits from drug smuggling and ex-

---

4. Gary Webb, "The Dark Alliance," *San Jose Mercury News*, August 22, 1996.

5. Campesinos are farmers on small plots of land.

6. Estimated deaths in Central American civil wars: 140,000 in Guatemala, 70,000 in El Salvador, 60,000 in Nicaragua. See Juan Gonzalez, "Timeline," *Harvest of Empire: A History of Latinos in America*, rev. ed. (New York: Penguin, 2011), 130. Maras are gangs. The term is primarily used to refer to MS-13 and Barrio 18, rival gangs that started in Los Angeles in the late 1980s and have spread across Central America's Northern Triangle. See appendix essay on "The Rise of the *Maras*."

tortion, the gangs have grown into a multinational gang network. The legacy of these conflicts has had devastating effects on families, communities, and children to this day. Many of the narrators in this collection are the grandchildren and children of people displaced by those wars. Before the US interventions in the 1980s, youth migration from Central America was virtually nil. We were curious about why the wave of youth refugees peaked thirty years later. For answers, we went to the source, listening to young refugees share their stories.

◊

Jonathan approached the current crisis of Central American youth refugees with over thirty years of experience as a journalist who has investigated the wars in El Salvador, Nicaragua, and Guatemala; undocumented immigration across the US-Mexico border; and the struggle for undocumented immigrants' rights. After years of writing about migrants and analyzing their experiences, Jonathan began working as a writing mentor to refugee children from Mexico and Central America. And in 2014, he was leading a writing workshop at the City College of San Francisco when Professor Steven Mayers came to him with an idea.

As an oral historian, educator, and writer, Steven has explored ways in which fiction, as well as oral history, can retell so-called official histories and bring into question their underlying assumptions. His own nomadic childhood—moving from California and Connecticut to Spain and Switzerland—drew Steven to the stories of young migrants. In 2010, he participated in a project at a school in Juticalpa, an agricultural town in Olancho, Honduras. Engineers Without Borders had installed an internet tower and were looking for Spanish-speaking instructors to lead workshops with the local teachers. In a town where most of the people lived on less than a dollar a day and had access to one hour of running water per week, the lavish compounds of drug traffickers perched on the hills and the drug dealers drove around in brand-new pickups with machine guns drawn in plain sight. The maras had infiltrated the town and recruited kids on the schoolyards. One afternoon, a cook at the school got a phone call from her son, who was walking home on a dirt road and was being followed. "I think they are after me," he told her. "Maybe they want my phone." Within seconds, she heard her son's last scream before he was killed. Then the connection was lost.

The following year, Steven interviewed refugees in the San Francisco Bay Area who had survived the wars in Central America. As the youth migrant crisis grew in 2014, he started talking to some of his City College of San Francisco students from the region about how the situation affected them. An oral history project that focused specifically on youth refugees from Central America began to take shape.

◊

In 2014, the year we began this project, roughly sixty-nine thousand kids from Honduras, El Salvador, and Guatemala crossed the US border. Migrants and refugees from Central America now outnumbered Mexican immigrants. Many were unaccompanied children trying to join family members already living in the United States.[7] As reports of border agents being overwhelmed by the surge of immigrants reached Washington, President Obama declared a human rights crisis and ordered special "transit camps" be opened to house

---

7. D'Vera Cohn, Jeffrey S. Passel, and Ana Gonzalez-Barrera, *Rise in U.S. Immigrants from El Salvador, Guatemala and Honduras Outpaces Growth from Elsewhere*, Pew Research Center, December 7, 2017, www.pewhispanic.org/2017/12/07/rise-in-u-s-immigrants-from-el-salvador-guatemala-and-honduras-outpaces-growth-from-elsewhere.

them. In the month of June alone, twenty-seven thousand children arrived at the border. On July 2, when Department of Homeland Security buses transporting Central American refugees from Texas arrived in Murrieta, California, throngs of US flag–waving protesters surrounded the buses and prevented the children from reaching a processing center.[8]

As we read the news accounts and watched the protests on television, we asked ourselves: Why is there a surge of youth fleeing their homelands? Why are some Americans marching to protest against child refugees, while others welcome and offer them sanctuary?

We listed the many facets of this human rights crisis: the impact of the wars in the 1980s on the social and economic conditions in the present; the relationship between the demand for illegal drugs in the United States, the cartels in Mexico, and the gangs of Central America; the privatization of US prisons and the rise of for-profit detention centers. The aim to talk to young migrants in detention centers in the United States—young mothers, gang members, survivors of domestic violence—coalesced.

We began interviewing some of the young Central Americans we knew in the Bay Area. Soledad Castillo, whom we have both taught at City College, became our first narrator, and Adrián Cruz, whom we connected with through a small organization that advocates for people in detention, the second. We then made contact with organizations that offer pro bono legal services to migrants in the Bay Area as well as across the United States. We began conducting interviews at East Bay Sanctuary Covenant in Berkeley and Centro Legal de la Raza in Oakland, and from there we traveled to the National Immigrant Justice Center (NIJC) in Chicago and Kids in Need of Defense (KIND) in Boston. We were struck by the passion and dedication of the lawyers and counselors who represent

---

8. Sam Frizell, "California Protesters Halt Buses Carrying Migrant Families," *Time*, July 2, 2014.

clients at those immigrant rights and legal aid organizations. In the absence of federal funding, they mostly operate on grants and donations, and try to fill the giant abyss of legal representation provided by the government.

At first, we saw the story mostly from the US perspective, and we were focused primarily on the abusive treatment of mothers with young children and unaccompanied minors in detention centers. Their experiences prompted us to ask: How can the United States respond to Central American refugees in a humane fashion that aligns with the Universal Declaration of Human Rights? As we continued to talk with people, we became more focused on the complexities of the problems that Central America faces and that are forcing so many youths north. The scope of our questions widened: How can the United States pursue economic and social policies in Central America in order to help make Central America a livable place that people don't have to flee from? Although these narratives don't answer the question explicitly, they do shed light on the conditions these youth face, which may inform policymakers, community organizations, and others working with them.

In the early stages of our project, we learned about a boy of nine who was kidnapped by Los Zetas with his mother just south of the US border.[9] He recounted that he was forced to kill a man with a baseball bat. The cartel members told him that they would kill him and his mother if he didn't comply. Our source noted that the boy switched between deep sorrow and nervous laughter. After considering the potential for retraumatization, we weighed the ethical considerations of this project: At what point is a young person ready to tell their story? We decided to speak predominantly with people who are over eighteen but made their journey in their teens, as well as young mothers traveling with children.

---

9. Los Zetas is a Mexican criminal organization that is responsible for attacks on migrants near the southern and northern borders of Mexico. See glossary.

Our narrators share their earliest experiences, hidden traumas, and fleeting triumphs. They have faced more dangers than many thrice their age and reflect wisdom beyond their years. What can we learn from them about risk-taking and resilience? As Soledad said after reading an early draft of her narrative, "Sharing my own story has changed my personal life. Every time I'm sad or I feel like giving up, I read my story and think, *Wow, look at all the things that have come true! I can do it! This is only a bad day, a bad week. I can get up and continue my life.*"

The early factors that influence young Central Americans come primarily from within the family. Josué Nieves describes his great admiration for his father, his mother's savory fish soup, and his deep emotional attachments to grandparents and cousins alike. Yet the current state of the family in Central America is precarious, unstable, battered by poverty, ill health, alcoholism, and violence. As Pedro Hernandez's story illustrates, babies are coveted but often poorly nourished. Teenage parents who have been beaten, abused, or abandoned often lack the experience and wherewithal to support their children, perpetuating vicious cycles. They bear witness to catastrophes: Julio Zavala's mother kicks him out of the house when he's six; Noemi Tun grows up in a community fighting over land and water; Gabriel Méndez is sexually abused by his cousins and uncles. Fleeing an abusive boyfriend who has joined MS-13, Danelia Silva attempts to feed, clothe, house, and protect her children. For youth growing up in such conditions, the lure of El Norte, mythologized in popular media, is a compelling, promising escape.

◊

A work of oral history focusing on vulnerable children who have suffered much and may be traumatized presents difficult yet surmountable challenges at every stage. We ran into roadblocks. After planning a trip to interview migrants in detention in Texas, we were told by legal aid volunteers meeting with migrants in trailers outside prison fences that our presence could jeopardize their work to aid detainees, so we backed off and focused on meeting and working with narrators through legal organizations and migrant shelters. In a migrant shelter in San Luis Potosí, Mexico, Rosa Cuevas hugged herself as we explained the purpose of our mission. We assured her, "We can only imagine what you've been through and respect your courage to tell your story. We will do our utmost to both faithfully record and edit your story and protect your safety and privacy." We asked open-ended questions: We'd like to hear about your home, your parents. What was it like growing up? What was school like? Why did you come to the United States? Tell us about your journey. What do you miss about home? If you could do anything with your life, what would you do? Where do you see yourself in five years?

We were struck by the epic nature of their journeys: while what they faced in Central America is a human rights crisis in itself, their experiences fleeing through Mexico are a second crisis, and the treatment many receive in the United States is a third. We wanted to get a sense of what their journeys were like, so we traveled to places along migrant routes in Mexico, visiting *casas de migrantes* (shelters for migrants), where they stopped for water, a meal, a change of clothes, and rest. We invited Oscar Garcia, a student at City College who is a former youth migrant from Guatemala and an ex-marine, to accompany us and act as advisor and guide. In a shelter in Guadalajara called FM4, we met youths of thirteen and fourteen on their first journey. We also met Ernesto González, a man of thirty-one on his tenth journey. He showed us his cuts and scars, and photos of parents and children back home. Together, we walked along the railroad tracks of the notorious Bestia.

We visited a number of shelters in Mexico to conduct interviews, including La 72 in Tenosique, FM4 in Guadalajara, Casa de la Caridad Cristiana in San Luis Potosí, Casa del Migrante San Juan de Dios in Irapuato, Estancia del Migrante González y Martínez in Tequisquiapan, and Grupo de Ayuda Para el Migrante in Mexicali. Most of the people staying at the shelters cannot afford *coyotes* and are riding on La Bestia and begging their way north. In comparison to the people we interviewed in the States, who have gained at least a semblance of safety and stability, the young people we met on the migrant trail are in mid-flight, mid-trauma, speaking of deportations and assaults that have just taken place. We're haunted by the words of a young Honduran woman we spoke with, in transit, at the migrant shelter in San Luis Potosí: "So you guys are flying back next week? You'll just be looking down at all of us. I wish I could do that."

In Tenosique, just north of the Guatemalan border, we met people who had been assaulted while crossing the border the night before, by men in black masks who robbed them of their few meager possessions. One boy of fourteen or so was covered in bright crimson cuts from a machete attack. A twenty-five-year-old woman had been abandoned with her three children by the *coyote* that her parents borrowed money to hire. As with the staff of the US legal organizations we met, the people who make up the network of casas de migrantes work with little governmental support or protection. But in Mexico they face death threats by crime organizations and resistance from neighbors who don't want the shelters in their neighborhoods.

We made some surprising discoveries: the discrimination Central American refugees face in Mexico, where they are identified by their accents and clothing. The extreme conditions that they face in immigration detention centers. The high number of deportations during the Obama administration, despite Obama's executive orders and promises to protect them. The crucial wraparound services that organizations working with child refugees offer their young clients to help them find work and enter school. The resilience of young migrants who suffer so much and yet have the capacity to recover, grow, learn, adjust, work, and thrive, if given the chance.

As we revisited narrators, in some cases two years after we first spoke, we saw how their lives had changed. Never are their young lives static. We were only able to keep in touch with about two-thirds of our narrators, as the other third we met were in transit in Mexico without phones or contact information. We wonder about the fates of Cristhian, Ernesto, Rosa and her daughters, and many more whom we've spoken with.

◊

The title of this collection, *Solito, Solita*, which translates as "alone, alone," comes from Adrián's narrative. His mother was murdered in Guatemala, he was stabbed and left for dead by a gang, and his grandmother was dying. In our first discussion, his voice cracked, and he whispered, "*Solito, solito.*" Tens of thousands of girls and boys attempt the two-thousand-plus–mile journey, but in many ways each travels alone. No two stories are the same. We have selected these fifteen narratives because of their honesty, directness, and breadth. Thousands of others go unheard. Our subtitle, *Crossing Borders with Youth Refugees from Central America*, refers to "refugees" in the general sense of people fleeing danger and seeking refuge, rather than the strict legal definition. At the beginning of each chapter, we note the narrator's "age at crossing," whether they crossed the US border or borders from Central America to Mexico. The narratives of people we met in migrant shelters en route through Mexico are labeled "in transit." We hope to fill a gap in the impoverished knowledge base that distorts public discourse and causes greater harm. The myths surrounding immigration and the American Dream have spurred some of our narrators to achieve success while crushing others. We offer a cautionary note to avoid the savior complex that projects that there is only bad in Central America and good in the United States, that only the United States can help Central Americans work through violence and poverty, and that the United States is the only possible refuge. There are several Central American organizations engaged in reducing violence and protecting children.[10]

With the 2016 election of President Donald Trump, who promised to "build a great, great wall on our southern border" and have "Mexico pay for that wall," the political climate in the United States over immigration has grown more heated and divisive.[11] But the conditions that compel young people to flee Central America have not been alleviated; on the contrary, the migrant trail is more dangerous, and the threat of deportation hangs over hundreds of thousands of students—such as Ismael Xol—who have lived in the United States since they were children. While the political debate around immigration focuses on how to secure the US borders, the ethical challenge is how to secure the childhoods of millions of kids in Central America and the United States. Millions of dollars are flowing to build the border wall, yet scant resources trickle down to protect children in their homelands and prepare young refugees for challenges they face in the United States. They are speaking. Are we listening?

Steven Mayers and Jonathan Freedman
San Francisco

---

10. See "Ten Things You Can Do."

11. "Here's Donald Trump's Announcement Speech," *Time*, June 16, 2015.

EXECUTIVE EDITOR'S NOTE

The fifteen narratives in this book are the result of oral history interviews conducted over a three-and-a-half-year period between the fall of 2014 and the spring of 2018. With every Voice of Witness narrative, we aim for a novelistic level of detail and (whenever possible) a birth-to-now, chronologized scope in order to portray narrators as individuals in all their complexity, rather than as case studies. We do not set out to create comprehensive histories of human rights issues. Rather, our goal is to compile a collection of voices that (1) offers accessible, thought-provoking, and ultimately humanizing perspectives on what can often seem like impenetrable topics; and (2) can meaningfully contribute to the efforts of social justice and human rights movements.

In order to honor our narrators' experiences, Voice of Witness oral histories are crafted with the utmost care. Recorded interviews are transcribed and organized chronologically by our dedicated team of volunteers. Then, narrative drafts are typically subject to three to five rounds of editorial revision and follow-up interviews, to ensure depth and accuracy. The stories themselves remain faithful to the speakers' words (we seek final narrator approval before publishing their narratives) and have been edited for clarity, coherence, and length. In some cases, names and details have been changed to protect the identities of our narrators and the identities of family and acquaintances. All narratives have been carefully fact-checked and are supported by various appendixes and a glossary included in the back of the book that provide context for, and some explanation of, the history of youth migration to the United States from Central America.

We thank all the individuals who courageously, generously, and patiently shared their experiences with us, including those whom we were unable to include in this book. We also thank all the frontline human rights and social justice advocates working to promote and protect the rights and dignity of all people making their way to the United States. Without their cooperation, this book would not be possible.

Finally, we thank our national community of educators and students who inspire our education program. With each Voice of Witness book, we create a Common Core–aligned curriculum that connects high school students and educators with the stories and issues presented in the book, with particular emphasis on serving marginalized communities. As we continue to amplify a diversity of migrant voices in our book series, we are also committed to developing curriculum that directly supports students in migrant and English Language Learner (ELL) communities. At the time of writing, about one out of every ten public school students is learning to speak English. In California alone, ELLs account for 22.4 percent of the total public school student population, and this number continues to grow. In response to this need in our education networks and beyond, in 2018 we launched our first oral history resource for ELLs, and we continue to expand our offerings in this area.

Our education program also provides curriculum support, training in ethics-driven storytelling, and site visits to educators in schools and impacted communities. I invite you to visit the Voice of Witness website for free, downloadable educational resources, behind-the-scenes features on this book and other projects, and to find out how you can be part of our work: voiceofwitness.org.

In solidarity,
Mimi Lok
Cofounder, Executive Director, and Executive Editor
Voice of Witness

MAP OF MIGRATION ROUTES THROUGH MEXICO, 2016

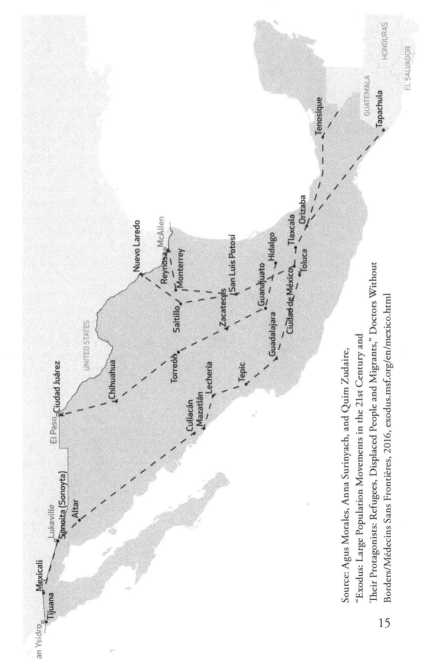

Source: Agus Morales, Anna Surinyach, and Quim Zudaire,
"Exodus: Large Population Movements in the 21st Century and
Their Protagonists: Refugees, Displaced People and Migrants," Doctors Without
Borders/Médecins Sans Frontières, 2016, exodus.msf.org/en/mexico.html

SOLEDAD CASTILLO

AGE AT CROSSING: 14
BORN IN: Tegucigalpa, Honduras
INTERVIEWED IN: San Francisco, California

We meet Soledad as a shy first-year student at the City College of San Francisco in the fall of 2014. A young refugee from Honduras, she is struggling to write an essay in Steven's English class. He suggests she get help in Jonathan's writing workshop. In the midst of a writing exercise, Soledad breaks down crying. "Are you okay?" Jonathan asks. She shakes her head and says, "My friend's husband is putting me out on the street in two days." Jonathan says, "Stop the exercise and write a letter to them." After the workshop, Soledad leaves in tears, and Jonathan worries that she may become homeless.

A few months later, we ask Soledad to share her story. Flushed with pride, she ushers us into the new, one-bedroom student apartment near

17

campus that she accessed through a housing lottery. The rent is subsidized as long as she maintains a 2.5 GPA. It's gray and overcast outdoors, but the apartment is bright with fresh flowers and shiny new furniture. "This was a gift from my Filipino coworkers at Round Table Pizza," she says, patting a lucky bamboo plant. The white walls in her bedroom are freshly painted and undecorated. Soledad is backlit by the window as she talks, her face cast in shadows. When she comes to a painful incident in her story, she rolls up her pant cuffs to reveal scars on her legs. As a girl, Soledad was subjected to multiple instances of physical and sexual abuse, medical malpractice, and abandonment. Through her own will and the help of others, she has been able to both succeed in college and engage in legislative reforms to help other migrant children in the foster care system.

WHY AM I NOT DEAD INSTEAD OF MY GRANDMOTHER?

My mother had her first baby, my older sister, Angela, when she was about sixteen, and she was about nineteen when she had me. I was born on June 6, 1992, in Tegucigalpa, Honduras.[1] My parents broke up before I was born and they lived apart. We were really poor, the poorest family in our little neighborhood. My mother got together with Faustino, the man who would become my stepfather, who had two younger daughters. My father left for the United States when I was five. Faustino always liked my sister, but he never liked me. I never knew why. My mother was scared of him, because he drank a lot and was a violent guy. He used to hit my mom and throw chairs at her. He never had a stable job. My mom was really weak and never stood up for me. She let other people make decisions for her. It was my grandmother who always took care of me. I was named after her, Maria Soledad. She never liked my stepfather, so she always took me on the weekends so that my mom wouldn't leave me alone with him.

---

1. Tegucigalpa, the capital of Honduras, is a city of approximately 1.2 million people. Soledad's family lived in a remote area on the outskirts of the city.

I was ten when my grandma died. It was a shock. Some people said that she took medication that had expired, but nobody knows exactly what happened. When she was sick, she told my cousin to bring me to be with her in her house. She hugged me and died in my arms. After that I didn't have anybody there for me, and my life changed completely.

One day when I was twelve, my mom went into the city and stayed overnight. She left me with my stepfather and his daughters. I slept in a bed next to my little stepsisters, who were six and seven. Faustino got drunk that night, and he came over to my bed and touched me. I started yelling. My little sisters cried, "Oh, Papá, leave her alone, leave her alone!" They hit him, so he'd leave me alone. I ran out of the house. I didn't take them with me because I was so scared. It was really late at night. I ran barefoot up the hill to his parents' house, crying, screaming, and asking for help. One of his brothers opened the door. I said, "Faustino was touching me." The brother brought me inside and told me, "Just go to sleep and we'll talk in the morning." I cried myself to sleep.

When my mom got there the next day, I was scared. I didn't know what she would say. I told her about what Faustino had done to me, but she didn't believe me. She tried to hit me. I left the house, crying to God, *Why am I not dead instead of my grandmother?*

When I came back to the house, my mother was packing all my clothes. She made all the plans without asking me. She sent me to another part of the city to work for relatives of my stepfather. I stayed with them and I cleaned their house, took care of two babies, washed clothes. I was their servant. They didn't pay me, but they gave me food to eat. I was only twelve.

NOBODY WANTED ME

A month later, I woke up with a painful red swelling on my left ankle. I had a high, high fever. The bones throughout my body were hurting. The family I was staying with called my mom and told her I was sick. She didn't come for three days. She only came to get me when I was really, really sick. She took me to the Hospital Escuela Universitario.[2] I passed out on the way and woke up in a bed with curtains around me. The nurses did blood tests and said I had dengue fever.[3] But the same night, I got worse. I had terrible stomach pains, and I cried all night. Then the doctors changed my diagnosis to lupus.[4]

The doctors gave me fifteen pills a day and blood transfusions. I lost my hair, and there were black blisters on my mouth. I had a lot of bruises on my body, and I was really weak. There were months when I didn't even eat. My body was really skinny, like a skeleton. I was dying. My mom, little sisters, and aunt visited me, but most of the time I was alone. It was a really lonely hospital. I cried and cried.

After about five months, I was stable enough to leave the hospital. But the family I'd been staying with said, "Oh, we don't want to take care of her because we know she'll be dying in a few weeks. We don't want to deal with that." Because of the situation with my stepfather, my mother never asked me to come home. I no longer had my grandmother, and my mom didn't believe me. I just wanted to die.

I went to my aunt Consuelo's house in Tegucigalpa. She was my father's sister, and she didn't know me well. She lived with her husband and their baby girl. But she was the only one who said, "I'll take care of her." She was pregnant. But she'd go with me back to the hospital for checkups. She has a strong character. She always said, "You don't have to be like your mom. You have to be strong." She used bad words when she was mad. She called me stupid. But I

---

2. Hospital Escuela Universitario is a medical teaching hospital in Tegucigalpa.

3. Dengue fever is a debilitating viral disease of the tropics, transmitted by mosquitoes, that causes sudden fever and acute pain in the joints.

4. Lupus is a chronic autoimmune disease that can damage skin, joints, and internal organs.

think that even though she was really strict with me, she has been an important person in my life. Many little girls out on the street made fun of my swollen face, calling me "Bear Cheeks," and throwing things at me. My aunt would say, "Don't be stupid. You have to go out. This is nothing to be ashamed of!"

I was still taking fifteen pills a day, and my medicine became expensive. Consuelo and her husband had a furniture store in Tegucigalpa, and they weren't poor, but they weren't rich either. Consuelo asked my father, who was in California, for money. He sent money every month. I was still really sick and I was getting worse again. Many days I wasn't able to get out of bed, because my legs and feet weren't functional anymore. I didn't eat. Every night I went to bed wishing, *Oh, I don't want to wake up tomorrow. I don't want to wake up.*

A doctor came to the house for a checkup. I heard him and my aunt talking behind the door, and the doctor said, "Soledad has only two or three days left. If anyone wants to see her, they have to come quickly." They never told me I was about to die. When Consuelo told my father on the phone that I was going to die, I overheard her. I was crying. But I'd been waiting for the day.

I woke up in the middle of the night and was determined to get out of bed. I went to take some of my niece's wet cloth diapers, which had been drying near my bed on the ground floor, upstairs. I don't know how I got up, but I pulled myself out of bed. I made it part of the way up the stairs, but I fell, hands first. I was bleeding a lot, but I didn't feel pain. The stairs were cement and all the skin on my lower legs was torn off. I just felt cold, really cold. After quite a long time, my aunt heard me, came down the stairs, and asked, "Why are you up?" I said, "I was taking the baby's diapers upstairs. I fell."

My aunt called one of her employees from the furniture store to help. He rolled up my jeans and my skin just peeled off. My bone was sticking out of my leg. Then my aunt called her neighbor Lourdes, who had a car, to come and drive me to the Hospital Escuela.

When we got there, we had to wait. When the doctor finally came, he asked why I was big in my face but skinny. Lourdes said, "She has lupus." His reaction was like, "I don't want to touch her," because maybe he thought lupus was contagious.[5] He said, "The only option is to cut off her leg. It doesn't make sense to keep the leg." Lourdes said, "I don't want her to be without her leg. If she needs to die, she needs to die with her two legs." And so the doctor walked away.

Lourdes decided to take me to the private hospital, San Jorge, without asking anybody. She took me there and called my aunt Consuelo to explain. In the car on the way to the hospital, I was peeling the skin off my leg. I was numb. I didn't care anymore. *Cut off my leg. I will die.* When I got to San Jorge the new doctor asked me why I was in that condition. I said, "Because I have lupus." "Okay, let's do surgery," he said.

I think the surgery lasted five hours. When I woke up, my first thought was, *So, do I have my leg or not?* I had my leg! There were a lot of bandages, a lot of blood. My mom was there with my sister Angela, who I love so much. Angela started crying. The surgeon had pinned my broken leg bones together. After a blood test, the doctor said I didn't have lupus. I was okay! Wrongly prescribed medications might have caused the symptoms of lupus. They may have mixed up my file with another patient who had lupus. But I believe I had lupus, and it was a miracle!

When I stopped taking the medicine, I started getting better. I went home to Aunt Consuelo's and had to stay in bed for my leg to heal. After six months I started walking a little. My hair began to grow back. I was thirteen and a half. My mom and the rest of my family contacted my father because the surgery to save my life cost thousands of dollars. His job was collecting bottles on the street in

---

5. Lupus is not contagious.

Hayward, California.[6] He ended up paying for all my surgeries and medications. Even though I didn't grow up with him and had never lived with him, I think he was the one who helped me the most.

"CAN YOU TAKE ME TOO?"

After I got better, when I was about to turn fourteen, my father decided to return to Honduras to see me. I waited by the door for him, wondering, *What will he look like? How will I feel after all these years?* I hadn't seen him since I was three or four. My only memory was as a little girl riding horses with him when we visited his parents' ranch in the south of Honduras.

My dad came in a car, and when he got out, I went and hugged him. He's really short, like me. He cried when he saw me. I just felt happy. But I was mad at him because he had left me alone, you know? When my stepfather abused me, my father wasn't there for me. But after seeing him and knowing he had helped me a lot with my medications and surgery, and knowing how hard he worked in order to pay for everything, I started feeling something for him. He stayed for about three months.

My father is a womanizer. He met a woman named Evita and decided to bring her back to the United States. I asked him, "Can you take me too?" At first he said no, but I explained to him that I didn't have anything left there. I wanted to start a new life. So I convinced him, and he said yes.

I JUST REMEMBER THEIR HANDS

It took more than one month to get to the United States. The three of us left Honduras and went to Guatemala on the bus. My dad sat

---

6. Hayward is a city in Alameda County, in the East Bay of the San Francisco Bay Area.

in the front seat, and I sat behind with other people. There were gangsters on board. First, one guy took out a gun, and then the other guys did too. They put a gun to my head, telling me to give them all my money. I didn't have money, but they didn't believe me. They took my pants off. I don't remember their faces. I just remember their hands. I remember hands touching me all over my body, and I couldn't say anything. At that time, I was fourteen.

The gangsters took money from my father, so we didn't have enough money to eat for the rest of the trip. We stayed in Guatemala for one day and then got in a van to go to Mexico. We went from van to van. We had to lie down with many people, one on top of the other. The *coyotes* put cardboard on top of us so *La Migra* wouldn't see us if they pulled us over. It was hard to breathe, and we didn't eat either.[7] They didn't want to stop.

Then, we had to walk through the desert for seven hours to get to a ranch house. It was really hot in the Mexican desert. There were like twenty or twenty-five people in our group, with many people from China, from everywhere. The *coyote* gave each of us a liter of water and a can of beans. So we walked and walked. My shoes were really bad, so my feet were covered in blisters. We finished the water really fast. After that, we had to look for water, and we found a well. We stopped to rest in the middle of the night. The *coyotes* ordered all the women on one side and all the men on the other side. My father said, "No, they're coming with me." He didn't want me or Evita to be separated from him. We ended up staying with my father. That night, one of the *coyotes* tried to abuse one of the girls. Then someone cried, "The police are coming!" You know, La Migra. We had to throw ourselves onto the ground, where there was a lot of cactus. My body was covered in cactus spines.

After being at the ranch house, we walked for three more days, I think. To be honest, my memory is really bad. Many people got lost,

---

7. See glossary.

and some didn't make it. The *coyotes* left an Asian girl on the ground to die. That was really sad. On the second day, I became too weak, so my father paid the *coyotes* extra for a little pill to give me energy. It was strong. It felt like I was starting from the beginning again.

Finally, we reached a house, somewhere in Texas, a really nice place. A guy with his wife and their little daughter lived there, and they spoke Spanish. We were really hungry, and they gave us food. They just told us, "Don't go outside."

After that, someone came in a van to take us from Texas to Sacramento. It was a long trip. They stopped to pick up other people at different houses, and the police stopped us twice. There was a hiding place under the floor where they put people in the van. There were air holes, but there were too many people. I was next to my father, and we were holding our arms in and we were curled up, and it was really hard to breathe. We had to stay quiet the whole time. They'd say, "Here come the police. Stay quiet, stay quiet!"

"NO SCHOOL, YOU HAVE TO WORK!"

We got to Hayward, California, where my father lived. It seemed really fancy. I looked at the glass buildings, and I was like, *Wow!* We stayed with my father's sister, who I'd never met before. She cooked carne asada for us. I was happy, but at the same time I felt scared and weird because I had never lived with my dad or known his family. I asked him, "Can I go to school?" and he said, "No school, you have to work!"

We went to the Mission District in San Francisco, and I got fake papers that said I was twenty-one, even though I was really fourteen. Then I started working at a laundry shop in Hayward. All the hotels, like the Hilton, sent laundry to the shop—sheets, towels, and everything. There were a lot of laundry machines. The guys would wash the laundry, and we had to move all the sheets from where they came out, fold them, type names on cards for each one, and send them out.

It was hard work. I felt lonely because my father had fallen in love with Evita, and he forgot about me. He started telling me, "You have to pay me back for the trip."

To pay my father back, I began working two shifts a day at the laundry service. I started at seven in the morning and I got out at one the next morning. I'd sleep for four hours. I was also sending money to my mom. When my check came, I didn't even see it. My dad would just take it. I didn't have any money to buy things for myself.

One day, someone invited Evita to San Francisco. She told me to come too. We went to the Embarcadero in San Francisco, on Pier 39. There were two guys there, and she started kissing one of them. She said to the other guy, "You can kiss her," meaning me. I'd never had a boyfriend. He kissed me and started sucking on my neck. I was like, "No, I don't even know you." Evita said, "Oh yeah, you can take her." She was kissing the other guy, and I was like, *Hmm. This is my dad's girlfriend.* Later, I told my dad about it, but he wouldn't believe me because he was in love with her.

Once, after a long day at work, I called my dad and asked him, "Will you pick me up?" He said, "Evita will pick you up." I waited, but she never came. I was really tired so I asked a coworker to give me a ride. When I got home, Evita was at the laundry service. My dad got mad, and Evita too. He said, "She was waiting for you," My dad hit me on the back with a belt. I don't know why. That was a stupid reason to get mad at me. I cried, "Why do you have to believe everything she says? She was with another guy over there in San Francisco. She doesn't love you. It's just for the money." Then he got really mad. I felt so frustrated, and I said, "I'm really thankful for you helping me, but you don't have to hit me. You don't even know me well!" I didn't think he had the right to hit me. And for no reason.

That same night, I ran away. I called one of my friends from work. I asked her, "Can I stay with you? My father hit me and I don't want to see him again." I was fourteen and my friend was thirty-four. After I moved in with her, my father went looking for me. He thought that I was kidding, that it was a prank. On the phone I told him no, I didn't want to see him anymore. He'd left marks on my body. I got really mad because he was outside my friend's house, waiting for me. I was also scared of him. I was thinking, *I don't know him. Why did he have to hit me? I don't want to see him again.* I told him, "If you come to the house again, I will call the police." He said I hurt his feelings, because he brought me to the United States. I said, "You had no reason to hit me."

"WHERE IS SOLEDAD?"

So after that, I felt really alone. I didn't have anyone. I was still working a lot, paying back my father and sending money to my mom. That summer, this guy, a friend of my friend, started talking to me. He was older, like twenty-five. I was only fifteen. His name was Sergio. He was very romantic and would come to my job and bring me flowers. I felt like, *Oh, here's someone who cares about me!* I don't know if it was love or if it was just the need to be with someone. He would do everything to get me to bed. My first time was with him. I gave him all of myself; I was so desperate to find someone to love and care about me. We started a relationship in July. He had plans to go to Mexico in August or September. Before leaving, he said, "I'll come back for you." I cried because for me, oh my god, he was everything!

After he left, I tried to call him. The first time he answered, the second time he answered, but after one week, he stopped answering. I discovered that he had gotten married in Mexico. That took everything from me. I went into a depression and lost my job. I didn't want to work or eat. A friend from work saw my condition and said, "Do you want help?" I said, "Yeah, I want to be far away. Bring me to an orphanage. Bring me somewhere. Bring me to a school." She took me to a place in Oakland, and they said, "We can't do anything for her.

Go to San Francisco Human Services." She took me over there, saying, "I can take care of her. Can you help her find a school?" I told the
counselor my story—that I was here alone, that I didn't have family,
because by this time my dad had gone back to Honduras with his
girlfriend. But the counselor said I couldn't stay with my friend. At
that time, my leg was hurting a lot. So I told the counselor, "I had
surgery and I think I need to go to the hospital." She took me to the
emergency room and told my friend to leave. She told her, "She's with
us, not with you anymore, so you don't have to worry about her." My
friend was crying because she didn't know what they would do with
me. I later found out that my family in Honduras was calling relatives
in California, asking, "Where is Soledad?" Nobody knew where I was.

The doctor checked my leg and said I was okay. He said, "Just
take some pills." Then these people—I think they were from child
protection—took me to an office here in San Francisco.[8] There were
a lot of kids there, seven, eight years old, maybe like thirty kids in a
kind of dormitory in the basement. There were bunk beds. I was crying all night because I didn't know where they would take me. There
were offices, a lot of phones ringing. The people who worked there
were speaking in English, and I didn't know what they were talking
about. The next day they said, "We have a family for you." I didn't
know why, because I didn't need a family. They said, "You will be put
into the foster care system."

So they took me to a house in Rohnert Park.[9] It was dark, with
a lot of masks and deer heads on the walls. The foster woman was
from Mexico and she was kind of old. The social worker introduced
us. The foster mom said, "Go to your room," and that was it. She
had a daughter, who had one son and one daughter. The grandson
was around three years old. The foster mom also ran a daycare in her

8. Child Protective Services investigates reports of child abuse and abandonment
and works with other agencies to place children in temporary facilities.

9. A small town approximately fifty miles north of San Francisco.

home, so kids would come every day, little babies, from six-, seven-month-olds to three-year-olds. The first day, she treated me well, gave me food, but after that, she barely gave me anything to eat. She made me clean the house. She said, "Today, it's your turn to wash the bathrooms, to mop the floor." So I was working for her without pay. She put me in summer school, and I passed out three times in school because I was starving. One day I passed out in the middle of the street, and the neighbors called an ambulance.

USED CLOTHES WITH HOLES IN THEM

I was fifteen, and this was the first time that I was back in school since primary school in Honduras, when I was eleven.[10] I was trying to find someone to talk to, to make some friends. I didn't speak any English at all because I was really shy. I was going to class, but I was outside of everything. In gym class, I heard two guys speaking Spanish. I was like, *Yes!*

Back in Honduras, I was always the one who didn't know anything, the one with bad grades, the one who didn't do the homework, the lazy one. So I had that idea of myself, but when I came here, I was happy to go to school. I had new ideas. I met new friends, like Paz, who always brought me apples and sometimes gave me her lunch. One time, Paz brought me to her house and her mom tried to help me. She said, "Why don't you call the social worker? Tell them about the situation that you are in, without food to eat."

The foster mother didn't know how to cook, and always gave me instant soup cups. She never gave food to the babies she was taking care of either, so the babies were crying, crying, crying. The foster program paid the foster mom around $600 per month to take care of me. She'd take me to garage sales and buy me used clothes with

---

10. It's common in Honduras for children's education to be interrupted by illness or the necessity to work.

holes in them, for one, two dollars. Then she used the money from social services to buy things for her daughter at the mall and gave the receipts to the social worker. I saw all this, but she'd say, "You'd better be nice to me because the other homes are worse. I'm treating you right." I didn't know how the system worked, because no one told me that foster parents are not supposed to treat you like this. Even though the social worker spoke Spanish, she never asked me, "Soledad, how is everything going?" They're supposed to talk to the child first. But we never had a private conversation about what was happening in the house. I was scared, and nobody was there for me.

Another foster girl from San Francisco came to the house. Her name was Julia, and she saw the way that they were treating me. She spoke English and was born here, so she said, "No, this isn't right, Soledad." She told her social worker, "You need to talk with Soledad." I was in the hospital many times because I was passing out at school, so the doctor also told that social worker, "I don't know what's going on with Soledad, why she passes out all the time. She says she sleeps, she eats well." I didn't tell them because I was afraid that my foster mother would punish me. So finally the social worker took me aside, and I told her that it was because I don't eat, that the foster mom doesn't even give food to the babies she's taking care of, and the mothers don't know how their children are not being cared for. The social worker looked surprised and said, "We're not taking you back there." I never went back to that house. She picked me up from the hospital and brought me to Cloverdale to live with a new family.[11]

"THIS IS MY DAUGHTER"

My new foster parents greeted me with flowers, and I felt welcome. They had three boys, a nice house, and were really warm, clean, ed-

---

11. Cloverdale is a town in Sonoma County with a population of about 8,600 people.

ucated people from Mexico. Their daughter had died at age one and would've been the same age as me. Lucy, the new foster mom, was nice and I had a good relationship with her. I felt like I was in the family that I always dreamed about having. I went from having the worst experience to having the best!

They put me in a new school with many Latinos, and I had problems. Many girls didn't like me, and I had a fight at school. I compared myself with other people and felt that I was the least, the worst. It was kind of sad, but I had two excellent teachers who encouraged me. I started learning English and worked hard. My new social worker was more proactive, assigning a personal tutor who helped me pass all my classes. My foster parents were proud of me, and always said, "This is my daughter," when introducing me.

When I turned eighteen, I didn't have enough credits to graduate from high school. My academic counselor told me, "You can walk on stage, and we can give you a fake diploma." I said, "No, I don't want that," feeling bad that I had worked hard but didn't get the chance to graduate. Meanwhile, my social worker helped me get my immigration papers approved before I turned eighteen.[12] So by the time I got out of foster care, I had my residence status, my green card, and my Social Security card.

My foster parents told me, "Now you're eighteen. You're independent." It was nice to be with my foster family. After two months of paying them rent, I made the decision to move to San Francisco. I had the option to stay with them, and to pay them rent and everything. I liked it there, but there wasn't enough for me. There weren't enough jobs, because it was a little town. So I told them that I would go to

---

12. Regulations for applying for asylum radically change when a youth migrant turns eighteen years of age. See "Minor Children Applying for Asylum by Themselves," US Citizenship and Immigration Services, www.uscis.gov/humanitarian/refugees-asylum/asylum/minor-children-applying-asylum-themselves.

community college, move on, and find my own place, get my GED.[13] They were really sad; they cried. We were really close so it was hard. I had a family, and my food was prepared, everything; I was treated like a princess with all the benefits.

IN THE SAME WEEK, I GOT MY CLASSES AND A JOB

I came to San Francisco in August 2011. Coming back to San Francisco by myself was hard, especially the first week. There's a program called Larkin Street for former foster youth.[14] My social worker connected me, and they put me on a lease for two years at a place called Holloway House. There were three floors, and both men and women stayed there. My foster dad drove me to San Francisco with my social worker and saw the house. It was really dirty because the youth didn't clean it, and it smelled bad, like drugs. He said, "Oh, Soledad, come back with us. This is not the environment for you. This looks really bad." I cried and told them, "I just want to move on, to explore, to meet new people." He cried too, and said, "Stay safe."

Rick, the manager at Holloway House, helped me enroll at City College. I was worried because I didn't have a high school diploma. He said, "You don't need your GED to go to community college. Just take classes for credit and you can get your GED later." But when I tried to register, the staff said, "No, it's too late, classes have already started." I found out students could ask teachers to let us in late, and I was like, *I can do this.* After I got into my classes, I started looking for a job. With Rick's help, I filled out an application at Safeway. In the same week, I got my classes and I got a job at Safeway, ringing up customers, cleaning the floor, mopping. After I got out of work at one in the morning, I'd walk nearly five miles back

---

13. GED stands for General Education Diploma, a high school equivalency degree.

14. Larkin Street Youth Services provides a range of services for homeless youth including housing, education, and employment.

to Holloway every night. It took me an hour and a half, and it was really scary. I always held my little cross that I wore around my neck. In high school, I'd only written like one essay a year. Coming to City College, I had to do an essay every two or three weeks—a big difference. The teacher was really tough. I cried many times. I'd say, "I don't know how to do it!" And my teacher would say, "Just try again." I would rewrite the essays like three times. The teacher would say, "No, this isn't good. Do it again." I didn't know any tutors then. I just worked by myself. I eventually got an A in the class, and B's in the others. I didn't pass math because math is always my most problematic subject.

I WAS SELECTED!

So, the first semester went well, but the second semester, my family was having problems in Honduras, so I had to work more, put more attention on working than school. My mom was sick, and I had to buy medicine and send her to the hospital. She had kidney stones, so she had a lot of pain in her stomach. I started working full time at Safeway and getting bad grades. I started getting C's and repeated the ESL course twice. I failed Math E3 twice. So for a year, I think, my grades really fell. I had too many responsibilities. While I was living at Holloway House, a guy who lived next to me stole my computer. It was a really bad environment. There were people smoking dope, and I don't smoke. There was a lot of noise, music, and weird people. I had never been in that kind of environment. So I was going through that, going through problems with my mom, feeling lonely.

I left Holloway House after almost two years, when I was twenty. I moved to a room nearby. The rent was $600 a month. I was working full time but living in bad conditions. There were rats, and I got a skin disease because it was so dirty. I lived with a friend for a while, but her husband doubled the rent. It was really bad for me, and I decided to ask Guardian Scholars, a support group for foster youth, to help me find another place. They told me, "There is an opportunity in a new building on Ocean Avenue, so let's apply and see." I had to write a statement and show my income and GPA. There was stiff competition, because there were hundreds of applicants, but I was the only one with a 3.0 GPA.

I was selected! But my new apartment wouldn't be available for a couple of months. While I was waiting, I worked at Round Table Pizza and met many Filipino coworkers there. It was good to work there, and I had a nice manager and really nice coworkers. The Filipinos have this custom: when someone gets a new home, they bring something new for that person. When I moved into the new apartment in March, they gave me a television table, a nightstand, a computer table, cups, plates, a plant.

This apartment is brand new, awesome! I always dreamed of having a kitchen, because I like to cook. It has a nice table to eat on, a big refrigerator, and a really big bathroom. It's clean, quiet, close to the college and Whole Foods. There's a beautiful view outside the window. And it's safe because they have a guard downstairs twenty-four hours a day.

WE DON'T CHOOSE OUR FAMILIES

My dream for the future is to graduate from City College, and that dream is very close. I will get an associate degree in sociology and social science in spring 2016, after being in college for three years.[15] I'm getting a certificate in Latino Studies this summer. My next

---

15. An associate degree is an undergraduate academic degree awarded by an accredited community college upon completion of a two-year course of study. In California, students with associate degrees are eligible to transfer to universities, where they can complete their final two years of college and graduate with bachelor's degrees.

step is to transfer to a university, graduate with a bachelor's degree in sociology, and find a better job. Right now, I have an internship working with foster youth, trying to make change, so the same bad experiences that I had do not happen to other youth.

I'm working with California Youth Connection, an organization that works on changing policy. I've been going to Sacramento to talk to state legislators. For example, in the beginning I didn't know what it meant to be in foster care. I think social workers should tell the youth what they can expect and what services are available. Another problem is that if a foster youth gets pregnant, they take the baby away and put it in the foster system as well. We're trying to change the system so mothers and babies don't go with different families. If I'm a foster youth, I don't want my baby to have the same life I had.

I'm twenty-three now. I don't want to bring a baby into this world until I have everything set up—a career, a good job. I want to have a baby with a person who I really feel for, who will be there for a long time. I don't want my baby to have a stepfather, because I don't want him or her to go through the same experience I did. I still haven't found that person, so I'm focused on starting a career.

My feelings about my mom are complicated. When I first came here, I didn't want to hear from her, but therapy helped me to understand. Even though we don't choose our families, she is my mom. What happened with my stepfather sometimes affects my relationships with boyfriends. I'm like, "Don't touch me, don't do that, don't do anything."

The hardest thing for me now is self-confidence. Sometimes I feel that I have everything, but I don't know; there's still something missing. I should be thankful for everything I have and everything I am. I still don't feel confident about what I can achieve. I think, *Oh, I can't do it*, or, *I'm not good enough*. I've been having trouble finding good relationships. Maybe it's because I have marks all over my body from the medications I was given at the hospital in Honduras, and I think that no one will love me because of that. Believing in myself is the hardest thing for me right now.

CHILDREN'S RIGHTS SUMMIT

Good news! I was invited to participate in a Children's Rights Summit at Google in Mountain View, California. They asked me to speak about immigration and the obstacles many immigrants are facing in order to get higher education. Six youth were on a panel discussion. Two hundred people—engineers, lawyers—were in the audience. I was nervous because I don't speak English well, but my mentor told me she believes in me. I talked about my own experience when I immigrated to the United States, what factors pushed me; that I'd suffered physical abuse. People in the audience were crying. I had mixed feelings. It was good to feel understood. But I'm not telling my story to make people feel bad or pity me. I want us to work together to make changes in the system.

We return to Soledad's apartment nearly two years after she moved in. She is now twenty-five years old, attending San Francisco State University, where she is majoring in liberal studies and minoring in criminal justice, and working for John Burton Advocates for Youth, a civic organization that advocates for foster children's rights. She is wearing a mint-green sweatshirt and petite pearl earrings. Her heart-shaped face has become more sculpted, her complexion clear, brown hair falling to her shoulders. She greets us in the courtyard, her face glowing in the wan March sunlight. "Look, I got my US passport!" she exclaims, holding it up for a snapshot. She unlocks her front door and pauses. "Please excuse the clutter, I've been very busy going to school and working. And I like shoes," she says, blushing and skirting a closet. "They are my weakness." The blank wall we remember from our first visit is now covered with eight framed certificates orbiting a huge banner that reads, "Congratulations, Soledad!"

This is why I came to this country. This is why I walked for days in the desert: to have this! This is my associate degree from the City College of San Francisco. This is a certificate from the California State Assembly for my advocacy for foster children. All the struggles that I've been through have been worth it. Many Americans think that we come here to take their jobs, to do bad things, to take advantage of the country. I'm not a bad person. I came here to survive, to do better in this world, to help my family and other people. There was no way to survive in my homeland. I didn't choose to come here. I didn't have another option. I was suffering from poverty. I was physically abused. I want the president of the United States to see that we are not coming here to do anything bad. We come here to get educated and have a better life.

It's exciting to know that other people will read my story. Maybe I can persuade and inspire another view: that things are possible if you work hard. We're not alone. I believe that telling one's story is a way to healing. Sharing my own story has changed my life. Every time I'm sad or I feel like giving up, I read my story and think, *Wow, look at all the things that have come true! I can do it! This is only a bad day, a bad week. I can get up and continue my life.*

JOSUÉ NIEVES

AGE AT CROSSING: 16
BORN IN: Puerto El Triunfo, Usulután, El Salvador
INTERVIEWED IN: Berkeley, California

We first meet Josué in the basement office of the East Bay Sanctuary Covenant in July 2015. The cramped warren of offices buzzes with activity: weary travelers in discolored T-shirts, young mothers nursing babies, the sweet-sharp odors of honeysuckle and diapers, and the tap of fingers on keyboards. Lawyers and volunteers are serving a new generation of youth migrants fleeing the abuses that afflict the children and grandchildren of survivors of the wars in Central America. Josué is of medium height, with a round face, and is shy, soft spoken, and polite. We climb up a set of creaky stairs to the church annex and sit down at a bare table. As Josué describes his early childhood in El Salvador, his cheeks flush and his eyes rise to the ceiling, as he describes being seated

*on his father's shoulders and reaching for a coconut palm. Unlike many
youth refugees who were beaten or abandoned by their fathers, Josué re-
veres his father as a hero, and describes how the happy idyll of his family
life was lost forever after the gangs moved in.*

A CHILD'S MIND

I come from Puerto El Triunfo, on the Pacific coast of El Salvador.
My early life was very beautiful because my world was tranquil and
peaceful. I had a child's mind that only had happy thoughts. My
mother and father were the first loves of my life. When I was with
them, nothing bothered me. I'd pass the time playing with my little
sister. My house was only one room, a big one, but we divided it. My
father would sleep with me, and my mother would sleep with my little
sister. They had their bed, and then there was the living room and the
hallway. My older sister had a larger area.

My mother, Beatriz, was a glorious woman, very beautiful, very
friendly. She'd wake up at six in the morning and make us coffee, a
breakfast of plantains, beans, and cream. Sometimes we'd eat fried
eggs, hard-boiled eggs. She always took good care of us and made
sure to have a meal ready. For Christmas she'd bake *marquesote*, a
kind of sweet bread.[1] No one could make it like her. Everyone in
our neighborhood would say, "Your mom's marquesote is delicious!"
Everything was natural. She wouldn't use chemically processed cooking products, only natural oils, seasonings, spices, and herbs.[2] When

---

1. Marquesote is made from eggs, flour, sugar, yeast, vanilla extract, and dashes
of cinnamon.

2. Salvadoran spices include achiote, extracted from the seeds of the evergreen
Bixa orellana shrub, guaque chile, cloves, and ground coconut.

she'd make *caldo de pescado,* fish soup—oh, how delicious it was![3] Fish from the ocean! The fish gives the food its energy. Stewed fish is delicious, and the tortillas made the way we do there, with some salt and a bit of lemon—oh! I'll never have better. When I was with my mother, everything was beautiful, beautiful. She made sure of that. Looking back, I wouldn't change a thing.

Sadly, I only had a little bit of time with her. My mother died of cancer when I was eight. She was young, only forty. After that, my father, Agosto, was mother and father to me. I followed him around a lot. He had a dark complexion and was kind of short, kind of fat. He was everyone's friend. Sometimes he was very serious, but even then he was funny. Even if you didn't know him, he'd start smiling and say hello to you: "What are you working on? I'll help you." He was a very good person, generous and admirable. When people would visit from other places, he'd say, "Is there something I can do to help?" When I went with him to a new place, he'd have friends. Another place: more friends. And another place farther away: friends again. In those days, he never had any problems, only friends. So I said to myself, *One day, I want to be like my father.* And to this day, I want to be like him. He taught me that however dark life gets, you always have to hold your head high, think positively, pray to God strongly, and you'll continue forward.

As a child, work was a game for me. I'd climb the palm trees to get the coconuts. At first, I didn't know how to climb. But my sister and other people would help me. And I really didn't go to school. The only education I got was from my father, who taught me to live well. After God, he comes second to me.

---

3. The ingredients for caldo de pescado, Salvadoran fish stew, include native fish such as red sea catfish, shrimp, garlic cloves, finely chopped tomatoes, cilantro, dried oregano leaves, salt, pepper, and water.

THEY JUST KILL PEOPLE

My father worked with my mother's family, who had a business selling coconuts. We'd get the coconuts from a nearby island and bring them to the coast in a small boat. There were times when we'd bring two loads of coconuts. It was a big business. Then the gangs started to come and threaten us. The gangs wanted to make their own laws, charge people *renta*.[4] At night they left little pieces of paper at people's houses, threatening, "If you don't pay us, we'll kill your daughter or your son." They know that we go to school at six in the morning and get out of school at three or at four in the afternoon. How's someone supposed to pay $400 when it takes all day to earn $20? The gangs just want the money. They demand protection money from all the businesses, so the people leave. We had all these small boats. We left all that behind. All this was abandoned, lost, because of the gangs. That's how gangs kill legitimate businesses.

Bigger problems started from there. I was bigger too by then—about sixteen. They wanted to kill me because they thought that I was with a rival gang. I didn't want anything to do with those people. The gangs have a rule that if you don't join the gang, you have to move. If you call the police, it takes a long time for them to do anything, and then the gangsters find out. They'll just pass by your house and *boom!* It doesn't matter to them who you are or if they're right or not. They just kill people. They even kill the police.

I remember a beautiful day; the sky was clear and the *maíz* grew green and golden in the sun.[5] I was relaxing with my cousin, watching over my uncle's cattle. My uncle was out with my father. Some *chucos* came near and started laughing at us.[6] One of them was a

---

4. *Renta* is protection money extorted by a gang. Failure to pay triggers retribution. See glossary.

5. *Maíz* is native corn.

6. *Chuco* is slang for "dirty." It can also mean "gangster."

friend. We'd grown up together, eaten together. They said, "When are you guys going to join the gang? You'll have your own money. You won't have to wait for your father to give it to you. You'll have money, women, guns, drugs, whatever you want!" My cousin and I told them, "No, we're good." But they kept demanding, "You need to join the gang." And I was thinking to myself how happy I was working with my father. I looked at them. They all looked disgusting. Something in their eyes told me that if I wanted to be a good person, I shouldn't go with them.

They kept harassing us. Meanwhile, there were more and more kidnappings. One day, an older guy in his twenties threatened, "If you don't join us, you know what's going to happen." I'd seen him hanging around but didn't know him or where he was from. This guy was selling guns, drugs. So I said, "Who are you to give me orders?" And he told me, "I'm going to teach you to respect me!" I told him not to touch me. Not long after, my father came home and told me, "They just beat up your cousin."

The next day, I rode out on a horse, yelling, "Ho! Ho!" The cows started following me because they know what to do. Then I realized that some guys had heard me and were approaching. One had a gun, another a machete. I abandoned the cows, jumped on the horse, and fled. I hid between rows of sugarcane. Later I rode to my uncle's house to return the horse. He told me that the cows had come back without me and he asked me what had happened. I told him that these guys had been bothering me and following me. I left the horse with my uncle and went home. I told my father the story, and we were both terrified. I had a little bit of money saved. My father had a bit in savings too. He told me, "If you want, ask your uncle to loan you some money. I'm going to talk to my sister in Chicago and ask if you can join her in the United States." So I said, "Okay, Papá, I'll ask my uncle for help." I spent a week in the house with the door closed. The gang left a piece of paper under the door. I didn't know how to read. Nor did my father, but my little sister read it aloud: "We're coming for you tomorrow morning. We're not playing around."

I felt something hard in my chest, emptiness. Even now, I feel that terror. My father told me, "I have someone who can help you. He'll take you away." I was anxious, but I said, "Okay, Papá." He said, "You're sixteen, a man now." I looked at him, trying not to cry. He said, "You have a father who cares about you, and no matter what happens, I'm very proud of you. I know who you are, and you'll be a good man." I brought one pair of pants only, the ones I'm wearing now. I brought shoes, a pair of boxers, and three shirts. I still have the shoes and shirts. My dad gave me some toothpaste, a comb. I only brought a bit of the money that we had, in Salvadoran colones, to buy a bit of food or something I'd need.[7] The morning I left, I awoke at five, bathed, and put my clothes on. I was crying like a small child. I'd cried a lot when my mother died, but this was a different feeling. My grandmother sat in a hammock, weeping. "Are you going?" she asked, and I replied, "Yes, *Abuelita*."[8] We always poked fun at each other and got along great. I was worried that something would happen to my aunt and sister when I was gone. But at the same time I felt motivated. My father hugged me. He didn't want me to see that he was crying. He only said to me, "You're going." I warmed up some beans and said, "Papá, let's share a plate of *frijoles*." I prayed to God to give me the opportunity to return and see my father. I woke my sister up and said goodbye. A white car with black windows drove up. A couple of the gangsters who'd been giving me problems and threatening me came up to the car. But luckily I got in and drove off. Inside the car were a *coyote* and his helper, who was driving. The *coyote* wore a dress shirt and black shoes. He'd made this trip many times.

---

7. One Salvadoran colón is worth about eleven US cents.

8. *Abuelita* is a term of endearment meaning "little grandmother."

We reached Usulután and bought bus tickets to Guatemala.[9] It was now just the *coyote* and me. He had a light complexion and black hair. He was stocky, kind of tall, muscular, and very serious. I don't know if he was armed. We spoke very little. My father and I had paid him $3,000 to take me.

We got on the bus. The *coyote* sat in one seat and I sat behind him. I got on the bus first, looked for free seats near each other. I sat in one and said, "I'm saving this seat for my father," pretending the *coyote* was my dad. I was nervous because I'd never traveled anywhere before, but I made my way little by little. When we arrived at a place before entering Guatemala, the *coyote* said, "Take this bicycle and cross the bridge." It was raining. There were some big trucks, and I rode between them. Then, on the other side, the *coyote* bought another ticket, and I bought the same. When we got to Guatemala, we went to a hotel. The *coyote* paid for the room, and I went inside. We slept there, and the next morning we left.

We went to a bunch of places. When we arrived at a checkpoint, we'd walk around it. To ford rivers, we took off everything, even our shoes. There were cactus spines, sharp rocks, and muddy waters. Crossing rivers felt adventurous for me because I was only used to walking in the mountains. I was more scared in the cities, in case there were Mexican federal agents or police officers. Once, I got on a bus at seven in the morning and got off at about eight at night. All day on the bus! My stomach churned with hunger pangs because I hadn't eaten.

One morning, we got on the freight train—*La Bestia*, "the Beast."[10] I brought a bag to cover myself, and there were many people there. Some train cars were cylindrical; others had steel bars inside. People rode on top, and when there wasn't any more space up there,

---

9. Usulután is a city in southeast El Salvador. It is located in the department, or state, of the same name.

10. See glossary.

they'd climb down ladders and hang on the bottom step. I rode on top because I got on before many people. I grabbed a spot and stayed there. The *coyote* was ahead of me. I spoke with some of the other travelers. They'd ask me, "Where are you from?" and I'd say, "El Salvador." They'd say, "I'm from El Salvador too," or Guatemala, or Honduras. They'd say, "We want to go to the United States." I'd say, "Me too." One night, it was really dark, like nine or ten at night, and we got off and walked. Another time, we were accosted on a bus in Mexico, and thieves demanded money. We didn't have much, but it was something that I wouldn't want to go through again. The *coyote* protected me on the journey because strangers thought he was my father.

"WE DON'T WANT PEOPLE LIKE YOU"

It took us a month to reach the US border. We arrived in Nuevo Laredo, Mexico.[11] It was a big city, and I got separated from the *coyote* and became lost. I slept alone, trying not to get caught. I had no money, nothing to eat, and only drank water. Three days later, the *coyote* found me. He took me and another migrant to a small bridge to cross. I watched cars coming across it from Mexico with US license plates. There was a lane for trucks, a lane for cars, a lane for bicycles, and a lane for pedestrians. I saw that border guards were checking the people on foot, so we grabbed bicycles and rode across. When an officer standing in a booth turned toward us, I ditched the bike and ran. I thought there were just a few officers, but there were many. One yelled, "Stop!" but I didn't know what he was saying and kept running. The border guards surrounded me, grabbed me, and handcuffed my hands and feet. They took me away. I started to cry because I'd never been handcuffed before. They mistreated me. In retrospect I see they had a reason, since I'd entered in a way that I shouldn't have,

---

11. Nuevo Laredo, Mexico, is located on the southern bank of the Rio Grande, just across from Laredo, Texas.

so I respect that. He spoke only English. I remained silent and he said many, many things in English. Then the officers spoke with each other. One grabbed me from behind and lifted my cuffed arms up over my head. It hurt, but I was mostly worried they might take me to the prison. They grabbed me as if I were some object, some animal.

I told them I needed help, that I'd fled from gangs in my country. One agent said in Spanish, "All of them say this!" Another yelled, "And when they get here they're the ones that ruin our country! We don't want people like you." They asked, "Why did you enter this way? Why didn't you go to another country?" I told them that I had an aunt here and I didn't have anyone in other countries. Actually, my brothers were here, and some uncles, but I didn't have any contact with them at that point, only with my aunt. I'd only spoken with her a few times, but she and my dad got along well. The guards asked me, "What's your aunt's name?" I told them, "Antonia." Then one said, "Okay, okay. Sit down there, son." That's when they started to interview me. When I told them I was sixteen years old, one said, "He's a minor." Then they took off my cuffs and the officer who'd been yelling at me left. A kinder officer said, "I'm sorry the other officer treated you badly. What do you want, that we deport you, that we take you to Mexico?" I told them, "I want you to help me. I don't want to go back. I want to call my aunt." I had her phone number written inside my belt. I told them, "Here's my aunt's number." They took off my belt, my shoes, all my clothes, and searched me. Then they asked me, "Do you want to eat?" And I told them, "Yes, I'm very hungry." They brought some burritos and juice. I'd been so nervous, and after I ate, I became calmer.

An officer called my aunt, asking if she knew me. She said, "Yes, I know Josué and yes, he is my nephew." They talked to her a bit, and then she and I started chatting, although I could barely hear her. After I hung up, one of the ICE officers cursed in Spanish.[12] I was

---

12. ICE is Immigration and Customs Enforcement. See glossary.

told they'd send me to the shelter. I wasn't sick, but they made me take medicine and injected me. I don't know why.

We arrived at a shelter for kids in San Antonio, Texas. The staff gave me a bed and food. It was clean and they treated me really well. They had rooms for American children, kids from other countries, and kids like me. The staff took us out to play and to school. They were very good people.

At the shelter, I called my aunt again, and she asked me, "How are you? How are you being treated? How are you feeling? Do you have any problems?" And I said, "No, I'm well, Aunt," finding it hard to talk. She said, "I thought I was going to sponsor you." But she couldn't take me because she wasn't working and my guardian had to be employed. So my stepbrother agreed to sponsor me. He was living here in Oakland. But, as my mother had died young and he had another father, we brothers weren't so close. He was about my age, but I'd never actually spoken to him and only knew him from photos. My brother started to talk to me on the phone, saying, "Hello, what's up? How are you?" I talked to him for about thirty minutes, but I was anxious to talk with my father.

The shelter only allowed me a couple of phone calls while I was there. So a few days later I called my father in El Salvador. "Papá, I'm in this place that's very beautiful." When I heard his voice, it made me feel like crying. He fell silent, and then asked, "Do you feel safe?" And I said, "Yes, Papá, yes." It made me cry because all my friends were in El Salvador, but I wasn't with them. I just wanted to talk to my dad for the whole hour, talk and talk, telling him about everything, the whole story: how the Beast had treated me, what had happened on the journey. My father advised me to be "a quiet and well-balanced person, and hang out with good people you're going to learn things from. Don't be a crazy person who hangs out with bad people because it's going to end badly." I took his words to heart and stuck with older people and teachers who dedicated time to me and gave me advice.

I stayed in the shelter for a month. That's where I celebrated my seventeenth birthday. I attended a fun Halloween party. Then the shelter staff told me I was going to be with my stepbrother in Oakland. When my plane landed, I looked around at the people at the airport, and a guy I didn't recognize said to me, *"Hola! Hola!"* I kept to myself. Then he said, "Are you Josué?" And I said, "Yes, who are you?" He replied, "I'm Horacio, your brother." I still didn't believe him until he said, "Do you want to talk to your sister?" and I realized he *was* my brother. He signed some papers for me and took me to his apartment. My brother worked all the time, seven days a week. He supported me, his three children, and his wife, who was a stay-at-home mom.

At that time I wasn't working, so my brother put me in school. One day, I asked a teacher if she could help me find a lawyer. She introduced me to a friend who was a school counselor, and he gave me the number for a female lawyer. She took me to her office at the East Bay Sanctuary Covenant with a stack of papers and said, "Tell me everything that's going on." I began to tell her everything, and I was so happy. She went to consult with the other lawyers, and from there they began the process of applying for asylum. She said I qualified. They sent me a card reminding me to show up in court. I wasn't afraid because I was with my lawyers. They told me, "Nothing's going to happen to you." They explained the court process to me, step by step, until I understood everything.

When I came to the East Bay Sanctuary Covenant in Berkeley, I felt very happy because they helped me a lot. They weren't charging me a cent! Everyone said, "How can we help?" Instead of me giving them money, they gave me invaluable advice and support. There are people who spend a lot of money on private immigration lawyers. I didn't even spend five dollars. Sometimes I'd be interviewed for a whole day. They'd take me to eat or have a fruit drink. In my life, there have been good and bad people, but I never imagined a place like this, where I'd encounter such good people with kind hearts.

They'd take me to school and pick me up from school, help me with exams.

My brother came with me to an immigration hearing. The hearing officer asked me if I was okay with my brother being responsible for me until I turned eighteen, and I told him yes. We spoke through a translator. I told him I was doing well. He asked me if I wanted to play soccer, and I told him yes. He told me, "You're not going to have papers or anything." I still worried that the hearing officer didn't have confidence in me. But I knew in my heart that God was helping me. I trusted in myself.

In San Francisco I went before an immigration judge. I thought it was going to be a big court with many people, but in fact it was just a desk with me, my lawyer, and her two assistants. I felt a little bit nervous that the judge was going to say to me, "No, you don't have anything, you aren't going to be able to stay." But they kept telling me, "Everything's going to be okay." I got a work permit, and I got fingerprinted. And, *bueno*, I felt relieved.

THEY KILLED MY UNCLE

After I was away from Puerto El Triunfo for a few months, I found out that my uncle had been killed. He was a trucker and when he arrived at my other uncle's business to drop off coconuts, the gangsters were waiting for him. They demanded protection money. My uncle was a bit drunk and yelled back, "No!" A very big, strong guy came forward, bellowing, "You have to pay *la renta!*" My uncle yelled back, "How can you say this?" And they roughed him up. They all left, and after a while, my uncle went back to his house.

Those guys were known to my family. They pretty much grew up with us. My uncle was approaching his house one day when there were a lot of gangsters outside. I can't tell you exactly what happened because I wasn't there. I heard that my uncle stumbled and fell and they shot him. They killed him. My little sister saw who killed my uncle, and the gang leaders told her if something happens to the men who killed him, she'd be blamed.

Let me explain: Earlier, my sister had started going out with a *pandillero*, a gang member, against my father's wishes. She was about fourteen at the time, the youngest child, and the gangster was much older and took advantage of her. After she moved in with the gangster, my father told her, "I don't like you living with him. You need to come back home." She said, "No, I love him." And the gangster told my father, "You will have a lot of problems with the *maras*."[13] When my father took my little sister back home, big problems started for him. The *marero* told him, "You're going to have to repent for having taken my girlfriend." He spread the news and other maras started leaving messages for my father.

My father was very angered by my uncle's death. Once, one of the maras came by and said, "Be careful where you go." My father said, "Why don't you let people live in peace?" And the guy said, "You have nothing to say because you are no one, so if you keep looking for problems, we're going to kill you." They sent someone to tell him that they were going to kill him at a dogfight. My father had lots of enemies because the mara is big. He'd never just let it go, but always faced them and defended his right to live. I left because I didn't want the gang to hurt me, my family, and I felt they'd be safer without me there. The mara's threats against my father increased after I left.

I'm very worried because they threatened my father, and I'm scared that they're going to do something to my sister or my father, but I pray to God that nothing happens. It's been very difficult for me to be away from my father. I talk to him every weekend, and he says, "My son, why don't you come down here?" And I say, "Yes, that'd be great!" I wish I could give him a handshake, a hug. I tell

---

13. Maras are gangs; members of gangs are known as mareros. See glossary.

him I miss being with him, and he tells me how much he misses me. There's hardly any work for my father, and there are so many problems with the gangs.

PICTURES IN THE SAND

Last weekend, on the Fourth of July, something wonderful happened. Earlier, my sister, who had made it safely to Oakland, had posted photos of a girl on Facebook. I told my sister, "She's pretty." That's all I said. After that, my sister invited her to the beach. They had celebrated my niece and nephew's birthdays together while I was working, and the girl told my sister, "I want to meet your younger brother." I decided to put in a request for a day off, and I met her at the beach. I was calm but really nervous inside! She introduced herself to me as Miriam, and I introduced myself. We started to talk, asking each other, "What do you do? What do you like?"

We went swimming and drew pictures in the sand, joking around. We drew a big bear in the sand, and then she started drawing a house, like a castle. We decorated the castle with rocks and sticks from the beach. She drew a hill behind the castle, and I made a heart. She asked me, "What are you making?" And I said, "Nothing! I'm just making it more beautiful!" She started smiling and we both laughed nervously. After that, we ate, swam, and talked a lot. We bought ice cream, and the day went by really quickly. Finally, around six in the evening, she said, "Okay, I have to go," and she went home. Later, I sent her a message on Facebook, and we started chatting online, checking in on each other.

We don't talk again with Josué for more than two years. When we reach him by phone, his voice sounds somber. We meet him at noon on a hot Sunday in August 2017. He has grown brawny, with strong biceps and a trucker's suntan. His dark curly hair has been cropped short, and he looks more mature. He rests in a plastic chair under a shady tree, in front of a green rental duplex in the flats of Oakland, a barrio about a mile from International Boulevard. Josué greets us with a shy, sleepy smile. "Sorry, I woke up late. I was delivering furniture late last night," he says, hurrying off to put on a fresh T-shirt with red sleeves and black shorts. He tries a smile, but when we ask about his family his lips tighten and his Adam's apple bobs. He introduces us to his stepbrother and nephew, who pose for a photograph, then wave goodbye. We drive to a local Vietnamese restaurant to talk, but it's too noisy, so we park on a side street under the shade of an oak tree. A dog barks but calms down as we switch on the recorder. Josué describes events that happened two months after our first interview, but which he says are "still fresh, as if they occurred yesterday."

"BE STRONG AND HEAR WHAT I HAVE TO SAY"

My father liked dogfighting, and so do I. He called me at around eight on a Sunday morning in September 2015, to say hello. He'd sent me a photo of himself drinking coffee, eating beans and fried plantains. He said, "My son, how are you?" I told him, "Good, my father." We started talking and he told me that he was going to a dogfight. He said he'd call me in the afternoon.

I went to work delivering furniture with my work partner. I was just arriving at a house in Livermore to make a delivery. I called the client and asked him if he could come outside because I couldn't find his house. While I was talking to him, my stepbrother called me. I said, "Let me call you back. I'm just arriving at a delivery." He said, "I want you to be strong and hear what I have to say. You have self-worth and strength." I asked, "What happened? Why are you telling me this?" He replied, "I'm calling on behalf of all of our family. Your father was just murdered." I cried, "No! Tell me the truth. That didn't happen." He said, "Yes, it's true. He's been murdered."

I didn't believe it. I didn't even cry. I didn't do anything. I just called my father. I called him and called him and he didn't answer. After the call, my work partner asked me, "Do you want me to drop you off at home?" I told him, "No. We're going to keep working." We did the delivery in Livermore and were on our way back to Oakland. I told him that we were going to finish the route, even though I felt a deep depression inside me. After some time, I spoke with a doctor in El Salvador. At first he told me that my father wasn't dead, just wounded, and I became hopeful. I finally talked to my sister who lives in Oakland. She confirmed that it was true, that he'd been killed. Then in the truck, I saw on my phone the photos of my father, which he'd messaged me earlier that morning. In them he appeared calm. Then I saw the photo of his dead body on Facebook, and I started to cry.[14]

After my father had called me, he'd gone to the dogfight with his friends. In these dogfights, they do one session in the morning and then another in the afternoon in a different place. In the afternoon, he'd gone in a car to a nearby town. My father had bet on his pit bull in a dogfight and then went to another dogfight at a different location. He was on foot when someone walked up and shot him from a distance. He was shot with three bullets. Two hit his head and one hit his shoulder.

I found out about three hours after it happened. After he was shot, his friends ran away. They didn't do anything. He was left on the ground next to his dog. Eventually, other friends of his found out and went to where his body had been left for about seven hours out on the street. I never thought this kind of thing would happen to my father. I was afraid for my sisters who were still there, afraid that they'd be murdered too.

---

14. A newspaper in El Salvador published a photograph of a gun murder victim's body lying in the street. The photo was posted on Facebook and Josué recognized his father.

MIRIAM

Remember Miriam, the girl I met on the Fourth of July? The next year, my sister threw a birthday party for her son. Miriam was there, and we started talking again. This time she gave me her number. After the party, we went out to the street and talked for about two hours. She gave me a hug for the first time. I asked her for help. I told her I wanted to talk with her more and that I could see that she's a very good person. I told her that if she'd give me a chance, I wanted to see her more. After that, we sent text messages to each other back and forth. She sent hers in English and I sent mine in Spanish. I told her, "I want to work on writing my messages in English," and she told me, "I want to help you learn." This is how it all started. We started to talk more and more. We've been together for two, almost three years. She gives me books with English and Spanish text to help me learn. And she tells me, "It's pronounced this way." She assigns me homework to work on. Sometimes she puts guidelines down for me to do things a certain way. She's strict!

Miriam is my girlfriend. She has a degree in nursing and dreams of becoming a doctor. She's a good person who is Romanian-Jewish American. She helps and respects all people and wants to start a clinic for those without resources.

My relationship with Miriam is very beautiful. Like me, she respects everyone's rights. I've always been taught to respect anyone who shows me respect. We often cook together. She's learning how to make tortillas and *pupusas*, so she makes them, and I eat them![15] We eat breakfast in the yard with her parents. They have a very beautiful yard with many plants and trees. I get along really well with her mom and dad.

Miriam works in San Francisco and is studying at UC Berkeley. She

15. Pupusas are thick corn tortillas stuffed with various fillings of meat, beans, and cheese. They are usually served with *curtido*, a slaw of spicy chopped cabbage.

was born here. We do many things outside together. She loves nature and we go out into the countryside. We both love to ride horses. We go to the beach, to the mountains. Sometimes we take my little cousins in the afternoons and share many wonderful moments together.

AGOSTO AND BEATRIZ TRUCKING

I'm twenty now. I work Monday through Saturday doing deliveries. I wake up at four in the morning. Then I shower, down a quick coffee and a piece of bread with cream. And of course, I'm thinking of my mother's delicious plantains, beans, and cream. I need to arrive at the warehouse at 5:15. I drive to work in my car, a seventeen-year-old Honda Civic with a standard transmission. When I get to the warehouse, I need to load the truck. When I finish loading, I drive to San Francisco, to San Jose sometimes, Sacramento, Santa Rosa, or Petaluma. Sometimes I drive for three hours straight. My partner usually drives in the morning, and I drive on the way back to the warehouse. Sometimes we stop by a store to buy food for lunch, or eat tacos or burritos—but they're a far cry from my mother's savory pupusas!

At my current job, I'm in charge of talking to the clients. I put on my headphones and call them thirty minutes before arriving, saying, "I have your delivery of a bed, a table." When I arrive at the house, I speak with the client, "Hello! I have a delivery for you. Can you please show me where to leave it?" They tell me where to leave the delivery, and I start moving the items with my work partner. I open the truck's back door, take the items out of their boxes, clean them off, and make sure that everything's in good condition.

I'm trying to start my own trucking business. I want to buy my own truck, hopefully a 2008 Freightliner model with manual transmission and a Mercedes engine. It's twenty-four feet long and can carry 2,300 pounds of cargo. I have to shift through five gears.

I really have to concentrate and always pay attention to what's happening behind me. Some people find it difficult to drive, but I really enjoy it. My company will be called Agosto and Beatriz Trucking, after my parents. Everything I try to do is for them. I'm grateful for them because they've made me who I am.

At the end of our conversation, we drive Josué back to his home. He looks at the empty chair beneath the tree and talks about a visitation from his father.

A couple of months ago I was a bit stressed. I was sad, *solito*, while my two brothers were out working. My cousin wasn't home, and I was sitting in the same chair I used to sit in when talking to my dad, where you saw me sitting today. And I heard his voice. It just said, "Jos-Jos-Josué." He repeated this, "Jos, Jos," and it faded out, more and more quietly. He was telling me not to worry, not to be sad. And I told him, "Okay, Papá."

GABRIEL MÉNDEZ

AGE AT CROSSING: 15
BORN IN: Tegucigalpa, Honduras
INTERVIEWED IN: Oakland, California

*We meet Gabriel on a warm summer afternoon at Centro Legal de
la Raza, in the Fruitvale neighborhood of Oakland. The Centro was
founded in 1969 and aids the greater Latino community with pro bono
legal representation, access to education, and human rights advocacy.
Gabriel is wearing a stylish blue button-down dress shirt with red trim
inside the collar, gray wool slacks, and leather loafers. He proudly sports
a rainbow wristband on his right hand and a silver watch on the left.
His black hair is swept up over his high forehead, and his eyebrows
shield penetrating eyes that light up with a smile. Although he is seventeen and still in high school, he displays the composure and self-assurance*

59

of a youth leader accustomed to speaking out in forums about issues of importance to him, such as defending children and LGBTQ people from abuse. Yet as he reveals painful incidents of childhood sexual abuse in Honduras, his voice falters, his elbows draw inward, and his eyes seem to burrow into a dark place. Then he smiles and tells us his dreams of becoming a lawyer fighting to protect vulnerable children.

BORN IN THE DEVASTATION OF A HURRICANE

I'm from Tegucigalpa, Honduras, from a very dangerous neighborhood called Villa Franca. The people there are very poor. There are a lot of *maras,* many negative things happening with the government, and a lot of ignorance in the community.[1]

I was born in the devastation of a hurricane in 1998, during Hurricane Mitch. The country was torn apart, and the hospitals were in terrible condition. My mother was sixteen when she became pregnant with me. She only reached the third grade before she stopped her studies. My father, who was also sixteen, had wanted to join the armed forces of Honduras. But when my mother told him she was pregnant, he wasn't able to fulfill his dream. The pregnancy lasted the nine months, but there were many complications. They had to cut her open to get me out—a caesarean.

My mother took care of me for a long time. Things were going well. Then my mom started working. My grandmother on my mother's side took care of me. She fed me and gave me everything, because my mother couldn't afford all those expenses. Then Grandma got sick, but we don't know from what. We didn't have money for the medicine, so she died in 2001, when I was three. I remember seeing her in the coffin.

My aunt came to live with us. Everything was good for some time. Then problems began to arise between my mom and my dad.

---

1. *Maras* are gangs and *mareros* are gangsters. See glossary.

I was about four years old. My mother was working hard at street fairs, selling corn, tamales, and fritters. I helped her peel corn, clean the husks, steam and fry up tamales. My father was always drunk: lying down, drinking beer, and passing out. He never played with me. There was a lot of yelling at the house. My mom would cry and my dad would beat her in front of us—and beat me up as well. I felt awful because there was nothing I could do. I felt hate inside of me because he was hitting the person who gave me life.

I had two younger sisters, one born in 2000 and the other in 2004. I would take care of them when my mom went to work and my dad went out drinking. I looked after them all day, took them to school, and went to school myself. I had to wash clothes and cook. I did everything.

We had our own home, with a kitchen, living room, two bedrooms, and parking. There was electricity, but the power went out frequently. We had running water, but only sometimes, so we had to keep water in jugs.

I WAS MADE TO DO THINGS I DIDN'T WANT TO DO

Later, in 2005, other people began to live with us. My parents rented out some rooms because they needed the money. One of the bedrooms was for two of my cousins, two sisters, another girl, an older guy, and me. There were seven of us in one room. Another room was for my aunt, her husband, and her son. My cousins were all older, over eighteen.

I was just a boy of seven. My cousins raped me for a long a time—for a year. They raped me at the river, where they collected water, and in my own home. Some of the cousins were brothers. One had a wife and his own children, yet he raped me.

In separate incidents, my cousins would force me to do things in their house. They'd have me touch their private parts. I was made to do things I didn't want to do. I was a child and I didn't know what was happening. I feared for my sisters because they were younger than me. Something bad could happen to them. They were little, one and four years old.

I used to be on friendly terms with my neighbor's mom and I would talk with her. One day I went over to their house. My neighbor's son told me to come inside, grabbed me by the neck, and began kissing me. He started to undress. Another time one of my mom's cousins grabbed me while I was playing in the street. I had walked by an old, abandoned house, and he closed the door and took me by force. I started to bleed. I was just little. He then moved in with us. He lived next to my room. And every day he'd come and do the same thing, day after day. He was living in my house so he had more access.

Once, when the power went out, I took my sisters to my grandmother's house because I was afraid. The wife of one of the cousins who was raping me was at my house. She asked me if I wanted to stay in their room. I stayed there with the wife, his two stepchildren, and him. He slept with his two stepchildren and his wife. The wife left at four in the morning and I kept sleeping because the power was out. When I woke up in the morning he was lying down next to the boys completely naked. No boxers, no shirt, no pants. He took me by force and laid me down next to him and the boys. He did dirty things to me for almost the entire day. Then I left to go get my sisters and make them some food. I did all the daily chores and these things continued to happen—the same thing, day after day, for a year. Was this normal?

I didn't know how to tell my family. I didn't know how to act. You know how if your dad hits your mom, he might hit you too? He'd say that I was offering myself, so I was afraid to speak out. I never said a word.

MY MOTHER HAD LIED TO US

At the six-month mark of all of this, my mom decided for the first time to go to the United States. She left without giving us anything but money for lunch. One morning she said, "I'm heading to work." I said okay. I was taking care of my sisters, did what I did every day. We went out to the street to play. I took them to my paternal grandmother's. Everything was fine. It was five and then six in the evening and my mom didn't show up. People came by and asked for my mom, and, crying, I told them I didn't know where she was. Then my aunt came by and told me my mother had gone to the United States. I started to cry. I didn't know what to do. I was only seven years old.

My dad showed up much later that night. He began to collect all my mom's things and then he left to sell them. My sisters and I were left practically on the street. We went to go live with my aunt. My dad then took us from there to my grandmother's house. When I was living there, the bad cousins would chase me as I headed to school, but they usually couldn't catch me. Sometimes they did catch me and did the same unspeakable things.

During this period, I discovered my mother had lied to us. She had not actually left the country. One night I was taken to my aunt's house because my father's relative had died. My mother showed up. I asked her why she was there since supposedly she'd already left Honduras. She said, "The *coyote* didn't take me yet, I'm waiting for him to pick me up." I told her how much I was suffering with my sisters and how we missed her. "You can sleep with me tonight," she said. "Don't tell your dad I'm still here. Please go get some of my clothes." That's all she said about it. In the morning, she left. We were taken to my dad's house.

My family was hurt by my mother's decision to leave the country. I didn't hear from her for a while. Then she called me on my eighth birthday and told me not to cry, that she would give us a future. My mom was caught by La Migra and put in detention for six months.[2] Then she returned home. She took us back and the same things kept going on.

My mom decided to take us to live at my grandfather's house in a town near Olancho. The town was called Jiniapa in Cedros, near Talanga.[3] My dad's parents were separated. He lived in the town, and she lived in the city. We weren't given enough food. We ate once or twice a day. I had to work in the field there, harvesting tomatoes, watermelons, corn, beans.

My mom told us we would stay in the town because the city was too dangerous. I thought it would be good since nobody could harm me there. She took one sister to Tegucigalpa so that my aunt could care for her and left my other sister with me. I would work in the field every day and go to school in the afternoon sometimes. I preferred work to school, because I needed to eat.[4] My grandfather told me that my mom hadn't left any food and that I needed to work to buy food. So I kept working in the field. I was doing well. I didn't touch the money I made. I'd carry buckets of tomatoes on my shoulders. They saw that I was good at growing the tomatoes so I began to do that as well.

Five months passed and my mom went back to the United States. One day I got a phone call—I barely even knew what a phone was at the time—and I spoke with my mom. I told her that I couldn't stand it any longer. My sister and I were stealing food to eat. It was that or waiting to be fed at school, which wasn't enough. I was extremely thin. My mom told me we'd do something so that I could leave.

---

2. See glossary.

3. Talanga, in the state of Francisco Morazán, is between the state of Olancho and the Honduran capital, Tegucigalpa.

4. Primary school is generally free and compulsory in Central America. However, in rural areas poor families require children to work in the fields, pitting food against education.

Since I was working and going to school and not being given enough food, I lied to my grandfather and told him that Save the Children was taking me and my sister. It was an organization that helped the communities in our area. I told him we were going on a trip, but we went to the city. My maternal aunts in Villa Franca saw me at that point and began to cry at the state we were in. I was so emaciated, as was my sister. We began to live with my mother's side of the family again, and I began to get better.

My mother's oldest sister left for Spain. Then I went to live with another aunt, then back with my grandfather who lived near Talanga, then with my dad. There was a rotation of who was supposed to take care of us. I kept changing schools and going from place to place for two years. Many things were happening, and I couldn't concentrate in school. Finally, I went to live with a good nephew of my mom's, one who hadn't abused me. He took good care of us and paid attention to us. He spent all day at the house.

One day he took us camping. But one of the bad cousins who'd raped me came along. We went into a river and I began to drown. He grabbed me by the neck and stuck his finger in my . . . I was crying. Later when we were leaving, I headed to another part of town where mangos were growing. The bad cousin, who was visiting a family member in the town, took me to the river again and began to abuse me. He began to hit me because he said I shouldn't cry when he did that to me—I should enjoy it. He told me to not say a word or things would go badly for me. When we went back to town, I didn't want to live with my good cousin anymore because he'd brought this bad person along. My good cousin didn't know that the bad person had raped me.

I went to live again with my aunt who lived in La Rosalinda, and I changed schools. Then I went back to my good cousin's house, but the school was very far away. I had to walk a long distance. I went back to my aunt's house and began to attend school with more frequency.

I CARRIED IT ALL IN MY HEAD

When I was ten I began to notice that something was changing. Everybody at school was calling me "gay," "faggot," "homosexual." I didn't know what that was or what they were referring to. They wouldn't tell me. In time they began to say that I walked funny, that I walked like a woman. I didn't like it. This kept going on for a long time.

I finished sixth grade and went to a middle school in the center of the city. I went there for only half the year because the same thing began to occur there; kids were saying the same things to me.

Some of my fellow students who belonged to the maras took weapons to school. We would get searched by security, and I told the mareros that I didn't want to bring weapons to school. I was afraid of them. They also wanted me to bring drugs into school. They would smoke inside the school. Other mareros who weren't students began to give me drugs, and I began to get involved. But I didn't like it, so I left that school. I went to my grandmother's house in Villa Franca.

Now the maras were looking for me—to kill me. They wanted me to join the gang and were mad because I dropped out. They were asking my neighbors if they knew me. My grandmother told me it wasn't safe and sent me to Jiniapa, my grandfather's town. From there I went to my aunt's house. She asked me if I wanted to continue my studies. I told her I did. So I went back to the school where everyone was calling me gay and everything else. The name-calling continued. My friends would ask me to go play soccer, but I couldn't because I didn't know how. This also led them to call me gay. That's how things went. Every day the same thing. Even the teachers said it.

I hadn't told anybody about the rapes. I carried it all in my head. I kept taking care of my sisters. Nobody knew about the rapes—nobody saw anything.

ADIOS, HONDURAS

When I was fourteen, I told my mom I wanted to leave Honduras. I didn't want to celebrate or go out for my fourteenth birthday. I didn't like playing with toys. I didn't like anything. I was always inside my house making my sisters food or helping them with their homework and doing my own. I couldn't do anything else. I told my mom I wanted to come to the United States. She said it was dangerous. I told her, "If you don't send for me, I'll leave." So she paid a *coyote* $6,000 to take me on the journey. She also got me a cell phone to contact her from Mexico.

My good cousin took me from Tegucigalpa all the way to the Mexico-Guatemala border. We left Honduras on a bus at nine at night, on September 12, 2013. I didn't have proper travel documents. The Honduran police stopped me for trying to leave the country illegally and held me for a day. We paid them a bribe, they released me, and I paid a taxi to cross the Guatemalan border. In Guatemala, the *coyote* took us to dirty hotels and fed us food we didn't like.

I was traveling with my good cousin and a dark-skinned young woman who was also trying to get to the United States. She kept getting stared at because there's a lot of racism against people who look different. She was afraid and the stares made her uncomfortable. It was hard to get across the border because of the checkpoints along the road and harder still for the dark-skinned girl to cross the checkpoints because she could not pass as Mexican. We crossed the river from Guatemala to Mexico, and there we had the same problems. A *coyote* told her, "You won't be able to cross because you are dark-skinned." He said she would get raped along the way and told her not to turn around to look—she could be kidnapped. I didn't like hearing all the stuff they said about her. My cousin told me not to believe him and to always stay together. When we entered Mexico, my cousin left to go back to Honduras.

We continued on with a *coyote*. He was a racist and said that we wouldn't be able to go on with the "black girl." He said she'd have to go separately. He was very strange and had us stay in a hotel for a week. He sent her off alone on a bus at five in the morning. We went on a different bus, where we weren't asked for papers because we looked Mexican, and we met up with her in the next town.

We got to San Luis Potosí, Mexico, where they kept us locked in a house with eight other people for a week. The others left first, and then we left. We kept moving. Many days passed without eating or drinking water. We traveled by bus, intercity bus, not clinging to freight trains. Some of the migrants with us had come on La Bestia.[5] The things they'd gone through seemed terrible.

We got to Monterrey, and from there we went to Miguel Alemán, Tamaulipas. We ran into the Zetas there.[6] Another person and I were taken off the bus and asked who had brought us. We both said, "Mario," the name of the *coyote* who had brought us. They told us to get back on the bus. There were other people traveling on the bus, and the Zetas made them get off and took them away. We never found out what happened to them. In northern Mexico, my cell phone battery died. The *coyotes* carried cell phones and made me pay them to call my mother. They also used their cell phones to call her and demand money.

We were taken to a hotel with a lot of other migrants: Dominicans, Cubans, and people from other areas. We were taken to the river, where there was a raft, but we couldn't cross, because US immigration was present.[7] The next day, at five in the morning, they woke us up. We crossed the river into the United States and moved to a safe house. Then we went to McAllen, Texas.[8] This was on November 26, 2013.

---

5. See glossary.

6. Los Zetas, which literally means "the Zs," is a ruthless drug gang formed by ex-members of an elite Mexican army unit. See glossary and appendix essay on "The Rise of the *Maras*."

7. The Rio Grande is the natural border between Mexico and the United States, patrolled by US Immigration and Customs Enforcement (ICE).

8. McAllen is fifteen kilometers from Reynosa, Mexico, just over the border.

We stayed there for another week. On the first of December, a few days before my birthday, we went into the desert at dawn. We spent four nights in the desert including the night of my fifteenth birthday.

We carried beans, sardines, and both flour and corn tortillas with us. That's how we moved through the desert, with that disgusting food. We drank water that was meant for cattle. We drank from anywhere we could find it. It was very cold. The *coyote* took our jackets and sweaters and used them to brush away our footprints so as to not leave a trail. This made it impossible to put them on because they were covered in cactus spines. We had to keep watch for the border patrol airplanes and helicopters. Only once did we run into US immigration. They went by the road, but we ducked and hid so they didn't see us.

This *coyote* was called "El Diablo." He liked one of the girls in our group from Guatemala and he raped her in the desert. She was eighteen, I think. He was an older man, maybe thirty or forty years old. We slept every night in the desert. There was a woman with us who was six months pregnant. There was another man from Guatemala who couldn't walk anymore because of his swollen feet. Two people had to carry him.

We were all very tired. They would give us drugs to keep us awake, Ecstasy and I don't know what other types of drugs—different colored pills. I began to feel extreme anxiety from the drugs they were feeding us; every three hours was another pill. Pill after pill. We felt no hunger, no cold, no weariness. The last night they ran out of pills, and we were very cold. The cold was killing me. We bundled up together to generate heat. We kept walking, running, jumping fences, and dodging cactus spines.

We came upon another group of people who'd been traveling two days ahead of us. A young man, under eighteen, had perished from exposure and lack of water and food. Five family members stayed with the dead boy. Their *coyote* and the rest of the group had abandoned them.

We stopped, and then continued on our way. I got stuck in some barbed wire in the desert. The *coyote* kicked me, ripping my flesh to set me free. That was on my birthday, the night we got out of the desert. We ran to find the vehicle that would take us. A truck arrived and inside there was a harrow and a tied-up horse.[9] They crammed ninety people in our group in the back of that truck with the horse. The *coyote*, who had US papers, sat up front with the driver. We spent six long hours in the truck to get to Houston. The *coyote* told us that the family of the dead boy had been taken out of the desert by La Migra.[10]

We were taken to a warehouse where a lot of people were making phone calls asking for more money to send for other people. A young man from Olancho, Honduras, escaped. So they took us to another house, where I stayed for a day. The *coyote* called my mother, demanding more money. Finally, she paid them to bring me to San Francisco, where she was living. They loaded about nine of us in a van bound for California. There wasn't a checkpoint in New Mexico, so we kept going. We got to Los Angeles on December 17, 2013, where they dropped off most of the people. The only ones left were me, the dark-skinned girl, and a guy who wanted to go to San Jose. The *coyotes* demanded more money to take us to San Francisco. If we didn't pay, they threatened to cut off our heads and all kinds of horrible things. My mom said she'd give them another fifty dollars, and they agreed. They piled another eight people in a van and brought us to San Francisco. That was on December 18, 2013.

A TERRIBLE PANG IN MY POUNDING HEART

I was sitting in the back of the van when I first saw my mother. She was standing in front of the house where I now live. I felt a terrible

---

9. A harrow is a farming tool with spiked teeth used to break up soil.

10. See glossary.

pang in my pounding heart. The *coyote* ordered me to stay put while money was being exchanged in case the police showed up. But I ran out of the van, hugged my mom, and we began to cry. I still have an image in my mind of that moment. The dark-skinned girl hugged my three aunts standing by my mother. We were all crying.

The *coyote* was angry because I ran out of the van before he got paid. My mom told him to take his dirty money—and he left. I never saw them again. It was six in the morning, and my mom hadn't slept all night. I spent the whole day with my mom. We were happy.

Our relationship started off well, but then I met my stepdad, and he wasn't so nice. He looked like he was thinking, *Who is this other man here?* The first days were difficult. I told my mom I wanted to begin school. To find a school we went to the district office and prioritized certain ones. San Francisco International High School had many Latino students, so I chose that one. I thought it would be easier for me to communicate.

I began in ninth grade. I thought they'd start me off learning English word by word, but I began reading a book about Manzanar, the concentration camp for Japanese Americans during World War II. It was difficult for me. I'd go to school one day and then the next I didn't want to go. I didn't really know English. It was hard for me to write. Passing through Arizona, I'd gone into a McDonald's where nobody spoke Spanish. I told them I wanted a hamburger. It's all I knew how to say. They gave me a hamburger and that was it.

I was embarrassed at school because the other students all understood English. But they helped me a lot to practice speaking and writing. I had a good experience there because the teachers were prepared to help recent immigrants.

After the joy of the initial reunion wore off, I didn't want to live with my mom anymore. When I asked her why she'd left us, she didn't want to talk about it. It was hard for me to accept her silence.

My mother took me to a therapist, who had been assigned to me after referrals from the school and teachers, to help me understand the new changes in my life and to talk with someone about my past and my bad experiences. The therapist I was seeing told her about the Instituto Familiar de la Raza.[11] They said it would help me adjust to my new life. One day, a social worker named Joey from the Instituto called me out of class. He asked, "Do you want to talk with me about anything?" I told him no, I didn't want to talk. We had about five sessions, and I never spoke.

Then, when I was having a hard time, I got in touch with him. I started by telling him that I'd been raped. It was the first time I'd spoken about it. I was then sixteen. My mom didn't know anything about this. After lengthy discussions with the social worker, I trusted him, and I confided that I was gay. The social worker said he didn't know what advice to give me; he was only a social worker, not a therapist. So he put me in touch with a therapist, who I began seeing.

This whole process of telling my story began in 2014. That was the most difficult year. I was talking to many people—my doctor, my therapist, and the social worker—while trying to come to terms with it all. Eventually, I told my mom about one person raping me, not about all seven. Mom didn't believe me. She still doesn't accept what happened. It was my own family, so she doesn't know what to say. I don't speak with her about that anymore. She knows about it, but doesn't like talking about the subject.

Recently, I spoke with my uncle's wife and told her about everything that had occurred. One of the men who had abused me lived in my house at the same time as my aunt and uncle. She used to be at home all day then and noticed the changes with me: I used to be happy; then I didn't like to be touched. After I explained what had

---

11. Instituto Familiar de la Raza is a community-based mental health clinic and outreach program dedicated to helping Chicanos and Latin Americans in the San Francisco Bay Area.

actually happened, she told me, "It makes sense now. No wonder you were behaving so strangely. You didn't want anybody to wash your clothes—they probably had blood on them—and you were afraid of men touching you."

OUR EYES MET

That same year I also found the person who became my boyfriend. I met him on Facebook. He was also from Honduras, living in Oakland, and going to school. He began to text me. He's older than me. He works in San Leandro but lives in San Francisco.

I was meeting with my boyfriend and hiding our relationship from my mother. I felt bad about it. Finally, I decided to tell her. She was cooking. I asked her to come with me where we could talk in private. She sat on a sofa. "What do you want?" she asked. I said, "I'm gay." She pleaded, "But I want you to give me grandchildren!" I said, "I'm sorry, I can't." Silence hung in the air. She sighed and said, "I suspected it. Okay, I'm not going to ask you to leave the house, because I accept you as my son." I went to school the next day, still feeling hurt, and three friends helped me deal with it. Then I found out that my mother had called my aunt in Honduras and told her I was gay. The news spread to the rest of my family in Honduras. Everybody was talking about it, and I didn't want people to be talking about it. So I was mad about my mom violating my privacy. I told her, "I don't trust you." "Look, I'm human too," she said. I couldn't handle it. Some people were calling my boyfriend. Eventually, some relatives came around. They said, "We understand your situation." Even my father called me from Honduras. "I accept you," he said. "I love you because you are my son." But I still felt uncomfortable talking with him. My mom sticks up for me now. "If somebody insults gay people, I will always defend you," she tells me. For example, yesterday, my sister called me a *maricón* and my mom was so mad at her.[12] She was just joking, but my mother got angry.

One day, I was walking with my boyfriend at the flea market in Oakland when I saw my neighbor's son from Honduras—the one who'd raped me. Our eyes met. He became red in the face, acted strangely, and began to laugh. Then he took off in his car. I've never seen him again. I felt terrible. I wanted to run away. Then I realized I was safe. If he wanted to do something to me here, I could now call the police and report him. He'd go to jail. I told my boyfriend what had happened to me in Honduras. He said, "I believe you." Sometimes I have bad dreams about it, but I try to laugh it off.

Another of my abusers lives in San Francisco. I sent him a message: "Do you remember what you did to me?" He wrote back, "Yes, I remember what I did to you." He has a son in Honduras and he's got a wife. I found him on Facebook since everyone in my family has him as a "friend." My account wasn't private at that time. Now it is, and my phone number and everything is private. My abusers are all free at the moment. It's against the law in Honduras to abuse a child, but I never filed a report.

If I met a young boy here who'd been sexually abused and was living with the pain, I would tell him not to be scared. I'd say, "Your family will support you. You can get help. The only thing you should do is talk. You have to talk." In Honduras, I'd say, "Tell your family. Don't be scared to tell them. Tell the police." In Honduran prisons the other prisoners kill people who've done bad things to children. Before they kill them, they beat and abuse them. For me, that's okay. They deserve that. The worst thing you can do is abuse a child.

PEOPLE ARE MORE OPEN-MINDED HERE

In May 2014, I began to write a paper in school. It was difficult, but I managed to conjugate some verbs in English. Then I was invited to

---

12. An insulting Spanish term for gay people.

attend summer school at Balboa High School in San Francisco. I participated in a program for gay youth called LYRIC.[13] My English improved so that by tenth grade I understood quite a bit more. From then until now, I've received straight A's in all my subjects—even English!

The people at school here are much more open-minded and less ignorant than in Honduras. There's much more communication. There's more openness to expressing memories here. In Honduras there's a lot of racism and ignorance. Everything is criticized. If you say that you're gay in school, everyone will call you a "faggot," they'll call you names, bully and beat you. I used to get beaten by my peers. The teachers in Honduras gave me strange looks. Here the teachers are supportive and try to get me involved.

I'm a member of the school's Gay-Straight Alliance to support students who identify as LGBTQ and others who question their sexual orientation. We also include students who identify as straight allies. I feel so fortunate that San Francisco International High School created a club to support this community. My first time talking in public about my experience was scary, but sharing my knowledge has also made me feel proud. Also, I made a plan with a teacher to make a rainbow flag to put up in the school. I want the best for the club and I like to talk about projects, to offer new ideas that can help the club. They don't have programs like this back in Honduras.

I don't see having children in my own family plans. I don't want to have to care for children in my home. But I want to protect children and work for them. I want to stay focused on helping others. I want to apply to UC Berkeley and maybe San Francisco State to continue my studies. I also won a scholarship from an organization in downtown San Francisco. I applied, and they gave me $7,000 for high school and college.

---

13. LYRIC is an organization for lesbian, gay, bisexual, transgender, queer, and questioning youth based in San Francisco whose mission is "to build community and inspire social change."

ASYLUM

When I was fifteen, in high school, I worried a lot about being deported to Honduras. I wondered, *How can I stay permanently in the United States?* First, I looked for help at an immigration lawyer's office in San Francisco but was told that the US government wouldn't accept my application because I didn't have evidence of abuse, police reports and such things. I was told that, without official documents from Honduras, it's as if it had never happened. I tried with other organizations too. I felt disappointed but was still unwilling to give up.

My younger sisters had gotten help from Centro Legal de la Raza. They'd crossed the border as unaccompanied minors in 2014, during the big influx of children, and were caught by La Migra. They were held for a while, then released. An attorney at Centro Legal de la Raza helped them get legal residency. I made an appointment with her. She listened to my story and wrote it down. When I told her I lacked police records from Honduras, she told me that my word would suffice as evidence. I applied for asylum—first, because my dad used to beat me, and second, for everything else that I'd gone through.

Applying for amnesty was a relatively quick process for me, about four months. We sent in papers in February 2015 and by March they asked for my fingerprints. By April they wanted an interview. I met with an official from US immigration who listened to my story to confirm that everything was true. My lawyer and a translator were with me for the interview. The interview lasted about an hour. Although it had been difficult for me to tell my story before, it was no longer difficult at the asylum hearing. By then I'd told my story to two therapists. I'd also spoken with the social worker. I returned to the US immigration office on May 5, 2015. Everyone congratulated me because I was given political asylum and then I got my Social Security card.

I SPOKE UP FOR HUMAN RIGHTS

I applied for the ACLU Summer Institute at Georgetown University.[14] They asked me to write about an issue in my community. I chose to discuss immigration issues, especially those involving children. Here's part of what I wrote: "My experience of childhood sexual and domestic abuse has shaped my dreams to become a lawyer to defend victims and fight for children's rights around the world. My immigration lawyer was a role model for me because she listened to my experiences. I want to continue studying to help children feel protected by the law, so they can believe they will not be hurt by anyone." I was accepted and we traveled to Washington, DC. At the conference, I spoke up for human rights and children's rights. As we walked around Capitol Hill, I saw Latinos participating in an immigration protest at the US Supreme Court. We talked with the protesters. Later we saw ourselves on the news!

I want to help my mom get US citizenship. I've focused on my goals and now I'm figuring out how to fulfill them. I'm more involved in school and completing all my work. My mentality changed quickly after I began to speak out in public; I realized what my dream is. I want to be an attorney in criminology and defend the rights of children. I want to protect those who've been sexually abused or mistreated by their parents. One day, I might even like to work with the Honduran government to help children, but they'll have to follow the rules of the US government, not simply agree and take money.

We call Gabriel one morning in September 2017 to see how he is doing. Before we get a chance to ask him any follow-up questions, he jumps right in.

I'm a freshman at UC Berkeley! I'm living in a dorm on campus and I go home on weekends to stay with my mother and boyfriend,

---

14. ACLU is the American Civil Liberties Union.

who are living at her house in San Francisco. I'm taking classes in English, majoring in social welfare with a minor in public policy. In four years, I'll take the LSAT exam for law school. I work at San Francisco International High School, translating and helping students study. My mother, boyfriend, and family support me, which makes me super-happy.

JHONY CHUC

AGE AT CROSSING: 17
BORN IN: Chicujal, Alta Verapaz, Guatemala
INTERVIEWED IN: Mexicali, Baja California, Mexico
in transit

We meet Jhony at Grupo de Ayuda Para el Migrante in Mexicali, the capital of Baja California, on a summer day in 2016, with the temperature breaking 115 degrees. He's sitting by himself on a bench eating a steaming bowl of chicken stew provided by the shelter. Due to an upsurge in Haitian and West African migration, we are the only Spanish speakers in a room full of the cadences of French and other languages. Jhony wears a sleeveless Superman shirt and a red cap that he removes to wipe the sweat off his brow. He holds his backpack, his only possession, close to his chest with one hand and with the other spoons the stew. The heat makes him drowsy, he says, and the stew isn't great. The

roar of industrial-sized fans meant to cool the moist air of the shelter,
a converted old movie theater, makes conversing difficult. We head to
a nearby café, where Jhony sips an Italian soda through a straw while
he starts sharing his story with us. He taps the table as he speaks and
looks at his cellphone from time to time, waiting to hear from a friend
who also plans to cross the border. Like Jhony, many migrants work and
save thousands of dollars to make the journey, only to be assaulted and
robbed, leaving them desperate for money to finish it. Jhony's narrative
is recorded literally on the border, where he must make a decision about
whether to llevar la mochila—*"carry the backpack"—an expression*
used in reference to carrying drugs into the United States.

IT'S BEAUTIFUL IN CHICUJAL

I belong to the Indigenous people of Guatemala. We speak our own
language. I am Q'eqchi' and that's also the name of our language.[1]
Spanish is my fifth tongue. I learned it when I was ten—I sometimes
still have trouble speaking in Spanish. I didn't even know "yes" or
"no" in Spanish when I was little.

People call me Jhony. I was born in 1993 in the state of Alta Verapaz, in the district of San Juan Chamelco, in a village called Chicujal. It's a village of about two hundred people in the mountainous
highlands of north-central Guatemala. It's beautiful in Chicujal. The
weather is pleasant. There's a lot of green forest. There's a river where
the water is blue and cool—we'd dive into it to escape the heat. We
never had to carry water from afar because there was a spring right
by my house. It's very different here in Mexicali. Everything is desert
here, and it's very hot. I don't really like it here.

I'm proud that I learned the Spanish I have. I learned it on the
street. I have friends back at home who can't speak Spanish; they only

---

1. Q'eqchi' is an indigenous Mayan language spoken by the Q'eqchi' people in
Central Guatemala. See glossary.

speak our language. I know I don't speak Spanish 100 percent correctly. There are still words that I can't understand. But those of us who can speak different languages have an easier time learning English. Q'eqchi' is one of the official languages of Guatemala. I learned to read and write it at school. I also learned to speak K'iche', which is another native language of Guatemala. It's very different from my language. I learned it on the street as well. People from a different region spoke it. I also learned Poqomchi' on the street. I like English. I wanted to study it in Guatemala. I never could. I would also like to improve my Spanish. Some people really judge me because of my Spanish. It annoys me that they don't understand it's my fifth language.

In my home region most people work in agriculture. There are a few people who are able to get out of that life and begin careers as professionals. They get masters or doctorates. But most of us work in the fields. We grow radishes, cucumbers, cilantro, beans, corn. I'll be honest with you, for the people who live there, that life is good. But for someone like me who's been away, it's different. I saw the things other people had. It opened my mind and eyes. I saw a different path. I saw that people in the city were better off financially. They had their businesses, houses, and cars. I don't care about luxury, but I want to help my family. I want to have a business so that my family can work. I also want to keep studying to be somebody in this life.

WE DIDN'T LIVE IN MISERY

My father's name was Angel. He worked as a farmer and raised cattle. Our life was good, more or less. We had a modest but comfortable lifestyle. We weren't rich, but we weren't poor. We didn't live in misery. We had a house and owned our property. My dad had gotten ahead in life; he'd managed to work and own a home. After he made some money for himself, he began to go after other women. Or the women came after him.

It all fell apart because he went chasing after other women. He got into that, fell in love with a woman, and left us. Little by little his business fell apart. We were young then. I must have been five when it all started to fall apart.

He didn't provide for us to go to school. My brothers and I had to start working to keep our studies going. We were four brothers and one sister. I'm the youngest of the family. We all had to work to have food. We were little so we couldn't earn a lot. We made about ten quetzales, one dollar and fifty cents, a day. My mom made money by making *huipiles* and other typical traditional clothes.[2] She wears those kinds of clothes. She dresses like that to this day. Her name is Monica. She's a homemaker. We'd work outside in the fields while she stayed at home. She'd take care of us and had to sew to have money to support us. There wasn't always food at the house, but when there was my mom would make us stews, beef stew, or *kak'ik*, which is a typical turkey stew from our region. My mom raised chickens, turkeys, and pigs. Sometimes she'd sell them too.

I have very sad memories of my childhood. I must have been about ten when I left my home and went out on the street looking for work. I began selling plastic bottles of orange juice on the streets of Cobán. Cobán is the capital of the state, the big city of the region. I would put all my money together and go home on certain days to give it to my mom. These are moments in my life I don't like to remember. I had no choice but to go out and look for work because I needed to go to school. My mom had been helping me out with my studies with what little she earned. I'd finished primary school, but to continue on to the higher level, to secondary, you have to pay. But we had no money.

---

2. Huipiles are loose-fitting cotton blouses, traditional garments commonly worn by Indigenous women. They are hand-embroidered with brilliant colors, exquisite patterns, and symbols.

On top of this, we were thrown out of our home. We became divided as brothers. My two oldest brothers, Chico and Rony, stayed with my dad. They didn't care about my dad's actions, only his money. The youngest three—my brother Wilson, my sister Alicia, and I—went with my mom. We were the ones who suffered.

We had to start working hard to buy a plot of land and then build a house. The house my mom is currently in is the one we bought. My brother, my mom, and I paid for it through sweat and hard work.

A BURNING RAGE

Around 2006, when I was thirteen, my dad was found hanged in front of his girlfriend's house. He'd lost his family by that point and had problems with the other woman. He had no way out, didn't know what to do. So maybe he took his own life. He was about thirty-five.

I fell into a deep depression. When I think back on this time, remembering what I've lived through, I'm filled with rage. I had a burning rage inside of me and at the time I had some terrible thoughts running through my mind. I was angry at my dad, even though he was already dead. I was angry at the woman's family. It was her fault that he took his life. It was because of her that he abandoned us, that we had to leave our studies. This was where my fury came from.

When I was about fifteen and had saved some money, I began to sell oranges and other types of fruit on the street. I bought myself one of those big tricycles that I could load with fruit and move around the city. Around Christmastime I would sell apples, grapes—I was making a good living. By the time I was seventeen I was making one hundred quetzales a day.[3] I could buy myself a few things and support my family.

---

3. Roughly $13 US in 2009.

After working for a while I'd made a few friends from other towns who'd crossed to the United States. They'd come back and tell me that there was money to be made there. I could see all the things that my friends had. One had even brought back to Cobán a woman he met in the United States. All these things caught my attention.

In 2010, I decided to migrate to the United States and crossed into Mexico. Back then, there weren't as many Mexican migration agents. Even though I was underage, riding on the bus, I was never caught. There were checkpoints, but the agents saw me next to somebody and probably assumed I was related to the people next to me. They never asked me for documentation, which I didn't have. When I left Guatemala as a boy that first time I didn't know anything; I was only seventeen. I didn't know how the roads were, about the desert, or the way the cartels controlled everything. I thought it'd be like how it was in my country. I only knew about the Beast.[4]

I arrived in Arriaga by bus and began to ask around for information.[5] I said I was a migrant and asked about the train station location and schedule. It's not easy getting on the Beast. You have to watch out for the migration agents; you have to run after the Beast to grab on and hold on. You have to find a way to do it in one motion or else the wind current will suck you in and pull you under the Beast. You can die or have a leg or a head cut off. It can cut you in two.

Already back then, the mafias were present on the trains—like the Zetas, cartels that kidnapped people. If you said you had family in Guatemala or you had people in the United States who were going to help you, you'd be kidnapped. They'd take your money. If nobody paid for you, they'd kill you. That's why along the way you can't talk. You can make some friends, but you have to say that you have no help and you're on your own.

---

4. See glossary.

5. Arriaga is in the state of Chiapas.

I was on my own, but I had no fear because I didn't know what fear was. When I got to Ixtepec I went to a *casa de migrantes* and took a quick shower.[6] The casas de migrantes always took migrants in. Those people deserve to be in heaven because they truly are good people. I jumped on another Beast. After Ixtepec I wasn't able to shower again until I got to San Luis Potosí, three days later. You can imagine, I'd been wearing the same clothes for three days.

At Ixtepec I got on another Beast that brought me to Medias Aguas, Veracruz. Then I got on another Beast that took me to Tierra Blanca. From there I went to Orizaba on another Beast, then on yet another from there to Mexico City. You can't imagine how cold it was in Orizaba. You ride on top of the Beast and are totally exposed. I had no coat. I almost died from the cold. I remember that in Orizaba we got off the train and kind strangers gave us coffee and bread so that we could continue on our way.[7]

Once I got to Mexico City everything was fine. I didn't get a good sense of the beauty of Mexico City because the train only passes around the perimeter of the city. I couldn't tell what kind of place it was. On our way to Guanajuato in the afternoon, we came to a stop-light. Our train stopped in its tracks for this light. There was another train coming from the opposite direction toward us. It was empty except for two men in blue uniforms on top of it. They appeared to be federal agents, but their uniforms were missing the patches, and they had no badges. They were carrying nine-millimeter pistols. The train was slowly moving toward us.

The two men on top began to fire at us. At the first shot we all jumped off the train and began to run. The two men did as well.

---

6. A casa de migrantes is a migrant house. See glossary.

7. Ixtepec is in the southwestern Mexican state of Oaxaca, just north of the Guatemalan border. Veracruz, on the Gulf of Mexico, is 441 kilometers from Ixtepec. Orizaba is 132 kilometers west of Veracruz, and it's another 276 kilometers west to Mexico City.

They were about ten meters from me. They were aiming and firing their guns to kill me. I could hear the bullets ricochet off the train cars. *Ping! Ping! Ping!* I was short—well, I still am—so I was able to duck beneath our train and run out the other side into the fields. I scraped my forehead on the train car as I fled under it. I left a chunk of my skin stuck to that car. We kept running and running, but they kept firing at us. I could barely run. There were about fifteen of us who fled. They didn't manage to kill any of us.

Later, we came back around and saw that their train had left and they were gone. Our train had begun to move so we got back on it. That event left me traumatized. I'd never heard a gunshot before. Of our group on the train, I was probably the most scared because I was a minor. We didn't know why they shot at us. After we ran away we began to ask ourselves who they were. Some said they were federal agents; some said they were Zetas. We never found out. I don't think they were agents because we weren't doing anything wrong. They never said a word. They only shot at us.

That day of the shooting we stayed on the train and got to Guanajuato, and then the next night we arrived at San Luis Potosí. I stayed at a casa de migrante in San Luis for one day and was able to eat and shower. Then I went to Saltillo, Coahuila, where I stayed for a while.[8] In that moment I didn't feel anything about the shooting. I forgot about it at the time. I continued on my journey. The situation with my dad's death is what kept me going. In Saltillo, I stayed at a casa de migrantes called Belén. They helped me out. I was given clothes, shoes, and food. I could stay there however long I needed to recuperate—I was in bad shape. I'd made the trip in fifteen days. All the way from my house to Saltillo—all on the Beast.

I stayed in Saltillo for about six months. There I worked at a factory that processed recycled materials. I processed and organized

8. Guanajuato and San Luis Potosí are states in central Mexico. Saltillo is to the north and just west of Monterrey.

different types of materials. It was a large factory that collected cans and all kinds of plastics. I would work my way through the different materials and sort them. I earned eight hundred or nine hundred pesos a week.[9] I was able to save some money with that job.

I'd made some friends at that point—Central Americans like me who worked at the factory—and they told me that if you reached the border without any money, you'd be kidnapped by the cartel. You would have to pay them $500. If you paid it, they'd let you go. That's why I stayed in Saltillo, to save up the $500 in case I was kidnapped.

From Saltillo I took the Beast to Piedras Negras. That's where the problems arose. Mexican immigration agents caught me and took me off the train. They asked me for my documentation and what I was doing there. It was obvious to them that I was traveling on the Beast illegally. They deported me to Guatemala. That's when I began to get sick. My hands would start to shake suddenly. Any little thing, a noise, startles me now. I never went to go see a psychologist. I almost lost the ability to speak. I was always afraid. I couldn't sleep by myself. I didn't understand what was happening to me.

Back in Guatemala, I began to think differently about my father. To start with, I realized that my dad had gone looking for trouble. In time I began to mature and analyze the situation. He could have left that woman and sought us out. I still don't know if he took his own life or was killed. I let it go.

FEAR WAS IN MY BLOOD

When I was deported, I went back to my town and told my mom about all that had happened to me. I was still underage, so I waited to leave. I began to work and stayed there from 2011 to 2016. Then once I turned eighteen I moved to the capital, Guatemala City. I

9. Eight hundred pesos was roughly $761 US in 2010.

didn't spend money on anything but my studies. I saved almost $4,000—a large sum in Guatemala, about 30,000 or 35,000 quetzales.[10] In the beginning of 2016, on April 15, I quit my job with the intention of going back to the United States, or to Mexico. I took up my studies again to finish my high school degree. With the money I'd saved working in Mexico, I was able to buy a plot of land in Guatemala.

I began to work at a maintenance company and kept going to school as well. I would clean and fix things. I did paint jobs. So, I continued my studies, paid for them, and saved money.

Over time, the traumas I'd experienced in Mexico began to affect me more severely. I had to break up with a girlfriend because of my nerves. I also stopped studying once I was back because of this condition. I couldn't concentrate on anything and felt ill all the time. The only thing I kept doing was working. I began to think about why I was feeling this way. I came to the conclusion that it was because of the death of my father and being shot at on the train. The fear left me traumatized. Fear was in my blood.

I sacrificed a lot while I was working. I didn't go out to the movies or anything, though sometimes I'd go out with friends. I'd tell myself, *Each one with his own money.* If we went out, I'd only spend money on myself. I wouldn't spend money on my friends. So a lot of my friends didn't like it; they thought I was cheap. I didn't care. If I went out with female friends, it was the same. I'd tell them, "Okay, let's go out, but I'm trying to save my money." I wouldn't tell them I was thinking about leaving even though I already had that in mind. I didn't want to tell them. I'd tell them I needed my money and that's it.

I didn't tell my friends I planned on leaving Guatemala because they might bring it up later. I'm the kind of person that if I plan something, I don't want to get ahead of myself. I didn't want to hear their comments in case my plan failed and I was still there. I

---

10. Thirty thousand quetzales was roughly $3,931 US in 2016.

preferred to keep it private. If I didn't make it to the United States, and had to go back, I wouldn't have to hear anything because they wouldn't know.

My mom kept telling me, "Don't leave. Look at what happened when you left." I came back to Guatemala in a bad state. My mom didn't want this for me. But I'm back here now. To this day I haven't seen or lived through anything like that again. To be honest, I'm still not 100 percent. I'm not well. I'm a very nervous person. I used to be very strong. Now people ask me why I'm so afraid.

I'm older now and I'm aware of the things that I need. I need a home, a job, and I want to be a dad. All of those thoughts came together. I thought, *I can't do these things here.* I made many sacrifices. I didn't give my mom money. I had a right to vacation days, but instead of taking them I'd keep working and earn double the money. So I kept saving all my money. The only thing I'd spend money on was my schooling. Once I had finished, I wanted to continue to university, but I couldn't afford it. I didn't earn enough. I thought, *What do I do?*

Having saved all that money, I thought it better to leave the country. I had saved so I could pay a *coyote* to bring me into the United States. I quit my job, and after preparing, I decided to attempt the trip to the United States for the second time.

IF YOU DON'T HAVE A CODE, THEY KIDNAP YOU

After five years in Guatemala, I came to Mexico again. It wasn't like it had been before. It's harder now. I came back to Arriaga, but guess what? There was no train. The Beast only showed up every ten days. I went back to the same casa de migrantes that I'd stayed at in 2010. They only allowed me to stay for one night this time. They were sending people back out because there were too many people.

I didn't know what to do since I didn't want to spend my money. I didn't have a lot. I didn't have a choice so I began to walk. I followed the railway from Arriaga to Unión Hidalgo, in Oaxaca. Imagine that. It was something like four hundred kilometers. I walked and walked for days with a fellow *chapín* and three Hondurans.[11]

We had no possessions. All we had with us was water. When we went by a city we'd go out and ask for food if we were hungry. We'd get a bit of food that way. People would give what they had from their homes. There were no casas de migrantes from Arriaga to Unión Hidalgo. We'd knock on doors and ask for a taco. We did that for three days until my feet were covered in blisters and I could walk no more. I ran out of water actually, before getting to Unión Hidalgo. It was a desert, nowhere to get water. I almost died.

I'd been robbed one kilometer outside of Unión Hidalgo. Just before entering the city, five guys came out with guns and machetes and took our possessions. They took the bit of money that we had, along with my good shoes. They took a thousand pesos from me. They take everything. Those sons of bitches leave you naked.

I'd wait until nighttime to walk. I only walked at night. At Ixtepec there is a casa de migrantes. Once there I got some medication for my feet and some rehydration salts. The staff there told us that the Instituto Nacional de Migración was awarding visas to any person who had been the victim of a crime in Mexico. We reported that crime in Ixtepec, Oaxaca. Based on that, the Instituto could give us visas. I had to wait for two months in the casa in Ixtepec for the paperwork to go through. We had food and shelter there. It was good. The visa would help me out a lot, I thought.

Then, on July 12, 2016, they gave me my visa. It takes a while for them to complete their investigation. They took us to the place where we were robbed. They had to verify all our facts. They gave me a criminal background check to make sure I hadn't committed crimes back in Guatemala. After this process, once I had my visa, I left Ixtepec and went to Monterrey. I was happy. Imagine! I had access—no

---

11. A *chapín* is a person from Guatemala. See glossary.

fear. I could just show my visa to the migration officers. I spent one
week in a casa de migrantes in Monterrey. I called my contact, the
coyote, and he told me to go to Nuevo Laredo. So I took a first-class
bus to Nuevo Laredo. During the trip, immigration took me off the
bus, even though I had my visa with me. They locked me in their
little office at the checkpoint. The officer asked me, "Where are you
going?" I answered, "To Nuevo Laredo." He screamed, "No, you son
of a bitch, tell me the truth! I need the truth!" These were Mexican
immigration officers—they were working with the cartel. I told him
the truth: "I'm going to cross to the United States." He answered,
"That's what we wanted to know." They let me go, but not before
telling me that my visa was worthless. He said that if he wanted to he
could rip up my visa.

When I got off the bus at the terminal, Los Zetas grabbed me.
They asked for the *clave* signifying that we had paid protection
money. The *coyote* gives you your code over the phone. If you say the
code when you arrive, then the mareros let you go. If you don't have a
code, they kidnap you.[12]

They knew how to identify me because they work with the immigration officers. The *coyote* didn't report me to the immigration
officers or the cartel: that's why Los Zetas came down on me. I think
the immigration officers called the cartel and told them what I was
wearing and where I was sitting. I was stopped at a checkpoint on the
road by immigration officers. They were trying to put me in a pickup
truck. But I dialed the *coyote* and told him my *clave* identifying me
as his client. I said, "They're trying to kidnap me." He told me, "Put
them on the phone." They grabbed the phone from me and began to

---

12. South of the US border, criminal organizations, primarily Los Zetas, demand
prepaid protection money from *coyotes* to allow migrants to pass though their
territory. Some *coyotes* have given migrants a *clave*, or code number, to identify
them as customers who have prepaid for the journey. Because of this, the prices
of *coyotes* have also increased significantly.

speak in code to each other. I couldn't understand at all what they were saying. They talked, then let me go.

TRYING TO KILL ME PSYCHOLOGICALLY

I got to the US border and paid the extortionist *coyotes* $2,500. I had to wait for five days to cross. Five days went by, and they took me to Laredo, Texas. We crossed the Río Bravo to the US side by swimming across.[13] We walked for three hours toward the city to the spot where we were supposed to get picked up. While we waited for the ride, US immigration agents showed up. So, there you go, back to Guatemala. The *coyote* got away though. He managed to escape because he knew the place. He knew where to hide. He was with us when the border patrol came down on us. There were seven of us in total, including the *coyote*, and we all scattered. We ran, but we got caught.

The US immigration officers were very racist. They were trying to kill me psychologically. They take you and lock you in a cold room, *la hielera*.[14] You're given a plastic blanket and kept there for five days. They give you a little juice and a cookie. They wake you up at 3 a.m. for a goddamn juice. They keep you sleep deprived. We couldn't tell if it was day or night, didn't know the day or the time. They'd give us a slice of bread with ham. That traumatized me, and now I can't eat that. Everyone they catch is kept together in a cold cell. It was a cement cell with a door. There were about fifty of us there, including all of us from my group.

After we got caught we were deported back to our home countries. There were three Mexicans, one Honduran, and a fellow Guatemalan with me in my group. The Honduran got to stay because they couldn't fill a plane and had to wait for more deportees to Hon-

---

13. In Mexico, the Rio Grande is referred to as the Río Bravo. See glossary.

14. See glossary.

duras. But they caught enough Guatemalans that they deported us in seven days.

It really is a sad event because they treat people so badly. We aren't animals. I know that I'm entering the country illegally, but they have no right to treat me that way—to toss a cookie at me, toss a juice. We're human beings. Also, I know perfectly well that the United States is dependent on many of us. You're not going to see a US citizen cutting lettuce or doing stoop labor in the hot sun. Yet they treat us so badly.

The US immigration officers, they're almost all Latinos. They're the children of Hondurans, Guatemalans, and Mexicans. They're so awful. Why don't they think, *My family could have suffered in this way*? We're treated like criminals. They chain us up and load us onto a bus. We're handcuffed from our feet to our waist to our hands. We're not criminals! That's how they load us on the plane, shackled. What if the plane went down? How are we going to swim if we hit the ocean? How will we put on that little oxygen mask? We flew out of Port Isabel, Texas, to Guatemala City. It was about a three-hour flight. They think we'll jump from the plane to stay in the United States? Don't they use their heads? I'm not going to jump out of the plane just to stay. Why don't they unshackle us once the airplane door is closed?

You have no idea how much anger I felt when I got caught and deported. I cried out of anger. To start, I'd sacrificed my mother's needs. I didn't give her money. I didn't know if she had food or clothes. I did hear from my brothers that she was sick. When I could, I'd give a bit, but the rest would come from somewhere else. That's what hurt the most. It's a pain I'll never forget. The day I was caught—I hate that day. I hate it with all my being. I sensed that with the money already paid, the *coyote* wouldn't care whether I made it across. And that's how it happened. It's been a month and fifteen days since I was deported from the United States on August 15.

I called the *coyote*, and I told him, "I've been deported back to Guatemala." At first, he said, "No problem. Come back over here. Once you're near, I'll tell you what to do." So, I came back over to Mexico. I took a bus to Monterrey, but I had no money so I worked a bit there. I worked at a sporting clothes factory. I pressed clothes with different images that clients asked for. I would move the clothes so that they sat just right in the press. It's not a press like an iron press. When I first showed up to inquire about the job, I thought I'd be ironing clothes, like a grandma. I had no idea.

I found that job by asking around. Over there you just have to inquire at different places and ask what requirements they have. Some ask for your Mexican social security information and if you don't have it, there's no way. But the guy I was working for didn't even ask for my name. He'd pay me 1,200 pesos under the table in cash. I did that in Monterrey for two weeks. I liked the job, but I knew that if I stayed any longer, I would get stuck there. I thought, *If I get a girlfriend here, I'll end up staying.*

Also, I'd already paid the *coyote* $3,100. I paid him $2,500 first in Nuevo Laredo. Then, in Laredo, Texas, my brother sent him another $600 when I was detained. The *coyote* asked him for that money because my brother couldn't get in touch with me. They ripped me off. The *coyote* told him I'd made it to the United States.

I called the *coyote* and told him I was in Monterrey. I asked him to tell me what to do because I was ready to go to Laredo. "No," he said, "you have to give me another thousand dollars." I told him, "I don't have anybody in the United States to help with more money. The money that I gave you was all I had." I told him exactly how much I had left. Then he told me, "The cartel has raised their fees, so you have to pay more." He needed more money to give to the Zetas.

Where was I going to get more money? I earned 1,200 pesos a week and had to pay for food and rent. At the end of the week I only had two or three hundred pesos left. This is what ran through my mind. I couldn't save that money there. I spoke with him again on Monday when I was in Monterrey, but he didn't give me another chance. I have no way to get a thousand dollars. So I made the decision to come to Mexicali. It's my only and last option. Actually, I do have one more option, which is what a lot of people do, but it's even more illegal. Many people enter the United States by "taking the backpack."

I've been asked many times to carry the backpack, you know. Carry some twenty-five kilos and get a pass from the cartel. On top of that I'd get $1,000 or $1,500. It's not something I want though. Many people have died doing this. You walk ten or fifteen days with the backpack. If you run out of water or food, you die there in the desert. It's hard walking through the desert, let alone with a load.

I look older now from all the stress. I'm twenty-three, but people think I'm twenty-seven. The stress is eating at me, killing me. Right now, I'm planning to cross on my own. I don't have money to pay a *coyote*. They charge a lot here—it's $4,000 and up. I'm sure I'll make it across. I won't give up. Everything I've gone through pushes me forward. And I'm not going to carry the backpack. I have morals that won't allow it. I plan on being a dad someday. When I am, I won't do what mine did. It angers me when I see fathers leave their children.

At the end of our conversation, Jhony reads a text message, holding it up for us to see, and with a tense smile tells us that his friend has decided to "carry the backpack."

NOEMI TUN

AGE AT CROSSING: 16
BORN IN: San Marcos, Guatemala
INTERVIEWED IN: Boston, Massachusetts

The video image on the computer screen is fuzzy, transmitted via Skype from the East Coast to the West Coast. In a wide-angle view, we see a young woman walk into a dimly lit room with a lively little boy of about two toddling behind her. It's March 2016, and Noemi is talking with us from her immigration lawyer's office in Boston. She sits down on a folding chair, smiles briefly at us, and then opens her arms, whispering in Spanish, "Rafaelito, come to Mamá." The little round-cheeked boy with bright eyes, wearing shorts and a T-shirt, scrambles onto his mother's lap. As we introduce ourselves to Noemi, she proudly introduces us to her son. "Hello, Rafaelito," we say, waving our hands. He stares confusedly at us onscreen and hugs his mother protectively.

We speak with Noemi in Spanish, her second language after her native Mam. In the 1980s, the region where her grandparents were born was the site of brutal massacres of Mayas by the Guatemalan military with covert support from the US government.[1] In the 2000s, Mexican drug gangs moved in, cultivating poppies to feed the growing US market for opioids. The forced displacement of native farmers provoked extreme fighting over access to land and water. A feud developed between two villages, with disastrous consequences for Noemi's family.

As she begins to recount the descent into internecine warfare, restless Rafaelito wriggles free from his mother's arms and runs to his aunt Glaisa, who fled to the United States with Noemi in the wake of violent attacks from strangers armed with clubs and guns.

LITTLE BIRDS WOULD START TO SING
WHEN THE RAIN STOPPED

I'll tell you, the place where I used to live was very beautiful. There were many trees and animals, little birds, rivers, and a lake that passed near my house. It was very green, and the little birds would start to sing when the rain stopped. Sometimes it was also foggy and cold. There were plantations of potato and corn—a little bit of everything. The landscape in Guatemala is beautiful, but it was not safe to live there.

I was born in November 1995 in San Marcos, Guatemala, but we moved soon after to a village called Finca Las Brisas.[2] My father and grandparents spoke the Mam language at home, but I learned Spanish in school. My parents grew beans, potatoes, and corn, in their *milpas*.[3] Growing up, I always loved nature. My father would teach me about

---

1. For more on the 1980s massacres, see "Historical Timeline."

2. Finca Las Brisas is a village that developed around a plantation.

3. *Milpa* has two senses: the system of farming used throughout Mesoamerica in which trees are cleared out to grow maize with other crops, and the field in which it is grown. Derived from a Nahuatl word, it roughly translates as "to the field."

how to use the plants as medicine. For example, there is a really tall tree called the eucalyptus. It is very beautiful. I wonder if they are still there. We would collect its leaves, boil them in water, and drink the tea to cure stomach pains.

One night, strangers from the other village came to our village, beat my father badly, and threatened to kill him. They cut him on the legs with knives. There were a lot of men attacking him. He couldn't defend himself. I didn't see this happen, but I saw him right after when he was all bloody. I was about eight at the time, and I don't remember the incident very well. My mom was also physically attacked when she tried to defend him. They punched her and threatened her. The attackers were Ladinos who spoke Spanish well.[4] She was terrified after that and wanted to flee. That's why they came to the United States and left us in the care of our grandmother.

I remember living in my grandmother's house. It was made of brick, with a sheet metal roof and an indoor kitchen. There was just one bedroom, and my grandmother and grandfather, my two siblings, and me—five of us at any one time—we all shared it. We were really young when my parents left us in 2004. I was eight years old. My little brother, Alberto, was seven, and my little sister, Glaisa, was six years old. At that age, I didn't understand why my father had to go away. But I do remember what he told me when he left: "I'm going to the other side to send you something, to send you money so you can have the best life." It wasn't like he could say, *Don't worry. I'm with you.*

My parents were now far away, but they sent money to my grandmother. I didn't have to support my little brother and sister physically or give them food. But when they needed somebody to hug them, I gave them affection. When my sister started school, I walked with her because she was little. It took us about half an hour. Sometimes we had

---

4. Ladinos are non-indigenous Guatemalans who may be mestizos—mixed Spanish-Amerindians or non-Mayan-speaking natives. Most Ladinos speak Spanish fluently, in contrast to Noemi's family. See glossary.

shoes, sometimes not. I think that was because my father was having trouble finding a job in America. But we didn't go hungry. We ate well. My grandfather planted maize and potato. He got sick with bronchitis and died when I was about nine years old. Afterwards, we stayed with my grandmother, but she couldn't support us or give us enough food.

PEOPLE FOUGHT OVER LAND AND WATER

One day, when my parents were still in San Marcos, our neighbors told us that we were supposed to fight against the bad men from the other village. Our neighbors had formed a small group of about six people, and they wanted us to be part of that group, but we didn't want to get involved. So we didn't join that group. To explain what happened to our family, I have to give you some background. Where I lived in Guatemala, people fought over land and water. The people of Ixchiguán didn't want the people of Tajumulco to drink their water, and the people from Tajumulco didn't want the people from Ixchiguán to drink their water.[5] They killed each other with pistols and Bowie knives. This feud had already gone on for thirty-five years, my dad told me. The *narcos* also fire guns on people who guard their *fincas*.[6] They use most of the water for this profit-seeking business while the people from both towns fight each other for what is left.

The fighting over water and land continued after my parents were gone, for the next several years as I was growing up. When the shooting would start, we'd run away to sleep in other people's houses. And my grandmother, because she was already old, couldn't defend

---

5. Many of the people who grow the poppies in San Marcos live in Mexico, and since San Marcos is right on the border, they cross back and forth easily. The narcotics traffickers, known as *narcos*, have stolen the water from both villages to grow poppies for heroin. Afraid of the *narcos*, the villagers have turned against each other in the struggle for water.

6. A *finca* is a ranch or rural property.

us. One day they were shooting at the house where we used to live and we—my grandmother, siblings, and I—ran and took refuge in another house for a week. That time they killed a man. I didn't see it with my own eyes, but I went to his funeral. We came back home after a week. They would fight every week, every month —there was no day when they did not fight. I was really afraid for myself and for my siblings. I was now about sixteen years old, and my brother, Alberto, was about fifteen. They threatened him, so he had to flee to the United States. That left my grandmother, my sister, and me alone.

They burned down our house and shot at us. They poured gasoline on the house and lit it with a match. I don't know if they were Mexican drug traffickers or men from the other town. They wear masks. They had come twice before and attacked my grandmother once. When they came to the house the second time, she tried to escape but fell when she was running, and they beat her. My uncles told me about it. They came at night, and she couldn't run fast enough. The night they set our house on fire, my sister and I fled and hid with our *abuelita* in the woods.[7] The bullets didn't reach us. From where we were hiding, we could only see the smoke rising up above our house. The woods were filled with smoke. It didn't matter to them that we were children. They wanted to hurt us, kill us. In the three months that they were threatening my grandmother, many people were killed in this fighting.

Because we didn't want to join the fighting, I grabbed my little sister and we ran to a mountain far away from there, so they couldn't catch us. My grandmother was too old to run with us. We kept running for about forty-five minutes, and then we hid in the mountains. We slept in a barn where the goats and sheep slept. I was really afraid, especially for my sister because she was a bit younger. After hiding for two days, we came back to our grandmother's house. The people had stopped fighting and we stayed with my grandmother for about two

---

7. *Abuelita* is diminutive for grandmother in Spanish.

months. We were in a very difficult situation because the group kept threatening to kill our parents if they came back. So my sister and I decided to go live with them in the United States. I told my grandmother, *"Abuelita,* we've got to get out of here." At first she didn't want us to leave, but then she raised her gray head and said, "Fine, go. It's for the best so those people don't do you any harm." At that time I was about sixteen, and my sister was maybe fourteen. I'd only attended school until fifth grade. I'd worked in the village and saved up something like five hundred quetzales for the journey with my sister.[8]

We didn't tell our parents that we were coming to America.

WE SUFFERED A LOT TO COME TO THIS COUNTRY

So we came with these *coyotes.* We walked for two days from Guatemala to Mexico. Then they put us in vans, like ten people at a time. We were traveling in a group of around thirty people. It was dangerous, really unpleasant. Sometimes people didn't give us food. We would go one or two days without eating. Sometimes we slept for two or three hours, and they woke us up to follow them. They didn't say anything to us. Over the whole trip, we showered once a week.

The *coyotes* abandoned us in the desert somewhere near the Mexico-US border. After two days of walking without food or water, we heard the engines of an airplane nearby in the middle of the night. My sister and I hid ourselves at the foot of a hill so that they wouldn't find us. In the darkness, I heard yelling that if we didn't come out, they were going to let the dogs out to find us. I think the *coyotes* might have known the immigration agents were coming, but I don't know. When the agents came, I actually felt happy because I didn't want to suffer more after being lost for two days and two nights without water. My sister and I were crying the whole time. When the agents caught us, I felt like they were rescuing us.

---

8. Five hundred quetzales was about $66 US in 2015.

So they brought us to a hielera in McAllen, Texas. Sometimes we were cold, hungry. It was really unpleasant. Sometimes all my sister and I wanted was to be with our mom and our dad. It was a huge sacrifice for us, and we suffered a lot to come to this country. La Migra held us for fifteen days. Sometimes they didn't give us food; sometimes we didn't sleep. There were around fifty people with us in the hielera in McAllen. Like all the people who come here, we suffered, endured a lot of things.

When I spoke with a male immigration agent for the first time, he asked me my age. I wasn't sure how old I was.[9] The agent told me that they were going to deport us. I was very scared and sad because I thought they were going to take us back to Guatemala. There were around ten kids in the hielera, a lot of people packed into this small room. They were all twelve, thirteen, fourteen years old, all girls more or less the same age as us. My sister and I didn't know any of the other people. Everyone was crying because they had told all of us that we would be deported to our countries. They gave us a thin mattress to lie on, but no blanket. The floor was cement and cold. They kept the lights on the whole time. At one point, they tossed some cookies and orange juices into the room.

A male immigration officer later said to us, "You're going back to your country." I started to cry and cry. I thought, *This is the end because they've already caught us and they will send us back to Guatemala.* Then a female immigration officer said, "Calm down. We found out you are minors. We will send you to your family in this country." It was the first time I heard this. We didn't know that a program to reunite children with parents in the United States existed. If I had known that back in Guatemala, I would have come with my sister a long time ago, but we didn't know. I felt so relieved and happy when she told us we'd be with our parents. Then they

---

9. Because their parents fled when they were very young, Noemi and Glaisa did not know their exact ages. They did not carry birth records.

sent us to take a shower and gave us food. We ate well, we rested, and I slept for I don't know how many hours; it felt so good. So, the people in charge said, "We will send you to a children's house." It was called La Casita del Valle and was somewhere in Texas. I was sad and afraid it would be like that place where they locked us up and didn't give us food. But when we got out of the bus, the people from La Casita del Valle were so nice. They made sure we had food, and we were able to go out and play. And we got four or five vaccines. Those people were really good. Although they wore some sort of uniforms, they said we should call them teachers.

The other people we'd been traveling with did not come to the children's house, just me and my sister. The adults were sent back to their countries. The immigration agents called our parents and asked them, "Are you the parents of Noemi and Glaisa?" My dad said, "Yes." The agent asked my father how old I was, and he told him, "Sixteen." And the agent said, "We are from ICE and we have them here." My dad was very surprised that we were in Texas because he thought we were still in Guatemala. We had never told him that we'd left home. When I talked to my dad and mom they said that they couldn't believe it. My mom and my dad started to cry, and I did too. I don't think they were angry that we had traveled without their permission because they found out after it already happened. And I believe my dad wanted us to come because he knew we had been suffering with the fighting in Guatemala.

I wanted to hug my dad and my mom, but I couldn't. I said, "I will be with you very soon," because that's what the staff member told me. So my parents talked to the people who worked at La Casita del Valle and they said that they would take care of us. They were not going to let us miss anything, and they were going to give us food. After that, we talked twice a week with my mom and dad. We stayed for a month and twenty days at La Casita del Valle. I turned seventeen there. I didn't have a birthday party, but we celebrated

Thanksgiving. Then they sent us by airplane to Boston to be with my mom and my dad.

I DIDN'T RECOGNIZE MY DAD

When we got off the plane at the Boston airport, we got lost. I was looking for my mom and dad and I was very emotional. I saw a group of people and recognized my little brother and my mom, but I didn't recognize my dad. I hadn't seen him for nine years and I couldn't tell if it was him or not. When he hugged me for the first time, I cried to myself, *This is my dad; this is my mom!* It was the most beautiful moment of my life to reunite with my mom and dad.

Afterward, we went to the apartment where they lived, and we hugged some more. My parents said, "God blessed us with joy to be with our family, with our kids." The apartment is very different from our home in Guatemala. It has three bedrooms: my little sister and I have a bedroom, my mom and dad have their bedroom, and my brother has his bedroom. My dad bought us furniture, clothes, new shoes.

My sister and I went to a public high school outside of Boston. In Guatemala the school was very, very small, while here the school was really big. There were people from many places: Africa, Asia, and Europe—all kinds of children. I didn't speak English when I came here, but people began to help me learn. My teacher gave me extra English lessons. It was very hard to learn to read and write in English because it's so different from Spanish. I still have a hard time understanding it. I went to Classical High for two years, and I worked at McDonald's during that time. The thing is, here in this town, the schools are not very friendly for immigrants. They put immigrants in programs that are so basic that they want to just quit school.[10]

I started seeing a guy named Mateo who's from where I come from, a *chapín*.[11] I got pregnant and he's the father of Rafaelito. We're still together, but we haven't gotten married. Mateo lives with his sister and little brother, but he comes to my house to take care of Rafaelito. Mateo is working, but I'm not employed right now. I'm taking care of my son, and my parents are very supportive. I think the United States is very good for people like us, who have been through a lot of things. Here we can get help, refuge, and schooling, which is free. The United States defends us, the police defend us, and my neighborhood is safe.

ASYLUM

In 2015 I went to my asylum interview. My lawyer went to court with us, as she had three or four times during the application process. She always helped us a lot; she's a very nice person. When we needed help and asked questions, she told us our rights. The interview was conducted by a man who was like a judge. He asked many questions about how it was in Guatemala, which brought up many bad memories. This made me cry, but my lawyer was with me. Then he asked how we were doing here, if we were doing well, and I answered all the questions. When the interview was over, I went back to our house. I was playing with my son when I received the good news. I was very happy because they gave us asylum!

I'm living with my mom and dad, my younger brother and sister, and my little boy. He's two and a half years old. We're doing very well.

---

10. Local public schools have been criticized for not providing courses to help immigrant students learn English or finish high school. Instead, English learners are often tracked into remedial classes that don't give credit toward high school, leading to a high dropout rate.

11. *Chapín* is a nickname for people from Guatemala.

My father, who is forty-seven, is working in landscaping. My mother, who is thirty-eight, is a little sick with diabetes and goes to the clinic once a week. My sister Glaisa, who is sixteen, is busy embroidering blouses in the Maya tradition and hopes to start a fashion business. My son, who is very lively, is keeping me quite busy! My hope is that I can see my son grow up here in this country, that he can be somebody here, a good student, something he likes. I don't want my baby to go through the things I've been through. I believe in getting married because I'm a Christian. So my dream is to get married here, in a white dress, to Mateo, with Rafaelito escorting me as a ring bearer. I think of working in the future, doing something. Buy a house, a car, go to work. I want to learn, to study, to speak English, to know how to defend myself really well so nothing can humiliate me, so I can be somebody in this life. First, I need to learn English.

I recently talked to my grandmother, who's living with my uncle in Guatemala. She's very sick. She has a sickness in her feet. They hurt a lot. She told me that about two weeks ago they killed another person for water and land.

If I could speak to the people reading my story, I'd tell them that a lot of good things happened to me and also bad things. The good thing is that I made it to this country, and the bad is that I suffered a lot before I came here. The people in this country treat us well. My hope is that in my native country there is no more war, no more problems, that they stop fighting over water and land, and that this whole thing ends so that I can be in my beautiful country someday.

We talk to Noemi a year and a half later, in August 2017, in her law-yer's satellite office. Noemi now has a green card. She is wearing a red blouse with her hair pulled back tight, accentuating her large brown eyes. Rafaelito plays with a toy train, the clickety-clack causing peals of laughter.

HAPPY TO HAVE ALL OF US TOGETHER

My son is good and growing a lot! Rafaelito is very happy. He's three years old and not in school yet. I am still with Mateo. Sometimes Rafaelito is a little troublemaker! He's playing with many trucks right now. He loves playing with Legos, building little houses, and everything. He speaks a bit of Spanish and a bit of English. My son always wakes up first, and then wakes me up, calling, "Noemi!" He calls my parents Mamá and Papá, probably because he hears me calling them that. He sleeps in his crib in the bedroom. As soon as he wakes up, he starts talking about toys. He just wants to play and play! Then he wants to eat. I cook him rice, eggs, cereal. It's very different from waking up in Guatemala, where we had to search for wood and make the fire. I am with him at home full time. I did work for McDonald's for a couple of months, but since Rafaelito was born, I haven't been able to work. I don't have time to go to school at this point. I am very interested in nature though. I'd love to learn more.

During the summer, we go out, but it gets so hot and humid that we stay inside most of the time. In the winter it is really cold here. This is the first place I've seen snow. It gets icy sometimes in San Marcos, but it doesn't snow. When I first saw the snow, I loved it. It was beautiful. But after it freezes on the ground, it's not so great!

My sister is still working at a Burger King. She's learning a bit of English, but she's not in school because she is working full time. My parents are very happy to have all of us together. My father is sad because my grandmother died a month ago in Guatemala. He is scared for his brothers, my uncles, who are still there in San Marcos. But he's happy to be with us.

ISABEL VÁSQUEZ

AGE AT CROSSING: 29
AGE OF CHILD: 9
BORN IN: Cantón El Rosario, Santa Ana, El Salvador
INTERVIEWED IN: Oakland, California

We first meet Isabel in winter 2015 at Centro Legal de la Raza, in the Fruitvale neighborhood of Oakland, California. She has recently arrived in the United States from El Salvador with her nine-year-old daughter, Diana. Diana stands next to her mother, her head nestled against her waist, and Isabel rests her hand protectively on her daughter's shoulder. The sounds of Spanish and English mix within the confines of the small room, and the smell of fresh pupusas and coffee suffuses the brightly lit cubicles. They are here to meet with Isabel's immigration lawyer to talk about a work permit.

Isabel grew up in poverty on a small coffee plantation. Her mother

109

came to the United States in 2003 while Isabel stayed in El Salvador, got
married, and had Diana. A few years into their marriage, her husband,
Ramón, started drinking, abusing drugs, and abusing her. The Barrio
18 gang started to kill people in her town, and she suspects her estranged
husband may have joined the gang. The tiny plantation village once had a
tight-knit community where everyone used to leave their doors unlocked,
but now that the maras have infiltrated even the most remote parts of
the country, trust in communities like Isabel's is shattered. In 2007, her
younger sister, who had gone to work in another city, was murdered.
When Isabel and her daughter started receiving death threats by phone,
they fled to the United States.

EVEN WITH ALL THAT FEAR, SHE LOVED HER DADDY

My mother is a survivor of the war, which was still raging when I
was born in 1987.[1] I was born in San Juan Opico in Las Lomas de
Santiago, about an hour and a half from Cantón El Rosario. When
I was a baby, my father, who had abused my mother, left us. We
moved to El Rosario when I was seven.[2] My mom had been working
there in the coffee fields and when the plantation owners gave her a
small house, we moved in.

I was sixteen when my mother left with two of my siblings. My
other two siblings and I stayed in our village. Then I came to the
United States in 2015. Her husband, my stepfather, had been mistreat-
ing her. My siblings and I continued to live in El Rosario. After my
mom left, I met a guy who'd grown up in that village named Ramón.
I didn't know him well, but once my mother wasn't around, it was my

---

1. The Salvadoran Civil War lasted from 1980 to 1992.

2. The village is located on the property of a coffee plantation in Santa Ana,
about sixty-eight kilometers northwest of San Salvador. Along with Finca Deli-
cias, Finca El Rosario is owned by the Don Miguel Menendez family and sells
beans to CREMA, Water Avenue, and the Rainforest Alliance.

opportunity to have a boyfriend. In Rosario, it's looked down upon to have a boyfriend before you're eighteen. Ramón didn't work. He was a kid, like me. He went to school because he was living with his mother, and she made him go. I didn't go to school. I was bored by school and I felt that I was an adult. I had my house, my work, and didn't feel like I needed anything else. Ramón came to live with me around 2006, when I was nineteen. He ended up dropping out of school like me and didn't do anything. His mom brought food to the house for us to eat.

When we first met, Ramón told me things like, "Oh, you're so pretty." He told me he loved me, and I thought, *Why should I say no?* Early in the relationship, it was really lovely. He brought me a stuffed animal, a pretty little bear. Candy. Chocolate. He looked at me with a lot of tenderness. It was unique for me, something that I hadn't known existed, that a person could come along and treat me so well. I said to myself, *Maybe there is nothing better than to be with him.*

Ramón and I got married in 2006, and our daughter, Diana, was born the same year. We had a normal life as a couple for about three years. We'd argue a bit, but nothing got out of control. Everything was fine. But after a time, he started taking drugs, drinking alcohol. The only two things that were really accessible there are marijuana and alcohol. Combining those was the worst he could do, a bad combination. Afterwards, he would say that he didn't remember that he'd gotten home, fought with me, yelled at me, almost hit me. We went on like this for a while. He'd always tell me afterwards, "Look, forgive me. I don't remember what happened." Back then, I didn't have my mind open to believing him or not. It was more like, *I love him. I'm in love with him.* Now I realize that it could not have been love. He came at me with a thousand and one promises that it wouldn't happen again, that he wouldn't do it again. It started to repeat every weekend. He drank the lowest quality liquor there was because it was the cheapest. There's a liquor called La Trenzuda. There's another one called Caña Rica. It's strong liquor, with a high alcohol content. He sometimes mixed the alcohol with beer. He excused his aggression, saying, "I did it because of the liquor." But in reality the alcohol wasn't to blame.

I think he started drinking because of his friends, the kind of people he hung around with. In the village there was no bar. They drank in the street, on a corner, a bunch of bums, with a little bit of liquor, nothing fancy, no table, just a disposable cup and a bottle. "Here's yours," one would say, draining the cup and then passing it. That's what it's like in the village. At first he did it for the company of other men, to feel like one of the group. But then when he started really drinking, he drank and didn't even make it home. Sometimes he knocked on the door and fell asleep right there in the doorway.

As time went by, Ramón started making a habit of drinking and drinking. Eventually, he didn't always come home and sleep. When he came home, he would start in with, "And what have you been doing all day?" He started to question me a lot. Afterwards, he briefly went out to work on the plantation. Any day he was drinking, he'd ask me who I had spoken with when he was gone. That's how things started, the jealousy.

I started to be a bit afraid. He yelled at me when he got home. More time went by, and he'd come home and start throwing the dishes around. He'd throw a glass, breaking it into pieces. I'd ask him, "Are you going to eat dinner?" and he'd grab the food and throw it. And the next day, he'd say he didn't remember. Things were getting worse. He came home and grabbed me hard by the arm. Sometimes he pushed me. He hit me many times in the face. A few times he left marks. There were times when he got out of control and came home very angry and wanted a Korbel brandy. And he said that I had someone else, that I was cheating on him. His friends told him things, said his woman had another man. "So-and-so says you're cheating on me." Where we're from, most men are gossips. They go from one to the other saying, "Look, your woman . . ." In our village, if someone saw a woman talking with a man, they would say, "Why is she talking to him like that?" If they aren't related, then she's his woman. And for that reason, things exploded between us.

Ramón came at me with rocks, with a stick. The moment came when I had to run for the first time, because he was going for a machete. I left with my daughter. At first when we'd leave, since it was usually nighttime, we'd hide ourselves where we could in the woods. But there were times when I couldn't escape. It was impossible. I tried to confront him a number of times. I'd work myself up to defend myself, but the strength of a man, the aggression! He hit me a number of times, but later he'd come to talk with me, to speak kindly, to say that he loved me, that it wouldn't happen again. I believed him because he stayed with me, but then a few days later the violence would resume.

Ramón always came off as right. He knew what he was doing. If he was yelling at me, and our daughter came up to us, he would say, "What do you need, my love, what's up?" He'd speak affectionately with her while he yelled at me. In the same house! It was small, just one room. Our girl was sitting there, frightened, but the aggression wasn't toward her. It was directed at me. She was scared, but even with all that fear, she loved her daddy.

THEY ARE LIKE A PLAGUE

Right around the time we got married and Diana was born, scary things started happening in the village. We heard that when people went to the woods to get firewood, they saw strangers. Then, more and more, we'd hear that people saw unknown people around, though nothing serious had happened. We thought they were thieves. They'd go into the stores at night to steal, and once they left the owner of the store tied up, but that was it. Once the gangs dominated in the city, they started coming to the *finca* as well. As my grandmother says, they are like a plague. We have a pestilence, like worms, flies, or leaf-cutter ants. I think there isn't any part of El

Salvador where they don't appear. It's practically all contaminated with them. Before, a village like ours was so beautiful, and suddenly things were ruined.

On October 17, 2007, I got a phone call telling me that my little sister, Alma, had been killed. She was seventeen. It could have been the gangs. The police said they were going to investigate, but they didn't follow through. The day before, she'd told me she'd found a job and that she would go and work in the capital, in a house taking care of children. She'd left with a friend on the bus, supposedly to go to a job interview. The employer had told her that she should just come to do an interview and see the home. She was just checking out the job and then would return to El Rosario.

I tried her telephone, but nothing. The next morning, I kept trying her number, thinking she would answer and wondering why she hadn't come back. At the same time, I thought maybe she'd stayed in the capital to work. But if she were going to work in that house, she should've brought a change of clothes. She had stayed at my house the night before she left for Santa Tecla, and I remembered that she hadn't brought clothes.[3] So I asked myself, *If she didn't bring her clothes, how could she have stayed to work?* I tried to call her again, and a man answered the phone and told me she was dead. But it seemed to me like maybe it was a joke, or someone had stolen her telephone.

We didn't have enemies or anyone who'd want to harm our family. The person who picked up her phone seemed like someone who knew us because he said, "Are you looking for your sister? Your sister is dead." Right away I called my aunt, the one who lived closest to us. I called the police, and they told me they didn't know anything. We still didn't believe it. The police told me we had to wait twenty-four hours before they could start looking for her. We waited until the twenty-ninth of October. At around eleven in the evening the police called us. We had given them details, described her. She

---

3. Santa Tecla is a suburb southwest of San Salvador.

was thin, very pretty. The police called me to say they had found the body of someone who looked like my sister farther beyond Santa Tecla, in Lourdes. I identified her at the morgue—it was my sister. She died in the worst way I could imagine. Even now, I still ask myself why it happened.

Alma was my only younger sibling. Her death left us with this tremendous pain that will never leave us. We don't even have a reason, something to explain why this happened to her. Some say it could have been her boyfriend. He was with the gangs. But he was detained at the time she died. Perhaps he gave the order to kill her from prison. It could have been for jealousy, if he thought she had someone else. My family has always thought that. But for the police, it's just another case. That's how the police are in my country. Alma had her whole life ahead of her. Who knows what God had in mind for her?

My daughter was only one year old. Alma loved my daughter a lot. Even a year later, my daughter would ask, "Where's my Tia Seca?" We called her "Seca" because she was thin. My daughter is also tall and thin, as tall as my shoulder and just as thin as my sister. Starting around October 2014, almost seven years since my sister's death, I began getting strange phone calls. At first they were just missed calls, and when I tried to call back no one answered. After my sister died, no one called us or bothered us. It seemed like it was all over. One day I answered the phone and a voice said, "I've been trying to reach you, bitch." And I asked, "Who are you? Why are you saying that?" He didn't say anything and the line went dead. After that there were lots of calls, but from lots of different numbers. In El Salvador, we buy SIM cards, so you can buy a different card and have a new number. It could have been the same person making all those calls. The last two or three times, he said that he was back, that he hadn't forgotten our family. I thought, *What now?* He said, "We started this and now we're going to finish it." After my sister, one of my cousins was also killed. He had been deported from the United

States. Maybe he was killed because of the way he dressed—with his pants sagging—and they confused him for a gang member.[4]

After the man said he hadn't forgotten our family, I got a call from someone, maybe the same man, who said he knew I had a daughter and she could meet the same fate as my sister. At that point I understood what this was all about. The school she went to wasn't at all secure. It had an open patio where the children would go out to play, so after that call I didn't want to leave my daughter at school. She was eight years old at the time. I would take her to school, but I would stay there too, like her bodyguard. I stopped working because I would stay at school with my daughter, waiting on one of the benches while she was in class. When they went out to play, I would be right there next to her.

My husband was put in prison in 2014. According to him, the police had taken him in for extortion, to try to get money from him. They had accused him of mugging people, threatening that they would kill him. He had friends in the gangs, but he said he wasn't a gang member, that his friends weren't in the gangs anymore, just drunks. I really don't know what to believe, but I know he wasn't in the gangs.

"WE'RE GOING TO GO BE WITH MAMÍTA!"

I felt we couldn't go on like that. My mother tried to bring us to the United States legally, with tourist visas, but there were so many requirements: she told me you had to have a bank account with $6,000 in it or a car for them to issue you a visa.[5] You were required to have property in your name or to own cattle. We couldn't come that way, but I had to do something because what if something happened to my daughter?

---

4. When migrants return home from the United States, they are often known by the local gangs as *desconocidos*, or "unknowns," and are hunted down and murdered.

5. This is Isabel's recollection. We could not confirm this as an actual visa requirement.

We couldn't come with a *coyote* either because that was too expensive. A *coyote* would charge $7,000 to $8,000 to bring us all the way here. With my mother not working, we didn't have access to that kind of money. Instead my mother sent me a hundred dollars and told me to go to Guatemala because her friend there knew a man who takes people and supposedly wouldn't charge much. She had remarried in the United States in 2008 and her husband supported us coming to live with them, though he didn't have much money either. We left our house one morning, and a man we met took us to the border with Guatemala.

There's a dirt path by the river's edge, and we managed to cross into Guatemala. My mother called her friend to let her know we were coming and to see if she could meet us. My mom's friend and her husband came to get us and we stayed at their house in Quetzaltenango for about a week. She said the man we'd been told about was up in the United States, and we had to wait for him to come back so we could ask if he'd take us and how much it would cost. When he got back we asked him, and he gave us the price in quetzales. I think it was about $3,000 US. That was less than what we would have been charged in El Salvador but still more than my mother could afford. My mother asked him if he would take us and let us pay him back later, but he said no, that he had to have the money in hand.

And then the woman we were staying with remembered that a friend of hers had mentioned she knew some people, a couple, who were going to leave right around this time. We walked to the house where they lived and the couple said they were leaving in two days. It was a Sunday or Monday. They said they were going by themselves without a *coyote* because they only had about $500 US. My mother's friend said, "This young woman and her daughter need to go north," and asked if we could go with them and just pay for bus fare and transportation costs. They said it was okay if I could pay the bus fare because they would be going from bus to bus, traveling overnight. I thought, *Why not?* I didn't want to get stuck in Guatemala.

That day we went with them, traveling all day, for a while on a bus, a really big one, then a small car, and then on a bus again. We arrived around ten o'clock at night at a bus terminal. The man in the couple said to the bus driver, "We're going north. It's very late to look for a place to stay, and this poor young woman has her little girl with her. Is there any way we could stay here on the bus?" The driver said we could sleep on the seats, but the bus would be leaving the terminal in another direction at 5 a.m. and we'd have to get off before then.

Guatemala is really big! It took us another three or four days to cross it and reach the border with Mexico. I kept wondering how far the border was because I thought it was close. It felt as if we'd never reach the other side. Sometimes we would stop by a river to wash ourselves, and that would take some time before we could continue on our way. The man in the couple would tell me not to be scared—if the police stopped us in Guatemala, they would just show their DPIs, which is the same as our DUI.[6] At this point it had been almost two weeks since I had left home.

Diana was very patient, very calm. I told her, "We're alone here, but we're going to go be with Mamíta," which is what we call my mom. We kept going by car and by bus, and by the fifth day the man said we were almost there. Then we reached a border crossing called El Ceibo. I saw the name on a sign. We got off a bus and walked through the winding streets until we got to a boat landing on the river between Guatemala and Mexico, the Río San Pedro. Someone close to the couple had gone ahead of them to make arrangements. There were two motorboats hidden there, "pirate boats," as we call them. They didn't want quetzales anymore, so I offered them dol-

---

6. DPI stands for Documento Personal de Identificación, or personal identifica-tion document (the Guatemalan national ID card). DUI (Documento Único de Identidad) is the Salvadoran national ID.

lars—I still had ten to fifteen dollars left, so we gave them that and then paid the rest in quetzales. It took us just fifteen minutes to cross that little stretch of water. They said to us, "There's Mexico," and I thought it was going to be quick, that we were going to get to Mexico and then cross into the United States right away. It took us about two more weeks to cross Mexico.

You meet other people who are also traveling alone, without *coyotes*, trying their luck to see if they can cross or not. When we got to Mexico, the couple said they couldn't continue traveling with us anymore, that it was a big commitment taking a child north and they didn't want to risk getting caught by Mexican immigration authorities. By this time we had met another woman and other people traveling north, and the couple said they'd leave us there with them. We met a woman who talked of having seen people who'd lost legs or arms riding on La Bestia.[7]

One time we got into a truck that must have been used for horses, where they packed us in like sardines to evade the Mexican Federales, they said. It was a really big truck. It was awful. That was how we crossed Mexico. At one point we went to a restaurant and the woman traveling with us said, "You know what? We need to ask them to let us work for two or three days so we have a little bit of money to try to continue our journey." My mother had sent us some money, sixty, a hundred dollars here and there, which helped us a lot along the way to at least buy something for my daughter to eat. The woman I was traveling with was Mexican, from Tuxtla Gutiérrez, Chiapas, and was on her way to the United States as well. She was traveling alone and was about forty years old. I had just turned twenty-eight. Since I didn't bring any documents to be able to withdraw money, my mother sent the money in the woman's name. She would use her ID to withdraw the money. I don't remember exactly where we were, but when we were close to the US border, she said,

7. See glossary.

"Let's go look for work," and we were there for maybe a day and a half. We worked at a restaurant in Otay Mesa, near Tijuana, about a half hour from the border. We were paid 7,060 Mexican pesos.[8] With that we continued on our journey. We met up with some other people going north, a young man bringing a girl with him who was about eleven or twelve years old, a little older than my daughter. They were family members. We joined up with them.

We had to hide all the time. One time we spent about a day and a half hiding in some bushes to avoid the *perrera*.[9] We watched their cars going by one after the other until there weren't any more. I had some crackers and water in my backpack for my daughter and that was all. I was always concerned about making sure she ate; the last thing I worried about was whether *I* had anything to eat. She was the priority.

She was scared sometimes. She has a diary, a little notebook I bought her and she's been writing in it. She wrote about getting stuck with a thorn, and about when she had to dive into the bushes to hide from the police. She has her own story to tell, too.

When we got closer to Tijuana we went to work in another restaurant to make a bit more money, and the Mexican woman I was traveling with spoke to another woman to ask her what it was like close to the border, whether it was difficult to cross. The woman said she knew a young man who took people across, who does a good job and doesn't charge a lot. We asked him, but he said he charges $3,000 just to cross the border between Mexico and the United States because there were so many immigration agents patrolling the area. The woman said that since I had my daughter with me, I should turn myself in to ICE. She said to tell them that I was coming for my daughter's security, that I didn't have any alternatives. I was really afraid to do that. After everything I had gone through, how was I going to turn myself over

8. Roughly $516 US in 2015.

9. Or "dogcatcher," as immigration patrol cars in Mexico are called.

to them and say, *Look at me! Here I am!* So they can send me back? It seemed like it would be stupid of me to turn myself in after everything I had done to get there. It had taken me almost a month, and to risk being sent back home after all that seemed crazy. But the woman said, "No, it's different because of your daughter. Do it for her."

AS IF YOU BELONG HERE

My daughter and I approached the border in Tijuana. My friend said, "I'm going to show you. We're going to walk calmly. Don't act scared. The important thing is you don't want to fall into the hands of Mexican immigration. Go directly to the immigration services of the United States because if you get detained by Mexican immigration, they *will* send you back quickly." I bought some clean clothes for my daughter, and the woman said to walk as if you're from here, as if you belong here. She said, "Don't look at anybody. We're going to get on a bus and I'll go with you up until you get really close to where you'll turn yourself in." I was really nervous but tried to stay calm as I walked right past the police. She even said hello to them, but she's Mexican. She lives in Tijuana. She said, "Good afternoon!" and I was so scared! She went almost all the way, almost right across the border. Then she said, "Look. Here it is. Go right up there where you see those cars. That's US immigration. Go on! Say hello to them. Say good evening." And I said, "How am I going to say good evening to them if they're from the United States and speak English?" She told me, "Just greet them and tell them you are looking for US immigration, that you have family there, but you don't have a way to get there." After a while the woman said she had to leave me there because if they caught her, they would say she brought me there and then put her in jail, saying she's working to transport people.

I stayed hidden in the dark with my daughter, and an agent came along with a flashlight. It was really late at night by then, around ten o'clock. We moved to the side, because the woman said we had to be inside the United States. I thought to myself, *You have to cross the gate.* And the official with the light didn't see us. So we crossed over and went to the building on the border that our friend had pointed to. A very rude female agent spoke to me in Spanish and asked what I wanted. I told her I wanted to join my mother in the United States and we filled out some papers. Another guard took us down a hall.

There was a really big space, full of people lying on mats with white sheets on them. I sat on a chair with my daughter and asked myself, *What are all these people doing here?* I began to talk to other people. They shared their experiences. They told me that if immigration believes what you tell them about what happened in your country, you'll be released to join your family in the United States. But if they don't believe you, they'll put you in a car and take you back. We spent the whole day in the hielera because we'd arrived at night.

La Migra gave us a sandwich with frozen ham in it.[10] The food was really awful, so bad that people said, "We've been in here for two weeks and this is the only food they give us here." We slept some. I lay down with my daughter. She was a little calmer because we were inside. The next morning we were woken up when it was still dark— one wall was glass, and I looked outside and could see it was really dark. "Get up! Get up!" said a female guard who worked there. She just came to make us get up and sit.

The same guard put the heat on really high, so high you felt as if you were getting burned. I felt as if it was spewing fire in my face. At night when it was "lights out," the guards turned on the air conditioning, very cold. It seemed like the border patrol does it to pressure you into saying that you want to return to your country, that you don't want to be there anymore. One day my daughter's lips starting bleeding because it would be very hot and then very cold. The other thing was that the guards only took us to use the bathroom once a

---

10. See glossary.

day. We had to go the one time they told us to, and if we wanted to go later, we couldn't. They would take us in a group, and the whole group would be crowded into the bathroom. We would turn our backs when someone was using the toilet to give them some privacy. You can imagine how horrible that bathroom smelled!

My understanding was that according to US law, they have to treat people better, but my experience wasn't like that. It was awful. They only gave us food that was frozen. My daughter would wait until the ham in the sandwich thawed enough for her to eat it, but the bread would be soggy, like dough, inedible. But that was all they gave us. I didn't see anywhere for people to shower.

After we'd been there about two days, they took me out at night and put some kind of restraints on me, cuffed me. Another woman officer, wearing a black or navy-blue uniform, put them on me. She only spoke in English. I wanted to ask where they were taking me, but I couldn't. You can imagine the fear I felt, with my hands tied like that, thinking that they would send me back to my country, and my daughter cried, "Oh, Mamá!" She was with me but did not have those wrist restraints on. The cuffs were squeezing and digging into my wrists. And I thought, *What am I doing with these things on, like a criminal?* The woman told us to go with her. She grabbed the papers that had our fingerprints and photos on them, and I left with my daughter. More than one of the other detained women said to me, "You're going to your country. You're going back." That made me so afraid.

We went outside to a parking lot where there was a bus with bars on the windows, like the ones they transport prisoners in. The woman told me to get on, removed the restraint from one of my wrists, and locked it onto a metal bar in the bus, so I had one hand still attached and the other arm around my daughter, with the two of us sitting in one seat. We drove to another place where there were more people. This wasn't where they were taking us; they just stopped there to pick up more people—three women, a child, and a man.

They asked me where I was from, and when I told them El Salvador, they said they were from Mexico. I asked if they knew where we were being taken. The man said, "We're leaving the country again." I started to cry. "They're going to leave us at the Mexican consulate. And you? I suppose they'll take you to your country's consulate and they'll send you back home. They didn't give us asylum; that's why they're kicking us out." I didn't know what to do or feel then. They didn't take us to any consulate; they drove up to a kind of fence or wall, which I think was the dividing line between Mexico and the United States. They took the Mexican migrants off the bus in the dark and said, in English, "Let's go! Let's go!"

The female officer stopped at a door. The wall around it was really high and seemed like it was electrified. She took out a key, opened the little door, and pushed them through. I thought, *Isn't it dangerous to just throw people out like that at night?* As they left, the man said to me, "Maybe they'll let you go." The bus continued with just my daughter and me on board, but I was terrified, wondering if they were going to leave us in the dark like they did with those people. But then we reached another center where there were other people. The woman took the restraints off my wrists. It seemed just like the first place, with mats on the floor and people just sitting there. We went in. They said we were going farther into the United States. Imagine the relief I felt!

They held both of us there for several hours; we were in custody no more than four days in total. They asked for my mother's phone number and called her in front of me. They spoke to her and asked if she knew me and my daughter, and she said yes. The officer who called said to her, "You know what, ma'am? We have her here, and she is facing a deportation order." A deportation order! Who knows what my mother thought when she heard the man say that. They held us there for a while, and the next morning, they took us to a different office. They took our photos and fingerprints again.

We walked to another building that was very big, and from there they sent us in a big immigration bus to San Diego. That's where they let us go finally. When I was about to leave, they said, "You just have to go sign papers in the office." We went into an office and there were a lot of people sitting in chairs, waiting in line. There was an official there crossing back and forth and it seemed as if he was cutting a black tape. And then I saw them putting this electronic ankle monitor on someone's leg. Someone said, "If they don't put that on you, they won't let you leave." I asked, "Is it really necessary?" "Yes," he said. "If not, you'll go back to your country instead of staying in the United States." When there was just one person ahead of me, I didn't want to move from my seat. That thing was so ugly, so big! They gave me some instructional papers explaining that the ankle monitor needed to be charged, that when the battery ran out, you take it out and put a new one in. An official spoke to me on the phone saying that I was going to leave. They told me to go to an office, and there was my mother sitting with my stepfather!

I felt such a mixture of emotions: relief, happiness that I had finally made it here, but shame that my mother and stepfather had to see me like this in the detention center. I was thinking about so many things at once. My mom threw her arms around me, and we both started crying. She said, "Oh, my princess, they'll take it off you; we'll ask them to take it off soon."

SHE CHECKS HER DOLLS
WITH A LITTLE STETHOSCOPE

My mom and stepdad had driven all the way to San Diego from Oakland. They had already spent a whole day driving, and they turned around, and we spent another whole day driving back. My stepdad had to stop to rest at one point because he couldn't keep driving, so it took longer. We left around 9 a.m. and arrived at my mother's house around 10 or 11 p.m. Plus, the ankle monitor battery died halfway there and we had to stop and ask someone to let us charge it.

I had an appointment scheduled for about four days later at an office in San Francisco called ISAP.[11] At that office I had to watch a video explaining how everything would work: I would have to keep the ankle monitor on until immigration said I could remove it. I had to leave it on all the time, shower with it on, sleep with it on. They gave me a map that showed the range of the signal, how far away I could go, because they would be monitoring it constantly.

The radius is marked on the map. They told me I couldn't work because I was still in a deportation process and I couldn't do anything until immigration decided what to do with me. It was up to them. That's what happened for three months. I visited the ISAP office once a week to sign in and get fingerprinted. I had left my passport with them when I first got here, and they kept it until my case was closed. Then they told me I had to get a phone in my house, a landline. If I had the landline and always carried my passport, they would remove the ankle monitor. Otherwise, they wouldn't take it off.

I was wondering, *What's going to happen when I go to court? What will they say to me?* On May 26, 2015, with the help of my lawyers at Centro Legal, I won my asylum case.[12] I have documents that prove that I called the police many times trying to stop my husband's violence. I have photos of my sister's death. I have forensic medical reports, reports that describe how she died. My mother had them. When I got to my mother's I was able to retrieve all those documents. I felt my anxiety lift.

I would like to be able to make my dream come true now that I'm free to be here. I'd like to be able to work freely. I can't cash a check. My lawyers submitted the application and say I have to wait. They

---

11. ISAP is the Intensive Supervision Appearance Program.

12. Centro Legal de la Raza.

don't know how much longer it will be. I work a little bit, taking care of a little boy. His parents bring him to my house and give me one hundred dollars a week. I also tried to apply for food stamps, which my mother suggested, but they rejected me. They sent me a letter saying my application had been denied because I didn't have legal status in the country. I haven't talked to the lawyers yet to try to resubmit the application and see if it will be approved now that our legal status has been clarified. It would definitely be good since I don't have any sort of stable job. We also went to see if we could get food stamps and Medi-Cal for my daughter since she has a rotten molar that really hurts a lot.[13] They did issue the Medi-Cal, but it turns out it's very restricted. It doesn't even cover the basics like teeth cleaning.

My daughter is very happy to be here, though. She wants to be a doctor. When she plays, she pretends to be a doctor. It would be wonderful for her to fulfill her dreams even if I can't fulfill mine. She plays with some plastic doctor's tools I gave her and she checks her dolls with the little stethoscope, listening all over. She cures them and everything. While I am dedicated to my daughter's future, I fear it won't really be possible for me to pursue an education. I always dreamed of studying at university to become a lawyer, to work toward creating a safer and more just society. Now that I am a bit older and I have to work to support my daughter, this seems like a distant dream.

I've been in the United States for nine months. We live in Richmond, California, with my mother and my two siblings. For the moment, I haven't seen the good side yet because I don't have work, and I need money. My daughter needs things—clothing, shoes—and I haven't worked to be able to give them to her. I don't feel very good. I'm in a strange country and I can't do anything.

Diana started fourth grade just a week after we got here. At first she didn't like it because the language made her very uncomfortable. She cried whenever I left her at the school, for the whole first week.

13. California's Medicaid program is called Medi-Cal.

The teachers and students spoke to her, but she didn't understand anything. Now, months later, she speaks a few words in English. We have neighborhood kids her age, and she goes out to play with them. The girls speak to her in English and she already pushes herself to answer. She's losing her fear. She's very adaptable and is getting used to things already.

We sit down again with Isabel in July 2017. We meet outside of a sprawling Walmart at the Hilltop Mall in Richmond, California, near where she lives. She's with her mother, her daughter, and a four-year-old boy named Diego, whom they look after. As we make our way through the fluorescent-lit aisles, Diana speaks English without pause, telling us about her success at school. When we enter the main part of the mall, we sit on a leather couch and talk while Isabel's mother takes the kids shopping.

Ramón has contacted my mother a couple of times, checking in on our daughter. He has her phone number, but he doesn't know where we live. He's still in prison for extortion in El Salvador but says he has converted to Christianity and that he's a "changed man." I still don't know if he had joined the maras or if he was just involved in crime with his friends. He tells my mother that he still thinks about reestablishing his relationship with me, but I don't want this. Now that I see that I can lead a different life here in the United States, I don't want to return to him. He's lost my trust.

Diana is thriving, and I'm watching her blossom. She's quickly learning English and has many friends at school. Her teachers all tell me that she is very well behaved, very intelligent, and eager to learn. She recently won first prize in a science fair and is earning A's in all her classes!

DANELIA SILVA

AGE AT CROSSING: 25
AGES OF CHILDREN: 3, 5, 7
BORN IN: San Salvador, El Salvador
INTERVIEWED IN: Tenosique de Pino Suárez, Tabasco, Mexico
in transit

We meet Danelia at the La 72 shelter in Tenosique in July of 2016. Danelia had planned to flee from San Salvador to the United States with her three small children. A coyote led them across the border into Mexico but abandoned them in Tenosique, where they made their way to the shelter. It's been a dry week in the area, and apart from some hard, short showers at night accompanied by loud booms and flashes, there is no rain. On the day of our meeting, the morning heats up quickly, and by nine it's humid and well above a hundred degrees Fahrenheit. Danelia is seated in the courtyard at a circular table beneath a thatched

129

umbrella with some fellow migrants, including a young mother from Honduras and a middle-aged farmer from El Salvador. Danelia's children play on the nearby basketball court in front of colorful murals, and the adults talk about their voyages and the stories of those who had been assaulted and left behind. Danelia's story touches on prevalent themes in the lives of many young women in Central America. Due to economic hardship, her parents were forced to leave her to parent herself and her younger brother. Now, as a mother of three, Danelia is making her own journey in order to flee life-threatening domestic abuse.

Back in El Salvador, Danelia's boyfriend Carlos had been physically abusing her. When she sought refuge with family members, he threatened her life and stalked her. He then joined the international criminal gang MS-13.

After being in the shelter for three days, Danelia is still in considerable shock and expresses her mixed feelings: on one hand, she feels liberated to be away from her abuser. On the other hand, she has only reached southern Mexico and has no solid plan to make it into the United States. Her parents live in Austin, Texas. Neither of them has documentation, though her stepfather's cousin is a citizen. They are scared because Carlos has been calling them and threatening their lives, saying that he knows people in Texas who can harm them. They have saved emails and photographs that document the words and actions of the abusive ex-boyfriend. Danelia is examining her options for keeping her family safe: she could apply for asylum in Mexico or at the US border, or her parents could apply for asylum from Texas and then help Danelia join them through family reunification.

HE COULD KILL ME

Our situation is very difficult. This is just a small piece of the terror I've lived in for almost four years. I didn't know how to leave with these three small children. I ask myself now how I ever gathered the strength to leave that house. But if I hadn't, I don't know if I would still be alive.

I was born in San Salvador. When I was twelve years old, my father moved to the United States, and my mother joined him when I was about to turn fifteen. So when I was fourteen, I was living alone with my younger brother. I became his mother in a way. I didn't work. I took care of him. My father sent us money monthly, as much as he could, so that we could survive. When I was almost eighteen, my parents sent for my brother. He made the trip to the United States with a *coyote*. So my father, then my mother, and then my brother all made the trip with *coyotes*.

When my parents left, the *maras* weren't really there yet.[1] We didn't know about them then. By the time I turned eighteen, the gang problem had grown and was very visible. I didn't know whether it was the MS-13 or the 18s, but then I started learning about them. My father was a soldier.[2] He was forced to join the army. It was a terrible war, but it's probably worse now.

I met a guy, a partner, in 2009, when I was eighteen, and I had a daughter with him, Sara. He really wanted a son, so when he found out that our child was a daughter, he left me. I never heard anything from him after that. About a year later, I met Carlos. For the first year and a half, everything was good. It was perfect. My second daughter, Natalia, was born and everything was still good. And then we had a boy, Javier. So Sara is seven, Natalia is now five, and Javier is three.

When our son was born in 2013, Carlos started to change a lot. I don't know if he had other women, but he started to mistreat me. He would hit me, yell at me a lot. He didn't drink. He smoked marijuana, and this made him crazy. He would insult me, say many

---

1. Maras are gangs. The term primarily refers to MS-13 and Barrio 18, also known as the 18s. See glossary.

2. Most likely a soldier in the army of the military-backed government of El Salvador fighting left-wing guerrillas in the Salvadoran civil war. See "Historical Timeline."

things to me. He would smoke marijuana in front of the children and say vulgar things to his friends in front of them. And because children copy their parents and imitate their habits, they started to say bad words and learn bad things that children don't need to learn.

While I was with him, he wouldn't allow me to talk with anyone. When he and I were with a group of people, I would just stand there trembling. He wouldn't let me say anything. He told me that he was the man and I was the woman, so it wasn't my place to speak. I was especially not allowed to speak with men. If a man spoke to me, that would be a beating for me. This happened for about three years: Carlos mistreated me. I endured all this for my children. They saw all this. When Sara would play, she'd start to pull the dolls' hair. She was very violent until we left that house. She's changed a lot. She used to fight with her friends. She was very aggressive. Now that we've left the house, she's not like that anymore. It's been sixteen days since we left and she's changed completely.

It's better that my youngest doesn't remember this. After the first year of assaults, it wasn't just one punch. It wasn't just one insult. It was more violent. Carlos would grab me, throw me to the floor, and kick me over and over. He hit me a lot. One time, he grabbed a baseball bat and hit me. He hit my entire right side with it. Sometimes, when it's cool or cold out, my feet hurt so badly that I can't walk.

At this point, Carlos became a gangster and continued to abuse me. He chose this. I'd had it. I couldn't do this anymore. So I prepared to leave. I just took my children, dressed, and left the house without anything. It was one morning, at about ten. I have a scar from when he threw a chair at me. Also, I still have pains in my elbow. It was very different at that point. It was too much and I started to realize that the way he was hitting me in the head with his hands, he could kill me. That was when I left—I grabbed my kids and went to stay at a girlfriend's house. On that same night, I called my mother in the United States and I cried, "Mamá, I can't stay with him anymore. I don't want to be in this country." And then, at that exact moment when I told her that I didn't want to be there, he called me. He asked me where I was because this was the first night that I had slept away from the house. He asked me, "Where are you? If you've left me, then go alone, but leave the children with me." I told him no. They were my children. They'd always slept with me. I'd always taken care of them. He told me, "Well, then I'm going to look for you everywhere if I have to." He was thinking that I'd perhaps gone to another district, another state.

I told him that I was leaving and that he wouldn't see the children again. He replied, "Yes, I'm going to see them because I'm going to look for you and when I find you, I'm going to kill you. You've taken the children without my permission and you're going to do what I say."

I tried to look for other places to live, but he always found me. He told me, "I'll come to wherever you are living whether you like it or not." I even went to places pretty far from where we were living, thinking that maybe he wouldn't look for me, wouldn't find me, but he always did. He'd break down doors and come through the windows, or, if not, from the roof, up the fire escape. This happened many times. Afterwards, he'd ask me why I left and he'd hit me, insult me. And sometimes I had no choice but to return to him. Sometimes we'd even have—I can't call them sexual relations. This was rape, because I really didn't want anything to do with him at this point. This happened many times. And I didn't want it. I just wanted to take care of my kids, leave him forever.

The last time I left, it was late June. I said I was going out and I told him to give me some of the money that my mother had sent for me and my children. He gave me some money, said that I could go, but I'd have to leave the boy there with him. I left and went to my aunt's house with the two girls. He felt it—that I'd be leaving. I was at my aunt's house for quite a while, but I was going to return home since I couldn't leave my son. His sister, who also had a son, ended up taking my son out with her. Right when I was about to leave, his sister arrived with my son and her son. This was the moment we left El Salvador. God had arranged everything so that I could leave. You have no idea how I started to cry when I saw all of my children there without Carlos! I'd been thinking that I'd have to leave with only the girls and leave my son behind, because otherwise I'd be in that situation forever. When I saw that my son had arrived with Carlos's sister and her son, you can't imagine! They were all there! It felt so beautiful. She asked me if I was going home. I told her that I had an errand to run. She asked me if I wanted her to look after the kids while I went out, and I told her that I'd take them with me. I left. I left everything there: my television, my bed, my clothes, everything. I left with what I had brought with me, nothing more. We only had one change of clothes. As we traveled, sometimes we would clean them in the street, in a church.

HE WAS GOING TO KILL ME

We took the bus from San Salvador to the border with Guatemala. My mother was sending me fifty dollars, one hundred dollars, from time to time, transferring money to me online. It is really difficult to arrive in a country and not know the currency. In Guatemala, the currency is the quetzal. I didn't know how much ten dollars were worth in quetzales. In El Salvador, we use the US dollar. There, a bottle of water costs fifteen cents, at most a quarter. In Guatemala, a bottle costs five quetzales. Sometimes people would charge me twenty, and I never knew what it was really worth. Here they have charged me two dollars for a bottle of water. We travelers like to have cellular phones in order to communicate with family and friends, to see how they are doing back in El Salvador. You have to buy a SIM card. For me, it costs at least eighty pesos: thirty for the SIM, and fifty for the charger. I've heard some say that it cost them one hundred, even one hundred and sixty. One Honduran couple even told me that they were charged two hundred pesos. They charge us what they want because they know that we don't know the actual value.

We had to pay $150 so that the Guatemalan border patrol would let us cross the river. My mother has a friend from the United States with family in Guatemala. They helped me, and we went to their house. The idea at that point was to be out of El Salvador because Carlos was looking for me. He sent my mother messages on Facebook, telling her that he was after me and that when he found me, he was going to kill me. I was in Guatemala for seven days.

In Guatemala, we stayed in hotels. Only when we met the woman who was a relative of my mother's friend did we stay in a house. I didn't have to worry about paying for another hotel. At that point, my mother said that she was going to try to find me a *coyote* to take me up to where they live in Texas. They found one, but unfortunately he only took me here to the ADO station in Tenosique.[3] My parents had paid him the initial payment at that point, $4,000. It would have been $14,000 for the entire trip. He had taken us with him in Guatemala, in La Ruidosa, Izabal.[4]

The *coyote* was from Honduras. He was probably thirty-five. He was friendly when he spoke with my mother. He told her that he was Christian. He also told my sister on the phone things about Christ. My mom would say things like "God bless you" to him. But in reality, from the time we met him, he was never like that. When we first met, he said to me, "*Oye, tu,*" and the way he said it, it didn't sound like a Christian.[5] I told my mom, "He is not a Christian." When we got to El Ceibo, he went out and never came back until

3. ADO (Autobuses de Oriente) is a major bus line in Mexico.

4. La Ruidosa is a town is in Izabal, Guatemala, 128 kilometers northeast of Guatemala City.

5. In English: "Hey, you."

the morning.[6] He would disappear. When we got to the border here
in Mexico, he arrived without his suitcase. I asked him, "Where is
your suitcase?" And he told me, "Well, I always leave it there in the
hotel." I asked him why, and he said, "Up here, it makes me stand
out." He would just walk around with his dark sunglasses on and
wear the same clothes. At that point, I started thinking that it was
very strange that he had left his bag. I felt confused. Since we met
the *coyote* and started the trip, he never stayed at the places we did.
He would just leave us at a hotel, get a room for us and another for
him, and then return in the morning. I would never hear him in
his room. He would always go out. I'd rise at four, five, six in the
morning eager to get going, and I would hear him just getting back.
And I began to worry that he might abandon us along the way. This
happens a lot with *coyotes*.

When we passed El Ceibo, we were in a van and the *coyote* paid
the driver some money to pay off the police. He told me that even
though there were police stops, we would always pass through them
because you just have to give them some pesos, and they let you go.
They all work like this. Through all of Guatemala he would pay
them, and we would pass. Even the border patrol between El Salvador and Guatemala. We just paid them off and passed through.

It was a bit dangerous at the border because there are lots of
rocks in the river. People get scraped up on the rocks. Sometimes
they can't hold themselves up and fall into the currents. An older
man was helping me cross, and another woman was helping my son
and carrying my bag. The current was strong, and the rocks hurt a
lot. But you have to do it because you can't cross in your shoes. This
was the most difficult part of crossing that border.

From there, he took us up here to a hotel called Luz de Luna in
Tenosique. The next day at six in the morning, he knocked on the

---

6. El Ceibo is on Guatemala's northern border, just south of Palenque, Chiapas,
Mexico.

door to our room and said, "Get up, get up, now! We are going now! We are not going to travel together. You guys are going on one ADO bus and I'm going on another one." He told me, "You are going to get into a taxi and tell them to take you to the ADO station. I'll meet you there." We got to the terminal at almost seven and began to wait for him. It became eight, then nine, the hours passing. And no sign of him. I had a phone that I had brought from El Salvador, but I didn't have a Mexican SIM card. I didn't have any contacts, nothing. Pretty soon, it was one in the afternoon, and we hadn't even eaten breakfast. My children were asking me for water.

When he left us at the bus station, I thought he would arrive quickly, but I guess he had all this planned out, to get rid of us. Easy money. We were in the terminal the entire night, and at nine the next morning the Mexican immigration police arrived. The woman who ran a restaurant there—she had noticed that I was a migrant—she told me, "Come in here, come with me! They're going to come take you. Come inside so they won't see you!" She helped me, brought me inside, and she asked me, "You've been here since yesterday, right?" I told her, "Yes." She asked me what had happened, and I told her that we had been traveling with a *coyote*, but he had left us there. I said, "I don't know where he went."

At one in the afternoon, I asked her if I could borrow her phone to make a call to my mother. I called her and told her what was happening. She then called the *coyote*, but he didn't answer. He also didn't answer on Facebook or on WhatsApp. The woman running the restaurant really helped us. She noticed that we hadn't had breakfast or lunch. It was almost four in the afternoon on the second day. The children were hungry, dirty, sweating from the heat, and anxious because they'd been sitting all day. I asked the woman at the restaurant if she could loan me some money because I didn't have anything, and she said sure and sent me to a little motel near the bus station. She loaned me one hundred pesos. She also told me about the migrant shelter here in Tenosique, and I told her no. I was scared that they would perhaps send me back. I didn't know.

The next day, she urged me again to go to the migrant shelter. My mother told me that day that she was going to contact some family members in Veracruz and ask them if they could come for us. We were in the streets for three days. The place we were staying would only have us at night. We couldn't stay there during the day. I didn't know what to do during the day. I visited the woman at the restaurant and told her that I was thinking about going back, and she finally convinced me to go to the La 72 shelter. I didn't know what it would be like, but thank God they have helped us a lot. I've spoken with the psychologist and the doctor here, and told them about everything that I lived through. I know that I'm not a perfect person or a superperson, but I want the best for my children. This is the most important thing for me. I don't want to know anything about Carlos.

THE CHILDREN ARE REALLY CALM NOW

I think that when people need something, they sometimes leave, and then they can get picked up by police outside this shelter. Here inside the shelter, the immigration police don't enter. They don't have permission. But you can imagine how we all feel here knowing that they are looking for us. Thank God, nothing really bad has happened. I would die if anything happened to these children.

I can free myself from Carlos, though I won't feel free until I'm further north. Even though I'm here, I still feel fear that he might come looking for me. Until I left, I kept this all to myself, everything. Before I left, I had never told my mother what was happening. I knew that my mother and father would feel bad. My father suffers from diabetes. I'd thought to myself, *Why make them feel bad if they can't do anything?* And if they returned to El Salvador for me, it would be worse because there is no work there. I kept it all inside. But when I left El Salvador, I told my parents everything. They didn't believe me. It really startled them. They told me it was better that I try to come live with them. And I understand that even though they are working, it's not like they have a lot of money. They gave $4,000 to this *coyote*. This was a huge loss. They're really tight on money. They had to borrow that money.

The children are really calm now, really calm. They know that we're on our way to stay with their grandparents. They sometimes say, "Mami, we're never going to make it to our grandparents." They've never met their grandparents. They've seen photos and videos and talked on the phone with them. My oldest daughter looks like my mom. Sara is calm now because she doesn't see Carlos anymore. The whole problem was seeing him. He'd just show up and start hitting me for no reason at all.

Leaving was the best step I've taken in my life. My oldest daughter would cry and say, "Mami, let's go. Let's go." I don't want to see him again. He wasn't a father to them either. "Mami," she'd tell me, "he just hits you. Let's go." I overheard someone here talking about how there were gangsters here in the shelter, and for a moment, I thought he might be here.

My birthday is in July, this month! I'll be twenty-six. I want to be with my parents on my birthday. We are going to travel quickly. In seven or eight days, we'll be there. I hope it's my first peaceful birthday.

My mother's family in Veracruz works a lot and can't come right away but are waiting for a day off from work to come pick us up. They'll come get us in a car. We'll stay in Veracruz with my parents' friends until my parents are able to save a bit more money for our trip. Supposedly, these very people know someone, so, although I'm a bit scared because of what happened with this last *coyote*, I think it's our only option. From what I've been hearing, I just need to get to the US border and turn myself in. With written proof of Carlos's threats against my life on Facebook and in emails, and with my three children, I think they will let me stay. So that is my plan, to arrive at the US immigration services.

We're treated very nicely here at La 72. There are many mothers here and many of us travel alone with children. The staff treats us very well and helps us, even playing with the children. They show movies for the children too sometimes. I'm excited to get to my parents, to spend time with my kids and celebrate my twenty-sixth birthday.

My only dream is to see my children grow up into adulthood. I'd like to be able to give them, not everything—you can't give them everything exactly—but at least what they need. This is my dream for the future, to see them move forward, to be able to move forward. I want to live with my parents. Sometimes people say, "I'm tired of living with my parents," but I feel that after being away from them for so long, I just want to be with them. Sometimes kids say, "I want to be older, to leave home, do what I want." But imagine, to reach an extreme where you can't imagine a better place to be than with your parents. I want to feel safe. My father never laid a hand on me. He never hit me. For me to get to a point where I was getting punched and kicked, by someone who supposedly loved me, someone whom I have a child with—this someone who was supposed to be protecting me was trying to kill me. He made me feel like I wasn't worth anything.

After a few more weeks in Tenosique, family members picked up Danelia and the children to stay with them in Veracruz, Mexico. Carlos sent text messages to Danelia's father and referred to himself as the devil, saying that he was very powerful. He also said he knew their address because before Danelia had left, her parents would send money for their daughter in envelopes bearing their return address, which Carlos would steal. In November 2016, within five months of our first interview, Danelia successfully arrived at the US border, where she turned herself over to Customs and Border Protection (CBP) and applied for asylum. A week later, with the help of a local priest who agreed to officially receive her from the CBP since her parents are undocumented, she reunited with them in Texas and began working at a tile company while her children attend school. Carlos is in prison in El Salvador and has not contacted Danelia's family since she arrived in the United States. Danelia is planning on filing an asylum case in the United States using the death threats that Carlos has sent her in emails as written evidence of the danger she faces in El Salvador.

ADRIÁN CRUZ

AGE AT CROSSING: 17
BORN IN: Guatemala City, Guatemala
INTERVIEWED IN: Oakland, California

*We're introduced to Adrián through CIVIC, an organization that sup-
ports immigrants in detention.[1] We meet him in March 2015 at a run-
down house in the Fruitvale neighborhood of Oakland, California, a
few weeks after he's been released from detention at a federal prison
in nearby Richmond. Boards cover the windows on the house, where
Adrián is renting a tiny converted closet to sleep in. He greets us at the
door with a warm smile and squints a little as he descends the rickety
wooden staircase. We walk to a local taco shop to eat and talk, but after*

---

1. CIVIC stands for Community Initiatives for Visiting Immigrants in Confinement. CIVIC has since changed its name to Freedom for Immigrants.

eating, we find it too loud and take a short drive onto the campus of Mills College. We sit on a park bench at the foot of Julia Morgan's campanile clock tower and gaze across the deep green lawns.

Adrián begins by telling us about his early life in Zona 18 of Guatemala City, a neighborhood notorious for gang activity. After he witnessed his mother being shot to death in her shop by a gang member when he was five, his grandmother, whom he lovingly refers to as "Mamá," raised him. When he was seventeen, he was shot and stabbed by gang members in his neighborhood after he refused to join them. The surgery to remove the bullets left him with a scar from his waist all the way up to his shoulder. He also has a scar across his neck, where the gang leader slashed his throat before leaving him to die. After the attack and a miraculous survival, Adrián rode cargo trains though Mexico to the US border, where he was caught by Customs and Border Protection. Prior to being released from detention, he applied for asylum and has an open asylum case. He's been moving from job to job and from house to house, and is struggling to start his life in the Bay Area. During our conversation, he describes his isolation in a foreign land and keeps repeating the words "solito, solito" ("alone, alone") in a low voice.

MY MOTHER WAS ALWAYS GOOD TO ME

My mother was always good to me. I didn't know my father, but I had an older brother and sister. My mother would buy me many things—she worked very hard to give me what I needed. We lived in the Zona 18 barrio in Guatemala City, where my mom had a business.[2] It was a store where people could buy household items, like things for the kitchen.

My neighborhood is very dangerous. The gangs there are very

---

2. Guatemala City is the capital of Guatemala, with a population of 4.5 million in the metro area.

dangerous. They've killed a ton of police officers. They'll even fire at soldiers. There was a gang that would sometimes come around to my mom's store and demand money. One day when I was five, I was with her at the store when a guy from the gang came in and asked for money. My mom said she didn't have it. She asked if she could pay part of what he was asking. He didn't answer her—he just shot her. And then he just left.

After my mom was killed by the gang member, I stayed with my grandparents. I was devastated because I missed my mother. But thank God I didn't really lack anything. My grandparents' house was very simple, but we always had food. My grandfather always worked—a lot. He grew tomatoes. He also liked to drink and spend money, but we always had enough for beans and cheese. Aside from me, my grandmother cared for three cousins, who were like brothers and sisters to me. I went to school. It was a public school, with uniforms and everything. All the teachers were good, but I was a troublemaker. I'd do things like throw paper at classmates, and the teachers would rap me across the fingers with a ruler. I was held back for two years in elementary school. I just didn't pay attention in class.

By the time I got to middle school, I did much better. I paid more attention because, back at the house, my grandma would hit me and tell me that if I didn't pay attention, they were just wasting their money paying for school.[3] I made it through sixth grade, and then I went to a high school called "The Cooperative." But then I didn't want to continue, because we didn't have much money. After I quit school, I worked as a painter. I had a cousin who was a contractor

3. Public school is free and compulsory in Guatemala for the first six years. However, expenses, including school uniforms, books, and supplies, are not covered. Partly because of those expenses, and also because public middle and high schools are not available for all students, the average years of schooling for a child in Guatemala is around four years. The country also has the lowest literacy rate in Central America at just under 75 percent.

who'd paint Domino's Pizza restaurants. So he'd hire me to help with the painting. I did that for about three years.

"YOU'RE DEAD NOW!"

When I was seventeen, there were some gang members who wanted me to join their gang, and, well, I didn't want to. The gang was part of the Mara 18.[4] They had about twenty guys in it, and I knew them from the neighborhood. One day about five guys came up to me and said, "If you don't join, we'll kill you." And I told them, "Okay." But I didn't want to do it! I didn't want to join that gang! So I tried to stay away from them. It's heavy, the situation in Guatemala with the gangs. They force people to join so they'll have more members to sell drugs, kill people, demand money from people.

One day after about a month, I went to the store and some of the gang members saw me. One of them yelled, "We're going to kill you!" I told them, "I don't want to join this gang with you." I was outside my house that night when four of the gang members approached me. They had guns, and one had a knife as long as my forearm. I knew the guy with the knife—he was a little guy called Ghost, or sometimes "the Rat." I was shot twice, and the Rat cut me across the throat with his knife. I remember one of the guys shouting, "You're dead now!"

There was a lot of blood! I heard someone say, "Leave him. He's dead." I stayed there like I was unconscious, and they left. When they were gone, I sat up, and very soon the emergency vehicles arrived and took me to the hospital. The pain was like torture. The doctor cut me open to see what had been damaged by the bullets.

---

4. Also known in Central America as La 18, Calle 18, or Barrio 18, this international crime organization started in the Rampart area of Los Angeles, California. See appendix essay on "The Rise of the *Maras*."

The bullets entered the ribs on my left and lodged inside, so the doctors had to take those out.

Afterward, while I was in the hospital recovering for a few days, I heard that the gang knew I was still alive and that they were asking around for me. So after I got out of the hospital, I hid, and then three or four months after that, I left Guatemala. I have a daughter who was about three months old when I left, and I saw very little of her before I left.[5] Her name is Cristina.

If I return, I think they'll kill me.

I WAS ASKING A LOT FROM GOD

When I told my grandparents that I was going to the United States, they were very sad, and they asked me, "Why do you have to leave? We don't know what's going to happen to you. It's very dangerous on the road." I replied, "It's better that I go." And so I left home with very little money, like fifteen quetzales.[6] This was January 6, 2012. I didn't say goodbye to my grandparents before I left. I decided that it was better that I left this way, secretly. I called them when I was about an hour away. I told my grandmother, "Look, the truth is that you know the situation here. You're sick. I want to help you, and if I stay here working, I imagine that I will not be able to buy medicine for you. I'm going to see if God lets me make it to the United States." And she told me, "And when you arrive, you will not have family there. Don't go."

But I made the journey. I took a bus to the Mexican border. Now the problem is that at the Mexican border there are immigration stations. That's where they ask for documents, and if you

---

5. In our expansive conversations with him, Adrián has almost never brought up his daughter. When we ask, he tells us that he is in contact with her and her mother, and that he sends her presents and talks to her on the phone.

6. About $1.92 US in 2012.

don't have any, you return to Guatemala. But I learned from other people making the journey that what you do is get off the bus at a certain spot before you get to the immigration station, walk into the hills and go around the station, and then return to the road on the Mexican side of the border at a certain spot where the buses will stop and pick you up.

From there, I made it to the train in Arriaga, Chiapas.[7] Then I went from train to train to train to train. I didn't have any friends from Guatemala who went with me, but I met many other Guatemalans making the same journey, and we stuck together. We call the trains La Bestia. What we'd do is we'd wait for cargo trains to pass, jump on, and climb to the top. There'd be many people up on top of the trains. We'd go through tunnels and have to tuck in and stay low. I did see accidents—usually with people trying to grab onto the train as it passed, since the trains move very quickly. Some people get hurt, and some die that way.

While I was traveling, I made a few friends, and one good friend. We'd all help each other. I lost my good friend along the way, though—I got on a train, and I think he couldn't make it in time. I waited up ahead, but he never showed up.

In between trains, I'd have to get off the car to find food. In Mexico, there are many good people—as in all places, there are good people and bad people. I'd ask anyone I met, "Look, Señora, could you give me a tortilla, and I can wash your car or something?" And then the woman I was talking to might ask me where I was from. I'd reply, "Guatemala." And she'd ask, "And where are you going?" And I'd say, "I want to go to the United States." And she'd say, "I hope it goes well," and give me some food.

On the way through Mexico there are houses that are called

---

7. Arriaga is a municipality of about forty-five thousand people in Chiapas, Mexico's southernmost state, about 260 kilometers from the Guatemalan border.

casas de migrantes.[8] They're in every state in Mexico. They give food to migrants passing through, and you can stay there for two days, three days, and then you go on your way. You can even find clothes and shoes there. I stayed in many migrant houses. Of all of them, the one in Ixtepec, Oaxaca, might be the best.[9] You can stay there for three or four days. They help a lot of people.

There's also a group called Las Betas.[10] They help all migrants—men, women, children, whoever. At every train stop from Arriaga to the capital, they give you a hand, group after group. If someone is injured near the train station, they arrive with an ambulance to care for wounded people. They have salve for the biting flies and sunscreen. They have crackers, tuna. They give you two blankets for the cold. They give you hoodies, sweatshirts, and this helps a lot! If you've been beaten up, they will treat you. And if you want to return home, they will take you to the immigration station, but if not, then that's fine. The whole trip, I was asking a lot from God. I asked that He would give me the opportunity to reach the United States and that nothing bad would happen. I asked Him to give me the opportunity to help my family.

Eventually I made it up to the United States, but I got caught by Mexican authorities and sent back to the Guatemalan border. I didn't return to my grandparents' house. Instead, I went to an aunt's house for about five days. My grandma came there to see me, and she told me, "I'm very old. If you go, you're not going to find me alive again. You're not going to see me again." She was seventy-six.

---

8. For more on migrant houses, see appendix essay on "Casas de Migrantes."

9. Ixtepec is a municipality of twenty-five thousand near Mexico's southern coast.

10. The Grupos Beta, or Beta Groups, is a service offered by the National Institute of Migration. Its main goal is to protect the human rights of all migrants, regardless of their legal status.

I CAME HERE FIGHTING, FIGHTING, SURVIVING

After five days back in Guatemala, I left again. On my second trip to the Guatemalan border, I went from Arriaga, through DF to Mazatlán.[11] And, thank God, everything went well.

I joined a group of twenty-five or thirty people of all ages heading for the border. Most people making the trip pay a lot of money to guides to help them, like 50,000 quetzales.[12] But we couldn't afford that. We made it very far together. We hopped a lot of trains, suffered hunger, suffered cold, and worried that gangs or cartels would catch us, would kill us. There is so much cruelty on this trip, right? I know that lots of things have happened on these routes through the desert, how many people have been killed coming from Central America. I came here fighting, fighting, surviving.

My group made it to Sinaloa, and one evening there we were waiting to catch a train. It was about six o'clock and already getting dark. Some men walked into the middle of our group, and the way they looked made me nervous. Then I noticed one of them had a pistol. Suddenly one of them said, "Everyone down! Everyone down, now!" So we threw ourselves onto the ground. I didn't have any money, but the rest of the group had some money and their phones. So the guys took everything and left, but, thank God, they didn't do anything else to us. They were bandits, gangsters. In Sinaloa they are called El Sufrágio.[13]

---

11. *DF* stands for Distrito Federal Mexico, Mexico City, the national capital of Mexico. Mazatlán is a city on the Pacific coast in the state of Sinaloa, 1,070 kilometers from Mexico City.

12. Fifty thousand quetzales was about $6,402 US in 2012.

13. *El Sufrágio*, or "the Suffrage," seems to refer to a street gang. It is not clear whether they are related to the Sinaloa Cartel, a group that the international security community considers the most powerful crime organization in the world.

"AN IMMIGRATION OFFICIAL
IS GOING TO COME GET YOU"

After what happened in Sinaloa, our group split up, and we all found our own ways to the border. I was *solito, solito*! I decided to try to cross by myself, and I didn't want to cross in the desert because I thought, *If I go into the desert, it's going to be really hot, and I'm going to die, right?* So I tried to cross the US border in Calexico-Mexicali.[14]

I went to the line at customs. While I was standing in line, I saw a little space off the line where nobody seemed to be looking, and I tried to sneak through across the border. But an immigration officer spotted me and said, "Go back!" I didn't go back. I just kept walking. Then the officer caught up to me, restrained me, searched me, and then put me in his car. The officer spoke Spanish, and he said, "Well, you're so young, so boyish. How old are you? Are you a minor?" And I said, "Yes, I'm seventeen." "Okay," he said, "why did you come to the United States?" I said, "I want to be here, but I don't have family or anything." And I started to tell him my story.

He drove me to a detention center.[15] The officers there spoke Spanish. They were very good people. They asked me what I was doing in the United States. I told them, "I want to work, to help my family." They only fed us soup. Every day, three soups, and always the same. There were very small rooms and there were a bunch of us there, one person next to another on the floor. There were young men together, fifteen to seventeen, around that age. Then there was a separate room with men, only men. In another area, there were women and children.

---

14. The Calexico-Mexicali metropolitan area is a major border crossing between the state of Baja in Mexico and eastern California in the United States.

15. For more on ICE detention, see appendix essay on "Arrests and Detention in the United States." For more on Calexico detention, see the appendix essay on "Arrests and Detentions in Mexico."

After spending more than a week in ICE detention near Calexico, Adrián was moved out of the federal system to a camp in Texas run by Baptist Child and Family Services (BCFS).[16]

I was locked up there for nine days, and after that the authorities sent me to Houston, to a camp with others from detention. We were all minors, and I was there for three or four days. The camp had small houses, six cabins on either side. It wasn't a prison, and there were no police, only normal staff, but we couldn't leave.

And then BCFS sent me on a plane to Fairfield, California.[17] Maybe they sent me here, to California, because it's the state, I think, where they help migrants the most. I was put in a house with other migrants in Fairfield that was part of BCFS. The director of the program was named Miss Nelly.

I was there in the house with Miss Nelly for six months. It was a normal house, but there were eighteen of us living there. Everyone else had family in the United States. Everyone stayed for one month, and then their families would come pick them up. They treated us very well there. We went to school—it was a big school. We had free time, and there was very good food! They would ask us, "What do you want to eat?" It didn't matter how much it cost. I had a very comfortable bed. Everything was great there. They even gave us MP3 players to listen to music, one for each of us.

---

16. Baptist Child and Family Services is a seventy-year-old global network of nonprofits that started as a small orphanage system. Today, BCFS establishes emergency shelters for children throughout the world, among other services. Since 2013, BCFS has received hundreds of millions of dollars in grants from the federal government to establish housing for undocumented minors who had been previously held in ICE detention. BCFS has established these shelters throughout Texas and California, though their locations are generally shielded to protect the safety of the minors.

17. Fairfield is a city of over one hundred thousand located halfway between San Francisco and Sacramento.

The program staff found me a lawyer, and they told me, "When you turn eighteen, two days before your birthday, you are going to enter a program in San Francisco, the Huckleberry House.[18] There are rules, but you'll be able to work and go to school freely." I even went to the house with them to see where I was going to live. We visited, and two days before my birthday, they said, "You are going to go tomorrow."

The next day arrived, and nothing happened. So I asked the program people and my lawyer about it, and they said, "We don't know what's happening with your case. We turned in your paperwork, but they didn't accept you." Then they said that since I was turning eighteen, I couldn't stay at Miss Nelly's because I would no longer be a minor. They told me, "We're sorry. An immigration official is going to come get you." I was so afraid of going to prison that I wanted to cry. I said, "I want to leave. It doesn't matter if they kill me in Guatemala. I want to go now and sign for a voluntary deportation."[19] Then I went to my room, and ten minutes after they told me that an immigration official was coming, he arrived. They said, "He's come for you. We're all very sad, and we hope that you go with God and that you have good luck." I wasn't crying anymore in front of them, but I was thinking, *I've now been locked up for six months. How much more time am I going to be detained?*

THEY TREAT YOU LIKE YOU'RE A CRIMINAL

The immigration official arrived and cuffed me and said, "Let's go in the car." I hadn't cried in front of the people at Miss Nelly's house,

---

18. The Huckleberry House is a transitional living residence for homeless teenagers in San Francisco.

19. Whereas a voluntary departure does not leave an order of removal on the person's record, it may result in the detainee forgoing relief that had been entitled to them.

but I cried in the car. We went to a place called Martinez.[20] They kept me there for one night and said, "You have to go to prison. You'll probably go tomorrow."[21] And then they sent me to Richmond, in Contra Costa.[22] I was very miserable. There were a lot of people there. And they detained me there and never let me make a phone call. Not one. You don't have contact with your family at all. I thought that we would at least be able to buy a calling card, but nothing, nothing. They treat you like you're a criminal.

I spent four months in jail, and it was very ugly. The guards treat people very badly. They're really racist. They don't hit us, but they treat us badly, especially the Chicano guards.[23] The Chicanos are really racist toward the Central Americans. I don't know why. There are times when everyone fights. A few of the dark-brown people start to fight, sometimes with lighter-skinned Mexicans, and they lock all of us up for two hours. It doesn't even matter to them if someone wants to go to the bathroom. Oh, the food, it's horrible! You can't even imagine. Not even dogs would eat it! No meat. They're like soups, but with no flavor and very ugly. If there's food left over from today, they make another soup tomorrow and mix the old one in. Almost everyone wants to work in the kitchen. They don't pay, but if you work there, you get more food and better food, like chicken.

There were two floors in each building of the prison. There were five buildings. In each building, there are probably two hundred

---

20. The Martinez Detention Facility is in Contra Costa, California.

21. Each detainee is supposed to be assigned to a deportation officer, who is required to meet a request by the detainee for a "voluntary departure." Adrián was denied this right.

22. Richmond is located on the east side of San Francisco Bay, in Contra Costa County. The West County Detention Center in Richmond is a major ICE detention center. For more on ICE detention centers, see appendix essay on "Arrests and Detention in the United States."

23. *Chicano* refers to a person of Mexican descent living in the United States.

people. In one building, half is for immigrants and the other half is for prisoners who are there for serious offenses, and we are not with them. The other buildings are all for prisoners. There are a lot of gangs there, Sureños.[24] They fight every day there.

To be locked up like that, well, I wanted to leave. If Franky hadn't arrived, I don't know what would have happened to me.[25] I told him, "Please call my family. I would greatly appreciate it. I hope my mamá doesn't worry.[26] I don't know if I'm going to be able to leave or if they're going to deport me."

CIVIC started to look at my case, and I told Franky, "Well, I don't know what I'm going to do. I don't have family or anything here. Can you help me?" And Franky told me, "Don't worry. We are going to look for a family for you." I told the people at CIVIC my story, what was happening with me. And they told me that with my scars and my story, I'm definitely going to earn asylum.

Finally, after four months, I went to court. They had me chained up—my hands, my waist, and my feet. Can you imagine? I told the judge my story, and she said, "Wow. All of this happened to you?" She was surprised. I showed her my scars. I had a lawyer who explained my entire case. The judge said, "Why didn't they let you go before you turned eighteen?" And I told her that there was a program and I was supposed to be placed in a house, but at the last minute, on my birthday, they sent me to the prison instead. So I told her this, and she said, "Okay, but you need to bring me your papers." And my lawyer got my paperwork. She asked for the minimum bail amount, $1,500, and the judge agreed.

---

24. Also known as Sur 13, or Sureños X3, the Sureños are a loose group of gangs whose stronghold is in Southern California and whose greatest rivalry is with the Norteños, whose territory is north of Bakersfield.

25. Franky is a volunteer for CIVIC who visited Adrián in detention.

26. As noted earlier, Adrián calls his grandmother "Mamá" because she raised him after his mother died.

Franky and CIVIC put my picture up on the computer and raised money from donations for my bail. The first day, they had raised $800, and by Thursday, more than $1,000. On Friday, Franky told me, "Look, now we have your bail! We actually have $3,600, and we're going to give you $2,000 to buy yourself a telephone and other things you need when you leave."

From the time I appeared in court, it took about ten days to process my paperwork, and then my lawyer called me in prison. She said, "Congratulations! You're free! Franky has paid your bail." I told her that she must have made a mistake. I was very calm, but the truth is that I wanted to be sure it was true. Then I heard someone say my name on the prison speaker. I was very happy, and all of my friends were cheering.

Then I was led out. Franky was waiting outside by the exit. I was surprised to see him! The first thing we did, he took me to eat. After that, he took me on a drive and then to his house. The next day, he gave me new jeans and shoes that he'd bought me in Fairfield so that I'd look good. Then we went to get my things from the detention center.[27]

IF I'M DEPORTED, I DON'T KNOW WHAT WILL HAPPEN

The couple I'm living with now are also from Guatemala, and they have their papers. I go to school, and the students at the school are from around the world. But I also work. I work for eight hours in construction and then I go to school for three and a half hours.

At work now I'm helping to remodel a very big house. The contractor is American. He speaks almost no Spanish. It's good pay, fifteen dollars an hour. I cut whatever they tell me to cut, with tools like the circular saw. I know how to cut, use the ruler, all of this, but to tell you the truth, when I started, I didn't know anything, not even how to hold a tape measure. I learned here. Even though I

---

27. Adrián was out on bail pending hearings on his legal status as an asylum seeker.

didn't know anything, they still paid me the same as everyone else, but I had to work hard! If not, they would fire me. The boss there fired a number of people because they were standing around. Here, like you know, they don't like to see anyone standing around. I've been working there for almost three months.

Everything was going well, and then I heard that my grandma had died. Everyone helped me out with money to get by, even the boss. He gave me two days off with pay. He was very good to me. Doña Elena, who took me into her home, is a good person. She cooks and prepares everything that I bring with me every day. I work with her husband, Alfredo. The other boarders are all older.

I want to stay here, working and studying, making a new life. I don't want to go back to Guatemala. If I'm deported, I don't know what will happen. I know what will happen to me if I go back and the gang members catch me: they'll cut me into pieces. Because they're young, they don't think. They think that because they're so big with the gang that nothing will happen to them. This is nonsense.

I'm going to give it my all because of the opportunity I have here. I'm alone. I'm doing well but still sad about my grandma. I'm motivated to work, though, and support myself. I'm going to go to school so I can convince the judge to let me stay. I don't have another option. I have dreams of learning English, living here, buying a car one day. And Cristina will be two soon. She says words, but she still doesn't talk.

In February 2017, we accompany Adrián to the immigration court off Market Street in San Francisco. Donald Trump is in the White House, and his anti-immigration chant to "Build the wall!" has sent chills through the Central American migrant community.

Adrián rides up the elevator anxious, hands sweating, eyes looking side to side. He tells us he is afraid that if his plea for a stay is not granted, he may be taken from the courtroom and deported to Guatemala, where the mara that stabbed and shot him will finish the job. Dressed in a black cap, shirt, and jeans, he stands in contrast to his attorney, who's wearing a gray suit and tie. The lawyer tells us he needs more time to gather documents from the hospital and police in Guatemala City, to prove Adrián was the innocent victim of a gang attack. But in the chaos of that country those documents may be difficult to find.

The bailiff calls Adrián to the stand. The black-robed judge questions the attorney in English, while Adrián looks on silently. Finally, the judge addresses Adrián: "I grant you a two-year extension." At first Adrián seems not to understand. But after the interpreter translates, Adrián's face breaks out in an ear-to-ear smile. Down on the street, the lawyer explains that the Ninth Circuit Court in San Francisco has ruled unfavorably in the past on cases such as Adrián's. It would take a change of direction for the court to grant Adrián permanent residence status. But Adrián wishes to celebrate. We accompany him to a street-side Mexican restaurant where we are joined by his sponsor, Franky. Elated, Adrián hugs Franky, exulting, "Gracias a Dios." Surrounded by friends, with a job and an apartment, Adrián has two years to prove himself.

PEDRO HERNANDEZ

AGE AT CROSSING: 17
BORN IN: Tzununcap, Huehuetenango, Guatemala
INTERVIEWED IN: Chicago, Illinois

To meet Pedro we travel from California to the heart of the American Midwest, Chicago. It's a rainy day in May 2016, and we take the L to South LaSalle Street. We ride the elevator to the offices of the Heartland Alliance's National Immigrant Justice Center, where social workers and lawyers are busy helping immigrants and refugees. In the Jane Addams conference room, a lawyer introduces us to Pedro, a young Guatemalan in his late teens. He shyly shakes our hands and sits down. Pedro is wearing clean but unpressed clothes; his black hair is neatly combed. His skin is sallow from lack of sunlight, and he has broad cheekbones and deep-set eyes. His eyes are red-rimmed with sleep deprivation—he just got off the night shift and has to go to school—and he yawns deeply and quickly covers his mouth.

In Guatemala, many Indigenous families struggle to survive through subsistence farming. Pedro's story highlights how many youth migrants bear the burden of paying off loans that their parents have borrowed, which come with exorbitant interest rates and also often require parents to put up their land as collateral, in order to pay for their journeys.

I WAS BORN BADLY

I come from the village of Tzununcap in the province of Huehuetenango, Guatemala. My first language is a Mayan dialect called Chuj.[1] My grandfather was a guerrilla fighter in the Guatemalan civil war, and afterwards, he settled in our village.[2] My father worked in a cardamom factory a great distance away and didn't live with us. Because we were very poor, my pregnant mother was forced to live with my father's brother and sister-in-law, who didn't like having to feed her. Eleven people were crowded in a small dwelling without windows or a kitchen, just a communal sleeping area and a wood stove. My grandmother said my mother suffered a lot from hunger when she was pregnant with me. My uncle would hide all my mom's food and wouldn't leave any for her.

I was born badly. On that day, the sixteenth of February 1997, my mother was home alone, and no one helped her. She couldn't take the pain. I just fell onto the ground when I was born. I don't know how many minutes passed before my grandmother picked me off the earthen floor, washed off the nastiness, and wrapped me in a blanket. The filth made the illness grow inside my mom.

I was very weak. I couldn't move my right arm. I couldn't breathe. We didn't have food or anything: no doctor, nothing. I was always naked as a baby. I didn't have any clothes, just a sheet. My grandmother bought me my first shirt and pants when I was three.

---

1. For more information on Chuj, and Mayan dialects, see glossary.

2. See "Historical Timeline."

"KILL THAT KID!"

That was around the same time our family moved to Playa Grande, where my father worked at a palm oil processing factory called Ixcán. I remember there was a big river nearby. My mom said that I had a problem with my hips. I didn't have the strength to stand up. I couldn't walk; I just moved around the floor. I don't know what illness I had. My family would have taken me to the doctor, but we didn't have money. When I went back to my village at age four, I still couldn't walk. My aunt told my father I wasn't good for anything. She asked, "Who will help you when you're old? What will you get out of him? Kill that kid!" She lent my father a pistol to kill me. He agreed. He said, "Give me the pistol. What am I going to do with this kid? How can he help me in the future? What is he good for?" My grandmother overheard and begged, "Why would you kill him? Pedro is a gift from God. He's not doing anything against you. It's wrong to kill him. I will call the police and have you sent to jail." She saved me.

My mom took care of me when I was a sick child. She never left me alone in the house. She always took me with her wherever she went. She didn't want anyone to hurt me or kill me. My mom is my most beloved person.

I'm the oldest son. I have four siblings, two brothers and two sisters. My younger sister and brother were born when I was in Guatemala. My youngest brother and sister were born after I left home and came to America. I've never met them.

Around age five, I got stronger and started to walk. At age six, I was put in primary school. I didn't have notebooks. I used crayons to write. My dad didn't support me at all. He didn't buy me anything for school, nothing, not even clothes. When I finished sixth grade, he took me out of school to work in the fields.

Back then our village was small, just fifteen or twenty people. When I was growing up, we followed all the Maya customs. We used traditional medicines. Our people planted herbs to use when they became sick. But when it's a serious illness, you need to go to a doctor. But no one has money for a hospital, and our government doesn't assist us at all. There's a hospital in another town, but you have to pay everything upfront. An even worse problem is that you have to walk for fifteen to twenty minutes to reach the road and then take transportation to the hospital. If someone is sick or dying, you have to carry them to the main road. It's very difficult living like that; if you're dying, that's it.

NO PERMANENT WORK FOR PEOPLE

I was ten years old when I started to work in the fields. In Guatemala, almost all kids are working by the time they are seven or eight: the boys with their dads in the fields, the girls with their moms in the kitchens. On a typical day, I got up at six in the morning to get to school by eight. It was far away and there weren't any buses. Sometimes it was raining, lots of mud. Class would end at 1:30 in the afternoon. After walking back home, I'd either go to work again with my dad or I'd gather firewood with my mom, cutting wood with a hatchet and then carrying heavy loads on our backs for a long way. I never had a good day.

When I was twelve years old, I was already looking for jobs on my own. I'd do odd jobs. When I began working, I only earned about fifteen quetzales, about $2 US. But when I was older and stronger, I earned twenty-five quetzales.[3] I planted corn, wheat, and beans. I used machetes and hoes. I would go to work on Saturdays and Sundays to earn some money to buy food for my mom and myself. Because my mom had no way of making money, I worried about her.

My father owned a small plot of land, about one *cuerda*, roughly

---

3. In 2012, fifteen quetzales was about $1.94 US and twenty-five quetzales was about $3.23 US.

one acre. But the people who own land are not rich. Most have two or three acres. They hire hands for a few days to harvest crops, but there's no permanent work for people, even those with land.

LOS NUDOS

The tough kids in my village hung out in a gang called Los Nudos.[4] My friends asked if I would join. I said, "Not me," because I wanted to be a regular guy with no problems with anyone. I never wanted to harm people, to rob or kill. Three times they asked, and I told them no each time. They asked, "So you aren't going to join us?" They threatened me, saying, "You'll see what we are going to do." Some time passed. One dark night I was walking from church to my grandfather's. I passed a run-down building and then I ran into the gang; some of them I knew, others were strangers. They asked me, "Where are you going?" and demanded money. I told them, "No, I don't have anything." They started to punch me. I only had fifty quetzales, about seven dollars, and they took it from me. They slashed my hand with a knife and left me. It bled a lot, but when I got to the house my dad said, "It's okay son, don't worry about that. That's how they are. We can't do anything to them, nothing, because there are so many of them." He was right, because there weren't any cops in our village. There was no one to help us. Then he said, "I'm very sorry." My father put alcohol on the bloody wound, that's all. This happened when I was around fifteen years old. If you look at my hand now, you can still see the scar.

When I was seventeen years old, those were very difficult times. We worked all the time, but bad weather and pests killed our corn harvests. We had nothing to eat. My dad was desperate. He said, "Son, you can go to the United States and help us." I looked down at the ground; I was surprised and afraid. Then my dad said, "Okay,

---

4. *Los Nudos* means "the Knots."

you're a minor, we know that, but the majority of people who go there are also minors. They go out of necessity."

I looked him in the eye and said, "It's okay. I will go." But we didn't have money to pay a *coyote* to take me on the journey. It costs a lot. I didn't know where my father could get the money. But on May 9, 2014, he told me, "I found the money." I said, "You're joking with me." He said, "No, seriously. You are going to the United States."

I never thought that one day I would come here. I was scared because people die on the way, riding on the Beast, which crushes their legs, their arms, and sometimes even kills them.[5] "Okay, I'm going," I told my father, but I was thinking to myself, *I hope that God is with me. If I am going to make it there, okay, that's good, but it's all luck. If not . . .* I said, "I'm going to leave here to work, to help you all, so that I can change your lives a little bit, so that you don't have to continue suffering."

For three months before leaving, I had a stomach illness. I'd gone without eating anything or sleeping, and I couldn't work. But two days before I was to leave, the sickness stopped, and I felt well.

I left around the end of May. I don't remember the exact date. My mother hugged me, crying. She said, "Take care of yourself, son. I hope we will see each other again here, alive, and that you will not be hurt or die. Remember us; don't ever forget how we are living here, how no one helps us with our situation. You're just a child, and I'm very sorry for sending you off to that country because of our problems, because of our poverty. One day you will help other people too, those who need it. One day we will see each other again, God willing."

I cried too. It wasn't like I was leaving for one or two days, but for years. I could have an accident on the way. I told them, "Take good care of yourselves. I will never forget you all, never. You will always stay on my mind because you guys are my greatest love in the world. Thank you for everything, and take care of yourselves. One

---

5. See glossary and appendix essay on La Bestia.

day we will see each other again; we will hug each other like this again." I left them in Huehuetenango.

"IF WE DON'T PAY, THEY COULD KILL ME"

Near the Guatemala-Mexico border I met up with my guide and twelve travelers from Ecuador. I was the only one who came alone; I didn't have anyone else who shared my Maya roots. My Guatemalan guide was a good man, but it was really hard for me because I didn't speak Spanish back then. We crossed the border to Mexico. The guide said it was dangerous for us to travel in a group. If we all came together, Mexican immigration police could catch us, and we'd have to go back to Guatemala. He had us go two by two, so we wouldn't be alone, and we walked all day and met the group at night. One day I got separated from my partner and got lost. Luckily, I reached the hotel and found them again. He sent us out again, every day or two, depending on the path. We only saw our guide at hotels where we were together at night. I had to be brave and resourceful to overcome hunger and fatigue. We didn't have money to buy food. I walked with fear about what would happen on my journey.

We rode on buses, enduring days of hunger and sleepless nights, worrying what would happen. We traveled west and on to Mexico City and northward without being harassed by the Mexican police or gangs. Finally, after many days, we reached a hideaway in Nuevo Laredo, Mexico, near the US border. Seventy people were crowded together. It was very hot, and I had to breathe deeply to stand the heat. Some people had been stuck there for two or three months. They couldn't leave because they didn't have sponsors—no one to send them money. The guide's "boss" told me, "You've arrived here already by your destiny. Give us all the money we want." I called my dad in Guatemala and said, "There are no beds, just one bathroom in the hideaway for seventy people. I can't stand it here because of the heat and hunger. The boss is asking for money. Please transfer money to the bank here so they'll let me out. If we don't pay, they could kill me. Please hurry." After he deposited the money, 4,000 quetzales, about $540 US, in the bank, I was released.

The guide led us through the desert until we reached the Río Bravo on the Texas border.[6] At three in the afternoon I crossed the river in an inflatable raft. Thirty minutes after reaching the other side, the US immigration agents caught us. We tried to escape, but they had helicopters, dogs, and guns. I didn't know if they would kill me. They shouted, "Stop!" and grabbed me. I was scared that they would shoot me. I thought, *What else can I do?* Nothing. So I let them take me, telling myself, *It's okay.*

LA HIELERA

The US immigration police herded us into cars and drove us to *la hielera*, the freezer.[7] It was very cold, and they didn't care about anything there. The guards were really bad. I was in a room with 180 young guys suffering because of the cold. There was hardly anything to eat, just an apple, a small burrito, and a bottle of water for each of us a day. We weren't allowed to bathe. We didn't have beds so we had to lay on the dirty floor with garbage and food. The guards didn't let us sleep at all, not even for a second. I suffered for six days and six nights without sleeping, and it made me feel sick. In another freezing cold room there were mothers who were suffering with their children—five years old, two years old, even seven or eight months old. I don't know how they didn't die.

I was eventually taken to a house for unaccompanied minors in Harlingen, Texas. I was there for two weeks. They treated us well.

---

6. In Mexico, the river running between the United States and Mexico is called the Río Bravo. In the United States, it's called the Rio Grande. See glossary.

7. See glossary.

They let us bathe and gave us food, clothing. I was learning English and studying, but I couldn't stay there. Next, they sent me to San Antonio, Texas. We had a very long trip, six hours by bus. We arrived at a larger detention house for minors. There were around a thousand young people locked up there.

I was able to call home to my parents. They cried, and I did as well. "I'm happy to hear your voice, to know that you're alive," my mother said. "We didn't know if you were alive or dead. We could barely eat or sleep. Thank God that you are okay." I got to speak with them for fifteen minutes twice a week. We had beds. We had food. Everything was good; I liked it there. I spent two months there waiting for someone to get me out. I called my cousin in Mississippi, and I told him I was in youth detention. I asked him, "Would you be my sponsor?" La Migra asked him for all his information, documents. He told them no, that he didn't want to have a problem with La Migra. *Well, what could I do?* I spent some hours talking with my dad in Guatemala, and I had to find another sponsor in the United States. My dad sought help, but no one wanted to help me. I had to stay in the detention house because no one could get me out.

After two months, my name was called. Seventy of us left in the morning; thirty went with me, and the others went to another state. We went at three in the morning to be on the plane at six exactly. The plane took off in San Antonio for Chicago. That's how they told us where we were going. I asked myself, *What can we do? We are under their control.* They took us to the Sears detention center here in Chicago.[8]

I still felt lost, alone, and powerless. You aren't free to do anything you want. You can't go out or leave your room or go for a walk or anything. I thought, *I came here for a good life, and I'm in*

8. Likely Homan Square, which is the former Sears building. See "Inside Chicago's Secret Detention Center," *The Takeaway*, WNYC, October 20, 2015, www.wnyc.org/story/inside-chicagos-secret-detention-center.

jail. I didn't know how long I was going to stay there. I always wondered because I spent a lot of time locked up. I was bored doing the same things all day, every day. We were locked up like that for eight months. My stomach problems came back.

While I was there, I got help from lawyers and social workers. My lawyer visited me at the house on my eighteenth birthday; I'd become an adult, so I couldn't stay in youth detention any longer. I told him everything. After that my social worker and another social worker named Marissa got me into the program at the Young Center.[9] I don't feel alone because I have people to help me and I owe them everything. It's almost like family. School started two weeks ago. I feel happy to live here. We have everything: clothes, food. The people who run the house look after us if we are sick or have something going on. People help us here in ways that people in my village have never seen before.

PACKAGING MEATBALLS

I'm nineteen years old now. I live in Hyde Park, Chicago. I've lived here for a year and three months and I'm very happy. It's a whole other thing to live here compared to where I was before, because I'm free and I have everything: food, a bed, and people who support me.

I'm going to school to get my GED![10] I'm attending Truman College.[11] I go there every day. I study in the mornings between 8:30 a.m. and 12:30 p.m. I'm studying science, math, English, and Spanish. In

---

9. The Young Center for Immigrant Children's Rights, at the University of Chicago Law School.

10. GED stands for general education degree, a high school equivalency diploma.

11. Harry S. Truman College is a campus of the City Colleges of Chicago, where working students can complete their high school classes and continue to community college.

the afternoon, I go to another class to learn English because that's very important.

Now I'm working at a food factory where they make sausages, meatballs, and hamburgers. My boss doesn't speak Spanish, but my coworkers do, and that's how I'm learning. I'm a machine operator for packaging meatballs. This is how it works: first they grind the meat, then they put it in another machine and meatballs come out, then they go into the oven. Afterwards, they go into the freezer so that the meat does not go bad. The machine I work on puts the meatballs inside bags that come out as sealed packages. You watch the temperature, make sure the meat doesn't stick, and adjust the settings on the computer. Then other people pack the product for shipping. I'm proud that I found the job myself. I've worked there for a month and a half now. I send money home to my family in Guatemala via Western Union. I start work at 4:30 p.m. and leave at 12:30 a.m. Since I don't have a car, I go everywhere by bus or train. During the day I study, and in the evening I work. I only get to sleep about three hours a day. On Sundays, I catch up on sleep, walk through the park, and look at the beautiful lake.

I have a lot of friends. We are like family at my group home. I also have a lot of friends at school. At work we're already friends. There aren't any problems; we just do our jobs. I'm very happy here.

THE DEBT IS GROWING SO MUCH

Let me talk about the debt hanging over me. I think it's very important that people understand how difficult it is for migrants to borrow money to come here. It goes like this: I borrow money from someone so that I can travel to Mexico. My dad gave the deed to his land to the moneylenders. The two men we borrowed the money from are our neighbors. We call them our cousins. They made the agreement with my dad; I wasn't a part of it and didn't know the terms. But I'm responsible for paying back the loan. I'm trying to find a way to do that because I owe a lot of money. And if I don't pay it back, the man will take my dad's land because he already has his deed. The lender has the right to go to the mayor or the police and say that he owns my father's land. That's why we can't do anything. I don't really know how much money I owe. The principal on the money is 50,000 quetzales, about $7,000 US, and I owe 15 percent interest every month, about $450. That's why the debt is growing so much, and I have to find a way to pay it back soon, so it doesn't grow more. Now, I can only send $500 a month, which is like 4,000 quetzales there. I have to pay off everything— the capital and interest—to cancel the loan. Then the lender will sign, saying that, yes, the loan is paid back, and then the deed will be returned to my dad.

The lender asked for the money the whole time I was in detention. After I got out, I told him that I didn't have a job here yet. He knew that I was in school and even though he said that it was okay— "take your time"—he kept demanding the money and threatening, "I'm going to take your dad's land." I would tell him, "I am going to pay back everything, but I don't have a job yet." I spoke to the lender recently. I told him, "Don't worry. I have started to work. I'm going to begin paying back your money, little by little." He said, "Okay, that's fine." I'm going to pay everything completely, the interest and capital—everything clean and that's it. So then my dad will get the deed back and have his land again. He'll be free and I'll be free, all the way free! Then I'll be able to send money to my village, to my family, and do other things that I want to do.

I'd like to continue my studies and graduate. After graduating, I'd like to go to a university. My goal is to become a doctor. I have always wanted to be one, ever since I was ill as a child in Guatemala and doctors gave me medicines and vaccines and I got better. I've decided to become a doctor in order to help people like me. I have dreams of one day having a family and children, but I'm not ready for that kind of responsibility.

What I want most is to continue studying and pursuing my career, and maybe I'll have a partner later on. I also want to build a house in my village so that my dad and mom can live there, so that they can have some money to start a store to sell things like food, building materials, clothing, and shoes. I want to make change in my village. To do this, I need to save money, not spend it drinking and smoking. I've never drank or smoked, and I don't ever want to have a vice. I want to do important things for our future. I want to save up some money to be able to buy a car and put some money together to give to my family. I hope that one day I will return to my family so we can live together. I can find a good job and work hard, so I can have a good future, live happily, and be free. But I'm not free now. I have a great debt to pay, that's why I'm worried. I hope to God it will end well.

We catch up with Pedro by phone in Chicago about a year and a half later, in the summer of 2017.

ONE DAY

I won my asylum case about three months ago. I have to wait nine more months to apply for my green card, my permanent residency. I can apply for a US passport in five years. Once I get my passport, I can travel to other countries, but not Guatemala, since I'm not safe there. I can apply to visit my family there once I get the passport and can also apply to sponsor my brother and sister to come live here. My brother wants to come live here, but I don't want him to come yet because I suffered so much on my voyage and during my first years here.

My dad paid the *coyote* half the money upfront, and then when we were ready to cross the border into the United States, he sent the other half. As I told you before, on top of the capital, we are charged

15 percent interest per month for that loan. Now that I've been working, I've finished paying off the 50,000-quetzal principal and have just started to pay off the interest. We have almost 200,000 quetzales in interest, and I've paid about 20,000 quetzales of that so far. Now that the principal is paid off, the amount I owe is not growing at all. So I'm sending whatever I can. I can pay about $500 a month for the debt aside from the money I send for my family to live. I really don't know how many years it will take me to pay off the debt entirely.

I make almost $2,000 a month. The saving grace is that I don't have to pay rent. I live in a boarding house for migrants and orphans, so I only have to pay for my food. Pretty soon I have to start paying rent though. My dad gets frustrated sometimes and doesn't understand why I can't send more, but I tell him, "Señor, I am working, but it's not easy to make money."

One of the men we borrowed money from is always asking about the money and the other isn't as much. One understands my situation, and the other doesn't. One says, "You can only send me what you can," and the other says, "Pay me more quickly!" Besides my dad possibly losing his land, the lenders could get angry and hurt my family. I worry, *What if I get sick and can't work, or what if I lose my job and can't find work?*

I'm studying here at Truman College, which is free. When I feel ready to take the entrance exams to transfer to the university, I can do that. Truthfully, though, I don't know how I can go to the university. Right now, I have to work full time in order to live and send money. I'm twenty now. I really appreciate the opportunity to live here, to work. One day, I'm going to reach my goals and be an important person. I want to help people in my life. I didn't come here with my eyes closed. I've seen the suffering in the world. God has a plan for me. I want to work hard so that one day my family, my parents, can be proud of me and say, "Thank you, son, for fighting for us. You are a good son." I want to hug them one day and have my family here. One day.

CRISTHIAN MOLINA

AGE AT CROSSING: 10
BORN IN: Florida, Copán, Honduras
INTERVIEWED IN: Irapuato, Guanajuato, Mexico
in transit

Cristhian comes through the doors of the San Juan de Dios migrant shelter at just after nine on a muggy July morning in 2016. He's holding a swollen face and tells us he's just been assaulted on the train tracks. One of his teeth has been shattered, and he's asked the manager of the shelter for a painkiller. We chat with him intermittently while he waits to shower, and we interview him after he has bathed and eaten. At twenty-eight years old, Cristhian's face has the weathered lines of a fifty-year-old. His eyes are red and swollen, his voice quivers as if he is about to unleash a floodgate of tears at any moment, and he speaks wearily. He talks in a quiet voice so as not to be heard by the other travelers in the entranceway. At times, he almost sounds as if he is chanting; at other times he takes on a solemn confessional tone, punctuated by moments of realization.

Growing up in severe poverty near Copán, Honduras, Cristhian felt that neither of his parents really cared for him. He suffered humiliations and abuse by all his family members and made his first trip to the United States when he was ten. Cristhian lived in foster homes until he went to high school in California, where he fell in with the Sureños and was deported.[1] He has been deported three times from the United States and eight times from Mexico. In Honduras, his brother is a gang member with Barrio 18, and Cristhian will likely be killed if he returns to his home country. Because of this, Cristhian has wandered in exile for years. To make ends meet, he makes sculptures out of aluminum cans and sells them in the streets. The hour or so that we talk with him is the only time we speak to Cristhian, since he has no phone, address, or any other way of keeping in touch.

AS I WAS GROWING, A ROOT OF ANGER
AND HATE WAS ALSO GROWING

Just getting off the train this morning, someone hit me really hard. He was some guy from Mexico. The first time I went up to the United States was when I was ten, in 1998. I told the US migration officials that my family had died in 1998, in Hurricane Mitch, and that I was homeless. I was lying to them. It's just that I didn't want to go back to my country. I was really poor. I was like eighteen when they first sent me back to Honduras. Now I'm twenty-eight, going on twenty-nine. I can't even go back to Honduras now because my brother is a gang member. He's with Barrio 18. If they notice I am there, they will come after me. I came across the border up to Puerto

---

1. A gang in Southern California. See glossary.

Barrios, Guatemala.[2] I have an aunt there. I started my first attempt to move north on my birthday, July 29, 1998.

I want to tell you about everything that I have suffered. Since I was born, my father has told me that I am not his son, that he bought me from a woman for one hundred lempiras. He says that my mother, who was very poor, stayed there in the hospital crying while he took me. This man beat me, kicked me, burned me with cigarettes when I was a child. My father never gave me any love. I never went out in public with him or anything.

And after a while, I went to stay with my grandparents. They were also very poor, and my aunt told me that I'd have to wash people's clothes to survive. I'd have to fix my own tortillas, because my mother was with another guy and my father was with another woman. As I was growing, a root of anger and hate was also growing. My family took me out of school because we were so poor. I had to chop wood so that we'd have fire to cook.

I was a child who liked a lot of things. I liked the army, the navy, the marines, all of that. When I was young, I wanted to be a good soldier when I was older. I wanted to be like Che Guevara, someone like that. But I changed my mind because man and God don't always think alike.

When I was a child and I wanted to play, my family would punish me. One day they burned my feet because I'd stayed away from the house. I was quite a wanderer. And when I returned, my aunts would hit me. That's why I left home when I was ten. My family was dead to me, and I didn't want to know anything about them. My family "died" with Hurricane Mitch. I came all the way up here to Tijuana.

I first entered the United States in 2000. I was put in CASA,

2. Copán is just south of the Guatemalan border in central Honduras. Puerto Barrios, Guatemala, is just over two hundred kilometers east of Copán on the Caribbean coast of Guatemala.

an immigration program in San Diego.[3] They work with kids who are eleven, twelve, and they put you in school. I was a little boy! I grew up there. I had a foster mother, and she told me, "My doors are always open for you." So I lived in the house with the American family. I lived in a group home, in different group homes. I lived in San Jose, San Francisco, the Castro Valley. I'd go to the BART station, and I'd go all over the place.[4]

So when I told my foster mother that I was going to leave, she almost died. It's just that I'm very nomadic. I tell her since they let me cross the border, I'm going to be good. When they deported me, I was arrested for "terroristic traits, and possession of marijuana." I was sixteen back then, and I'd hang out with anybody. When I was in high school, I met a ton of Sureños, with their blue bandanas. The Norteños were more Chicano.[5] The Sureños were mostly from Latin American countries. I regret joining them because if I hadn't, I would've had many more opportunities. But there's still hope for me. In the United States, La Migra has caught me three times. And here in Mexico, they've deported me like eight times. They take me to Honduras in a plane. You fly right into Tegucigalpa with two hundred and fifty other migrants.

When I was eighteen, I lived in Atlanta, Georgia. I was there for about two and a half years. I went to South Beach, Miami, Florida. I wanted to know more of the United States, but they deported me again. They put me in an immigration station where they had social

---

3. A CASA is a Court-Appointed Special Advocate who advocates for youth in foster care. They are volunteers from Voices for Children in San Diego. They act as fact-finders, learning as much about the children as possible through speaking with them and family members to represent them at school and in court.

4. BART is Bay Area Rapid Transit.

5. *Norteños* and *Sureños* refers to members of various gangs in California. See glossary. The territorial border that is thought to separate the gangs crosses Delano County and Bakersfield. For *Chicanos*, see glossary.

workers, therapists. In the United States I worked selling popsicles. I worked for a company putting roofing on American houses. I was making $120 a day in the United States. I painted, I washed taxis. I made a lot of money in the United States, and it's beautiful there. I liked to go see films. Every weekend, I'd go out to a movie. I'd walk in through the exit and watch two or three.

MAKING ART FROM ALUMINUM CANS

One time, a very racist police officer here in Mexico said to me, "You know what? I don't like damn Hondurans." And another time this guy had a lot of methamphetamine and took me up to Nuevo Laredo. We were picked up by the police, but he never arrived in court, and I wrote "Not guilty" on the form. "I don't have any drugs or use any drugs," I told them. And they searched me. They said I had an accent and put me in the hole for forty-eight hours. In the hole, there was a lot of shit. It stank! I had nothing to eat, and I had to try to wash myself at the sink! I had to pay 5,000 pesos to get out of there. I ended up locked up for ten months in Mexicali. They got me to Laredo and left me there with some boxer shorts and socks. And I didn't have any drugs. It was only because that officer didn't like me.

When I got to prison, I'd just wake up in my socks, and they'd start hitting me. I told them, "I'm going to file this with the Honduran consulate for human rights abuse!" I went to the doctor, and said, "Doctor, look at how these gangsters have kicked me and everything." I told him that they had put me in the prison without proving my guilt, without giving me a drug test. The doctor gave me a Coca-Cola and an apple, and said, "Eat it. Don't worry." I was put in a protected zone where you only leave once a month.

In prison, they feed you very little, a piece of bread perhaps in the evening. And I was hungry all day. While I was there nothing happened. There was the zone for the people with AIDS, a zone for the homosexuals. There were a lot of crazy guys who looked like women. There's a lot of drug addiction in Mexicali. In Tijuana, you see fifteen-year-old, sixteen-year-old girls working at night, all crazy with their fishnet stockings. I've seen how they lose their youth there. Because that's what they want for people, that they not be free. They kill us, beat us, because they don't want us to be able to do anything.

I met this guy in the desert, in Sonora. Last time I was there, I asked him, "How much do you want to take me through the desert?" He said, "1,800," then he asked me, "Are you sure you want to walk through the desert? It takes two weeks." And I told him, "Actually, I don't want to." Earlier I had gone to Mexicali and started making art from aluminum cans. I make beautiful art—marijuana plants and lots of other things. I make hearts. I make them shimmer. People buy them from me for twenty-five, thirty, fifty pesos for each piece. I've sold them here, in Sinaloa, in Matamoros, Tamaulipas. The guy loved them and had a bunch of them, my aluminum art. So he said, "When you want to cross to the other side, I'll take you."

Once, I spent six days with my eyes swollen shut. When I arrived there at the border, these guys asked me where I was from, and I told them I was from Copán, Honduras. They hit me with the handle of a .22-caliber pistol in the corner of my eye. Then their commander approached and was just looking at me, at the blood coming out from the corner of my eye. He asked, "Who did this to you?" I pointed to the guy who had assaulted me, and he said, "He works for La Letra, Los Zetas." The commander asked me, "Where are you from?" "I'm a *catracho*," I replied.[6] "And no one can take my nationality away." And the guy took off all my clothes and placed thirty *tablazos* in front of

---

6. *Catracho* means Honduran.

me.[7] Then he said, "Honduran, why are you laughing?" I was laughing because I knew that they had no right to hit me.

Getting off La Bestia this morning, I fell, running in the air.[8]

FOR EIGHTEEN YEARS I'VE WANDERED

I need a pill for the pain. I lost my backpack, everything. My molar is broken, this molar. It hurts! When I drink water, wow, it hurts! They took everything in my backpack. I need some scissors and an aluminum can. That's how I make my art. People watch me work. I make palm trees, everything very pretty.

In my heart, I come alone, with just God and me. I got off the train alone. I didn't even have a jacket. I was dying from the cold last night! I haven't eaten in two days. I caught the train, early in the morning, and took the train all day, with just a small amount of water. To arrive here, one has to suffer a lot. One has to get around La Migra in Palenque.[9] Sometimes immigration stops the train and all the migrants run from them. When this happens, people fall. They kill some. Thank God—He has helped me. I've been deported like eleven times.

I have two daughters in the United States. Their stepfather is Mexican, but they were born there. They're crazy, though, and like to take drugs. I see that all the kids do drugs up there, and I start to feel bad. The government took them away from me when they deported me. Yes, after ten years they sent me back. For eighteen years I've wandered from the bottom to the top of North America, trying to change my life. And I can't go back to Honduras,

---

7. *Tablazo* refers to both the form of torture used by Los Zetas and the wooden board or paddle they use to carry it out. The torturer uses the instrument, which sometimes has nails in it, to strike the victim in the back, chest, and legs.

8. See glossary.

9. An ancient Maya city and modern town in Chiapas.

because they say that San Pedro Sula is the murder capital of the world, right?[10] There, one's life is worth nothing, and I want a better future for myself. I still have dreams, hopes, and my faith in God has never stopped. I don't have anything here in Mexico or Honduras. I've always wanted to build my house in Honduras, in the woods, on the mountain. I worked for two years in the United States saving money to buy that land. American dollars have a lot of value in Honduras. I still dream of buying land near Copán. San Pedro Sula is dangerous, but Florida not so much.[11] But I'm not going back.

I'm going to put my life in His hands and see what He makes for my future. I need to try to be simple, humble, prudent, a person who doesn't let his mouth go, because perhaps sometimes I offend people with my words.

One day, I want to write my story on a computer—everything about my life, the life of a migrant. Cristhian, that's me. From Florida, a town in the department of Copán. And now I can't return to see my brothers, my family in Honduras. I want to apply for political asylum here in Mexico. I was stabbed here in Mexico. They cut me with a machete. And when I got hit with the .22 in the corner of my eye—that was the worst. That guy with Los Zetas. I know all of Mexico, from Tijuana all the way down to Tenosique, Tabasco. Mexico is huge, and it has many beautiful places, many tourist places—Puerto Peñasco, Puerto Vallarta, Monterrey, Nuevo León—many cities and many opportunities that don't exist in my country.

And do you know what I want to do one day? I want to reunite myself with God. I want to ask for His forgiveness for the many bad

---

10. San Pedro Sula is the industrial capital of Honduras. At the time of this interview it was listed as the "murder capital of the world," according to data compiled by Citizen Council for Public Security, Justice, and Peace, a Mexican think tank.

11. Florida, Copán, is a rural tobacco-growing region 140 kilometers southwest of San Pedro.

decisions I have made, realize that He made me Himself and that He wants me to complete a mission on this earth. They say that these are the final days. Noah wanted to make a huge ark to save the people, and they all yelled, "You're crazy! How is it going to flood when it hasn't even rained one drop?" And now people think that those of us who study the Bible are *loco*. I'm going to live here in Mexico, with political asylum. I mean, I can't go back to Honduras, and the United States has deported me multiple times. They just have to accept me here. I want to get Mexican papers. I need to find a good job.

I hope that we all see each other again. The world is small. My life is going to change. I want to work, perhaps with machines, and maybe I'll marry a Mexican woman. I can have a better future here. I wish I had some scissors and a can. You could see what I make. I once made a bicycle, and the people just stared, and I made a robot, like Iron Man.

I don't have a phone. I used to, but I had everything stolen from me. I had a speaker to play music as well. I met this guy, and he called out to me, "Hey, are you from Honduras? Do you want me to buy you a taco?" I asked him if he wanted to buy my speaker, and he took it and kept it. He robbed me, and I just said, "If you want it, take it. And take this charger cable as well, because you'll need it." That's how I am, because why fight over something that is insignificant?

ROSA CUEVAS

AGE AT CROSSING: 35
AGE OF CHILD: 12
BORN IN: Jucuarán, Usulután, El Salvador
INTERVIEWED IN: San Luis Potosí, Mexico
in transit

La Casa de la Caridad is a migrant shelter run by Caritas, an orga-
nization developed by the Catholic Church to promote social welfare.
The shelter is adjacent to the train tracks. We notice signs for a shelter
across the tracks that we later learn had been placed there by a crime
organization for the express purpose of luring migrants into being kid-
napped. On the outside, Casa de la Caridad is completely nondescript:
another cement structure with no windows and one door with a small
sign reading, "Ring bell 24 hours a day, Casa del Migrante." Inside,
it is the most expansive of the shelters we visit in Mexico. It takes up a

good portion of the block, with an outdoor basketball court surrounded
by a gigantic mural made by migrants, large sleeping quarters with
rows of bunk beds, and a full industrial kitchen.

   We speak with Rosa in a large meeting room in July 2016. Rosa and
her daughter, Alejandra, are traveling with Rosa's sister and her daugh-
ter, as well as Rosa's brother. Escaping threats by gangs and a death
squad, they fled El Salvador only to be assaulted in southern Mexico. At
every step of the journey Rosa and her family don't know whom to trust.
They are hoping to receive Mexican visas that will let them travel safely
to the US border, where they can turn themselves over to US immigra-
tion agents and apply for asylum. Rosa is the only one in her family to
speak with us at length. She is clearly traumatized by the recent assaults
but wants their story to be heard. This is the only time we are able to
speak with Rosa.

I DON'T HAVE A HAPPY MEMORY THERE

I was born in Jucuarán, a town in the province of Usulután.[1] In
Jucuarán, the people are peasants who work in the fields, growing
corn, beans. I moved to Chirilagua, San Miguel, as a child because
my mamá lived there.[2] It's very pretty. It's a village in the mountains.
To get to the town, it takes about a half hour.

   I lived in the city of San Miguel when I was with my late boyfriend, my daughter's father. I don't have a happy memory there.
I moved there when I was fourteen and lived there for fourteen
years. My boyfriend and I met at a store. He spoke to me and
invited me to go out to eat. We went to the movies, and then we

---

1. Usulután is the largest department, or state, in El Salvador by land and is
located on the Pacific coast.

2. San Miguel is the third most populous city in El Salvador, and is 138 kilometers east of the capital, San Salvador. It is also the capital of the state of the
same name.

started to fall in love. He'd call me on the phone, and I would talk to him.

His family would go around to *ferias*.[3] There were mechanical games, Ferris wheels, things of that sort. His mother, my daughter's grandmother, owned the mechanical games, and we also went around selling *enredos*, toasted plantains, fried potatoes with cheese.[4] I was working with his mother, and then I got pregnant and had my daughter. We always traveled from town to town. Then my boyfriend went to work in the United States, in a pizzeria. He got sick and came back to set up a pizzeria in El Salvador. I worked with him there. He eventually died of heart and kidney malfunction. He's been dead for seven years.

After he died, I rented a house and lived with another man for seven years in Capulín, about a half hour away from Chirilagua. It's a remote district. There are just a few houses.

I fought for my child. I started to sell potatoes, corn tostadas, enredos, soup, churros—I used to sell everything. I'd sell them from house to house. I'd go out at four in the morning to buy ingredients in remote places and come back to the house at ten. I'd make the food and then go out and sell it. During the *Annona* season, I'd buy the peeled Annonas and go sell them.[5]

We left El Salvador on May 22, 2016. There are a lot of gangs there. They said that they were going to kill us. They wanted to kill my brother, and because of this we all left. In El Salvador there is a gangster's code that minors and women who have communications with anyone are killed. For example, if they saw me, a woman, here chatting with you, they would kill us just out of jealousy.

The government also secretly sends around vigilante squads, like

---

3. Spanish for "fair."

4. *Enredos* are a fried Salvadoran street food, typically made with yucca.

5. Annonas are a Salvadoran fruit, also known as custard apple.

La Sombra Negra, to "clean up" all areas.[6] They go around killing young people, families. This is recent. It hasn't even been a year since it started. They dress like military police in green and black. They wear hats, black gloves, sunglasses, and tall boots. At first, they came close to my house. They only go around in armored luxury cars. With their tinted windows, they can see outside, but you can't see inside. They have a list of all the people they want to kill. They killed my friend. They killed seven people nearby. Then they came to our house looking for my brother. They go around killing mareros and also people who aren't even *pandilleros*.[7] They go looking for someone at one house and the people there tell them about someone else, and then they go looking for that person. They take people out into the street to torture them. They come by late at night, at midnight, and knock on the door when everyone is asleep. When they first arrive, they throw a canister of gas, and when the person walks by, they shoot him and cause an explosion so he burns.

The truces between the gangs began in 2012, so there wouldn't be more deaths. Salvador Sánchez Cerén, who became president in 2014, initiated the truce but changed his mind and called the truce off.[8]

My brother is twenty-one. Some men came looking for him like a week before we left, and then they came again the night before we left. I think they were La Sombra Negra, and they seemed to think my brother was a gangster. He was sleeping in the jungle. They went

---

6. La Sombra Negra, "the Black Shadow," was the name attributed to US-sponsored death squads during the civil war in El Salvador. There has been a recent resurgence of death squad–style slayings of suspected gang members, along with girlfriends, family members, and children who are not in the gangs. Some claim they are off-duty military or police, while others say they are law-and-order vigilantes. For more on the role of the United States in recent paramilitary forces, see May 2018 in the "Historical Timeline."

7. Both *marero* and *pandillero* are terms for gang members, though *pandillero* is more general and can refer to any type of gang.

8. For more on the truce, see "Historical Timeline."

to look for him but didn't find him. I told him that we should leave. He didn't want to go, but I said that I was going to go. I already knew the way to the Guatemalan border because I had traveled there before. My dad suggested that my brother go. He was the youngest son. Our father didn't want him to get killed. If they have someone they're looking for, they kill everyone in the family, even if you aren't in a gang. They set people on fire. They leave white pieces of paper stuck to the bodies with tape, put tape on people's mouths, and tie up their hands and feet with cables. They put photos on the internet, sometimes showing people with big holes in their chests. Look for the *pagina azul*.[9]

THE GIFT OF NOT KILLING HER

We left at dawn. We were a group of five: my brother, my sister and her daughter, and me and my daughter. My dad had already taken out a $500 loan from the bank so that we could flee. My brother usually held on to the money for our trip. We first paid for bus tickets from El Salvador to the Guatemalan border.

Approaching Guatemala, we climbed over a hill. It was raining. We walked almost all day to get to the border. Because my daughter is a minor, she doesn't have a passport, and I didn't have a parental permission form because I didn't have the chance to get one.[10] Because we didn't have the permit, we couldn't cross the border legally, and we had to go all the way around the checkpoint. We walked around lost in the mountains. We had to endure hunger, worrying that maybe La Migra would catch us, or that a pandillero would

9. Spanish for "blue page." Rosa is referring to a Facebook page, now closed, called "Héroe Azul" (Blue Hero), allegedly administered by policemen of the Policía Nacional Civil, which published pictures of murders as they happened.

10. The Mexican National Institute of Migration requires special documentation for minors traveling through the country.

rape or kill us. Then, at night, we stopped a tractor and some guys helped us. One guy took us to a gas station and from there to Tecún Umán.[11] We drove all night and then the next morning at ten, he left us there to get a *combi* to travel to the river between Guatemala and Mexico.[12] At first the van operators told us that we couldn't go in the van. I had to pay for the tickets. The van then took us partway to Tapachula, where we crossed the river.[13]

On the other side of the border, the Mexican Migra kept following us from block to block.[14] We were running like crazy. A guy helped us escape, and we got in another van to get to Tapachula. We looked for a hotel. We stayed a day, and the next day we left Tapachula. We made friends with another guy and kept going with him. We walked for days, through the jungle, risking our lives, not meeting anyone. We would take a van for a while, walk for a while. When there were immigration checkpoints, we went around, sometimes walking all day without eating. Our route was from Tapachula to Chahuites, walking through the jungle in the mountains at night.[15] We passed through Mapastepec, Pijijiapan, and Arriaga. Then from Chahuites we went to Ixtepec.

We had changed our money into Mexican pesos. I was carrying fifteen hundred.[16] My sister and brother were carrying two thousand each. I was with the kids, my brother, and another guy. These men came up to us, looked through our brother's backpack, and

---

11. A Guatemalan city close to the border with Mexico, named after the last ruler of the K'iche' Mayas.

12. The *combi* is a van-taxi that operates like a small bus.

13. Tapachula is Mexico's southernmost city located in the state of Chiapas, at the border with Guatemala. It is the main center of migration to Mexico from southern countries.

14. See glossary.

15. Chahuites is a Mexican city approximately 248 kilometers from Tapachula.

16. Fifteen hundred pesos was about $86 US in 2016.

said they were the police. They wanted to take our daughters away. They said, "You're trafficking minors." They asked me, "Are you her mother?" But they weren't the police. They were dressed like private citizens, like anyone else. Another man intervened and asked, "Where are you from?" Another said, "Don't move! We're going to check your bags. We're the police." After that they said, "Stay here. Don't move!" We were really scared. They told us, "Don't be scared."

We told them, "We can't stay here. We have to go on." After they let us go, we left at about noon for another town. It might have been Mapastepec. I don't remember what town it was, and there was a car following us. Every block we walked these men were following us in their white four-door car. We walked one more block, and they were one block down watching us. We walked another block and then started running. In the end we ran and walked so much that for a little while we lost them, and we got in a van. They followed us for many days. We walked in the jungle, climbed hills, mountains. We'd catch vans. We had to give the van drivers money so they'd let us off one kilometer before the checkpoints, and then we could avoid the men by going through the jungle. Sometimes the van drivers would tell us, "When you go, be careful because there are thieves. They assault, rape, everything. Especially taking your children, you are more at risk."

We were walking through the jungle at four in the morning. You couldn't see anything. Thank God the thieves were sleeping because they didn't come out. Later on, we arrived in Arriaga, where we stayed for five days.[17] We traveled on from Arriaga.

It was raining again. It was pitch black. Under a bridge there was a big lagoon. La Migra were going around in patrol cars. When we saw that they were turning around with their colored lights—blue, red, and yellow—we left the road and threw ourselves into the lagoon. We got all wet and ran to a hill. When we got to the other side of the hill, I realized my sister was still stuck on the other side

---

17. The distance between Mapastepec and Arriaga is 146 kilometers.

of the water. The immigration police were so close. Everyone was running, and I got stuck in a chain-link fence. It seemed like there was no way to get unstuck and everyone was running. All my clothes tore apart on the fence. La Migra was so close to catching me!

We walked all night and slept an hour.

I also lost track of Alejandra, as well as the others, when thieves assaulted us. They stole some of our money; they took everything. It was June 18, 2016, my sister's birthday. They gave her the gift of not killing her. I ran one way and my daughter ran the other way. Then I was lost in the jungle. I ran from the thieves and went to a gas station. The owner gave me a mattress so that I could sleep there. There were people coming in, and I was scared that immigration would come, that they'd see me sleeping there.

At dawn the next day I wanted to pay for a cab to get away because the thieves had left me two hundred pesos, but my heart wouldn't let me go because I had a feeling that my daughter was in danger. I was distressed for her and went to the hotel in Chahuites, because before we got separated, we had all said a prayer and planned to meet there. I paid a guy on a motorcycle to take me under the bridge past La Migra. I found my daughter at the hotel, all beaten up. She couldn't even stand up. And after a half hour, the rest of the group arrived as well. They smelled awful, with nothing, naked, as if they were monkeys. I was crying because I thought that they'd killed my sister. My brother was followed all night. I was the last to arrive. I found my daughter, sister, niece, and brother there. My sister told me that, after we'd all been separated, she had found her daughter and they'd met a man who took them into his home. For an entire day my sister and her daughter had stayed in that man's house, where they could take a shower and sleep, waiting for us to walk down that road. But we never did. We stayed at the hotel for twenty-five days because my sister couldn't walk. The hotel owners gave her pills for the pain. The night of the assault was the most tragic night of my life.

It turned out the thieves had assaulted both families that night. In the jungle, they'd grabbed my niece by the hair and tried to rape her, and ended up stealing 3,800 pesos. They were all dressed in black and were carrying machetes, guns, and a flashlight that was the same color as the flashlights of the immigration police. There were ten of them, and they formed a circle. My niece was held inside the men's circle. They were telling her to give them the money. "Where are you carrying *la lana*?[18] Take it out," they were saying. They lifted my sister high up above their heads in the air and then she fell front first. She landed very hard and cried out. My sister thought they were La Migra but asked herself, *How is it that La Migra is going around at this hour at night? It's scary to go into the jungle at night.* The hotel owner later told us that La Migra doesn't go there because they're scared that people will kill them there in the jungle. I asked a woman at the hotel who those men were. She told me, "They're not La Migra. They are a *pandilla*.[19] They assault and rape women and kill men."

MAYBE ONE DAY YOU CAN GET TO THE OTHER SIDE

Was it worth it? When you leave home, you never know that you're going to suffer so much. You think the road is going to be easy, but it's not. I think it's worth it to look for a better life because in El Salvador there's so much poverty. There are days you don't even eat because there's no work. There's no money. You always look for the best for your family, thinking maybe one day you can get to the other side and work.

Everything is in a legal report on the assault that the Mexican police wrote after questioning us. It has the same story I'm telling you. The government typed this up two days after we were assaulted. They said that they were going to give us a military transit visa. We went to

---

18. In Mexico, money is often referred to as *lana*, or wool.

19. Spanish for "gang." See glossary.

the immigration office today to get the permit, which we need before the visa.[20] Now that we have the permit, I can go to request visas for my daughter and me, and my sister can do the same for herself and her daughter. When we go, we'll leave our daughters here at the shelter. They're going to tell me how long it will be before we get the visas. Supposedly it will take thirty days. Then we can continue north. From here, I think we can go by train. It doesn't matter. As long as we have the permit, Mexican immigration won't touch us. The food here at the shelter is not very good. They cook rice and beans, but they do it very differently. In El Salvador, we don't use much chili.

I want to keep going until I get to the United States. I have a friend in Virginia from our hometown who's going to help us. She lived six houses down from where we lived in San Miguel. She's been in Virginia for a long time now, working at the Salvadoran embassy. She told me to turn myself in to the US Border Patrol, and then when I'm on the other side she will welcome me. We have some family in the United States, my mom's nephews, but we can't rely on them. We're not in contact with them. They are *mojados*, just like us.[21] When they were poor like us, we got along, but since they went to the United States they feel more important. My friend in Virginia who will pick me up with my daughter can submit legal papers for me. She's a citizen there. We want to apply for asylum. When I get to the United States, I want to work. I'll do whatever work I can do in order to care for my daughter. She was going to fourth grade, but before we left I took her out of school. She's twelve now. I want to put her in school in America, far from the dangers in El Salvador.

---

20. Victims of violence in Mexico can apply for visas that allow them to travel through the country. In the Mexican bureaucracy, they first get a permit and then have to go to another office to get a visa.

21. *Mojados* or *wetbacks* are derogatory slang terms sometimes used to describe (and sometimes used by) undocumented immigrants. See glossary.

ERNESTO GONZÁLEZ

AGE AT CROSSING: 14
BORN IN: San Esteban, Olancho, Honduras
INTERVIEWED IN: Guadalajara, Mexico
in transit

We meet Ernesto at FM4 Paso Libre in Guadalajara, Mexico, a day sanctuary for migrants located near the railroad tracks of La Bestia, which are stained with blood and littered with messages, scrawled on broken pieces of cement, from migrant riders to meet up.[1] Behind the gates, dozens of weary Central American migrants—most in their late teens and early twenties—sit down at long tables covered with floral-patterned plastic tablecloths to eat their first hot meal in days, cooked fresh and served by Mexican volunteers. The migrants are offered

---

1. See glossary for more on La Bestia.

a shower, a change of clean clothes, and first aid, but their mobile phones and valuables are locked up and they cannot stay overnight.

Few words are spoken as the migrants dig into heaping portions of scrambled eggs, corn tortillas, fresh vegetables, and steaming cups of strong coffee. Then they sit back and relax in plastic chairs, savoring full stomachs, exchanging travel information and stories of riding on La Bestia. Ernesto is one of the older migrants, his dark skin lined, broad cheekbones hollow, black hair flecked with gray. He's exhausted after nearly two months on the migrant trail. He coughs frequently and scratches rashes on his skin. His demeanor is serious, unsmiling, and impassive, but when he opens up about his wife and six young children, whom he left behind in Honduras to seek work in the United States, his dark eyes moisten and his voice catches. He wears a crimson T-shirt with the words "Walking for Health" printed on the back. His khaki trousers are stained with grease. He's about six feet tall, strongly built, yet his clothes hang on his body as if he has lost weight recently. His Honduran passport photo shows a younger man with round cheeks, cleanly shaven with a thick black mustache. His cheeks and chin are now covered with several days' growth of beard. He appears exhausted, but he seizes the brief opportunity to tell his story. Because he is in mid-transit and has no phone, we only speak with him this one time. In our intense brief conversation, he focuses on his dangerous journey and discloses only scattered incidents from his previous nine or ten sojourns to the United States. Ernesto's experience reflects those of thousands of migrants for whom repeat entries and itinerant work have become their main way of supporting families back home. He wants to provide food, shelter, and education for his children so they don't have to become migrants themselves.

I'M THE ONLY ONE STILL ALIVE

I'm the only one to live to tell the story. I was born on the ninth of August, 1984, in San Esteban, Olancho, Honduras. There were five of us kids in the family, my sister and four brothers. We had almost nothing, and my parents fought a lot. I left school after sixth grade and got involved with street gangs, with the *mara*. They told me to rob and kill, but I said no. They said that love for the gang was the most important thing, that to kill and to rape was for your own good. They said everything you could grab with your hands was yours. Yes, I robbed. I robbed a lot, but I never killed. I never raped anyone. Rapists are cowards. When I was thirteen and a half, I told the gang I wanted to become a boss. They told me to kill my mother and father. It was them or me. I didn't want to kill my parents, so I told them to get out, to leave home. That's why I quit the gang. My mom left for Grand Cayman. My father went to Panama and started a new family. After my parents left, it was really hard for me, my sister, and three brothers. We didn't have money for the rent. I felt alone without my mom and dad; I was living on the streets, selling water, and the mara would always come after me. There were thirty-six of us in the gang, and mysteriously, miraculously, I'm the only one still alive.

DIVINO PARAÍSO

Between 1999 and 2010, I made nine or ten trips to the United States. The first time I crossed the US border was in May 1999. I was about three months shy of fifteen. I lived in San Francisco and Oakland. I remember a beautiful day in San Francisco. We went in a caravan to the city center. There was a band and all that stuff. I liked it because it's a sanctuary area. Immigration doesn't come through there. If you're working illegally, they won't bother you, but if you're dealing drugs, they'll deport you immediately.

I also worked around Phoenix, picking grapes and strawberries. I got paid seven dollars an hour. I didn't have any difficulties at work. The boss treated me well and I thank God because in the United States there are bosses who push you hard without giving you much money and there are others who don't push you too hard and pay you well.

Back in Honduras, I worked as a moto-taxi driver until 2006. It didn't last because I only earned one hundred lempiras a day.[2] I didn't like being a taxi driver because you have to pay off the mareros—gangsters—who charge three hundred per taxi ride. They attack you. They try to kill you. I was driving a moto-taxi in Tegucigalpa, the capital, and behind my shoulder, they killed my assistant, who rode with me and collected fares. Just like that they killed him. It was on Holy Wednesday. It was our last trip, and we were at the Chivirito market, going to Divino Paraíso.[3] We went around like three times and were doing well because it was crowded with people standing everywhere. Each trip was four hundred, five hundred, six hundred lempiras. We did three trips and ended up with around three thousand lempiras.[4] When it was seven or eight and we were about to call it a day, three criminals in hoods jumped us. They took our money, all of it. Supposedly, my assistant had seen those guys kill someone and he'd told people what he had seen. And in revenge the killers came and shot him. There were three of them and one had a .38-caliber gun. They shot my assistant around eighteen times, his whole body. He was carrying a dagger, and it broke with just one shot. They shot him right in his face. The only thing that I could do for him was to get some firefighters in Puente Carrizal to take his body. Then out came the guy from the district attorney's office. They took me away, detained me, and put me under criminal investigation. I was questioned for five hours. They looked me over and brought me to the morgue to look at the body. They asked me if I knew the victim, and I told them that I did. I knew him well. I went with the police from

2. One hundred lempiras was about $5 US in 2006.

3. Divino Paraíso is a cemetery in Tegucigalpa where many gang slayings have occurred.

4. Three thousand lempiras was about $159 US in 2006.

the morgue to where his family was. The family said, "We don't want to see you here."

Since 2006, I haven't been driving in the capital city. I drive outside the city to places like Olancho or Trujillo. I thank God that, even though I didn't prepare myself in my studies, at least I prepared myself in some way. I can drive heavy equipment. My dad taught me how to drive tractors, excavators, and trucks with eight or ten wheels.

THEY DEPORTED ME FOR SELLING DRUGS

When I returned to San Francisco sometime around 2007, I hardly ever worked legally. I sold drugs—*piedra*, coke, crack cocaine—but I didn't use it myself.[5] I'd buy one hundred dollars' worth, which was a lot, and make two hundred. I'd sell twenty piedras. And then I'd buy two hundred and make four hundred. I'd send two or three hundred dollars home to my wife and babies in Honduras. Sometimes gangs would attack me, and I wouldn't send anything home. In San Francisco, there are a lot of Sureños, and they charge protection money.[6] I'd pay, but they'd still attack me. They'd take all my drugs, and I wouldn't have anything to sell. They'd beat me. The last time I sold crack was in October 2008. I'd brought three piedras with me. A policeman arrested me, grabbing me from behind and choking my throat. I hit him back, and they sentenced me to two years for fighting with the policeman. I was in 850 Bryant for six months, and from there they sent me to San Bruno.[7] The gangs never messed with me in jail because I never told anyone I'd been in a gang. I worked in

---

5. *Piedra*, which literally means "stone," is Spanish slang for rock cocaine.

6. The Sureños are a Southern California Latino gang. See glossary.

7. 850 Bryant Street is San Francisco County Jail. San Bruno County Jail is located ten miles south of San Francisco.

the kitchen. If you're whiter, you work in the kitchen.[8] I got a dollar a day. It's a way to survive, to buy a phone card so that I could talk to my wife, calling her long distance in Honduras. I got out of jail in August 2010. They deported me to Honduras, and I haven't tried to return until now, 2016.

"PAPI, DON'T GET LOST"

Now I'm coming with a clearer mind—no scars, no alcohol, no drugs—to make an honest living. I want to have a home that I really work for honestly because that's what my kids expect of me. Something honorable. I'm thirty-one. I have a wife and six kids in Honduras. I'm going for them, to give them a better life. I don't want to be a freeloader living under someone else's roof. I want to have my own house, a space for my kids where they can study and I can watch them grow. It's all for them.

I said goodbye to my family two months ago, in May 2016. My wife and kids stood on the street waiting for the bus to take me to the capital. My wife was sobbing. She didn't have the words to say goodbye. My kids did, because I just told them that I was going to work in the capital. I was talking to one of my daughters—she's just four years old—and she told me, "Papi, don't get lost." It was very painful. You need a lot of courage, yes, a lot of courage. God willing, I'll make it to New York. You can get good work there, make good money mowing lawns and that kind of thing. You don't live a good life there, but you can get very good work.

My friends and I—there are five of us who are traveling together—come from the same town in Honduras. I'm the one with a passport. I have a cell phone, and we've been videotaping

---

8. "Whiter," in this sense, connotes higher social status based on the racist tradition of judging people by the extent of their "white" blood or skin tone, dating back to Spanish colonial times.

the journey, waving our arms on top of the boxcar, passing jungle and mountains, ducking under tunnels. We take turns resting on the train, and one is the lookout. When the trip is long, lasting the whole night and I'm not tired, then I don't sleep. If I'm tired, I'll just wake up one or two of the others. One sleeps while the others stay awake because there are a lot of thieves who people say are from the cartel, from the Zetas. Once they came to collect a hundred dollars. Since I didn't pay them they beat me up and threw me from a train. But thankfully God was watching over me. I went to migrant safe houses in Palenque, Tierra Blanca, and Teozacoalco, Oaxaca, and they helped me. I'm really thankful there are migrant safe houses like this one here in Guadalajara where they support migrants, give us food to eat, clothes, shoes.

On June 24, we were riding La Bestia from Guadalajara to Mazatlán. A friend had sent me one hundred bucks from Canada. You know, I just felt happy that day and I got some Tonaya, a type of tequila. We bought four bottles and shared it among ourselves. One hour from Guadalajara, a guy who said that he came from San Pedro Sula, the murder capital of Honduras, invited us to drink in the carriage above. He saw the bottle of Tonaya and immediately was eyeing it. I let him have it because I had already drunk some. When he gave it back, the bottle was empty. We all drank some more from the other bottles. The next-to-last guy to drink had let an insect fly into the bottle and it just died. The guy from San Pedro Sula swigged the dregs and about five minutes later he was heading down the ladder, mumbling that he wanted to get off the train. He was wearing a neon orange jacket, the type that guys working construction wear. The train was moving fast. We were wondering, *What happened to him?* I was looking from above, and saw him put out his hands. He grabbed a long bar, did half a somersault, and fell under the train wheels. He got cut in half on the tracks. One leg was still stuck on the ladder. That was a disaster. And that's something that sticks with you. If you're strong, mentally, you can forget, but if you're weak, mentally, it sticks with you. You have to be mentally strong.

DEPORTED FROM CABORCA

On June 26, we arrived at Caborca, Mexico, near the US border. Two days later, Mexican immigration officers caught us and deported us. From Caborca they sent us to Hermosillo. From Hermosillo they sent us to Tapachula, Chiapas. They forced us all the way back to the border. I couldn't bear to go home to my family in Honduras. I called up a brother I have in the United States and he sent me a hundred dollars so that I could cross the border again. So we turned around and headed north. On the way, we ran into people we knew from our hometown who'd joined the maras and were preying on other people. We were robbed by some guys—one fat, the other skinny—who pretended to be guides but just took our money.

Later on, we learned the fat guy was from El Salvador or Guatemala and the skinny one was a neighbor from around where we lived. Another neighbor I saw under a bridge in Veracruz had joined La Letra.[9] It's not right for someone from the same town to steal money from another on the Mexican trail. A lot of Hondureños get stuck halfway along the Mexican path and end up messing with their own countrymen. It's sad because they sometimes end up killing their own people. If a neighbor stole from me in Mexico and asked me for *charlo*, I wouldn't help him because he had left me barefoot.[10] If he drew a weapon on me in Mexico and I saw him in Honduras, I would ask for help from God. There are good people and bad people, too. There are a lot of Mexicans who will say, "I'm from Honduras," because maybe that'll win them sympathy, and

---

9. *La Letra* is slang for Los Zetas. See appendix essay on "The Rise of the *Maras*."

10. *Charlo* is slang for alms or a handout.

then they start to beg for charlo. But most Mexicans hardly give anything to *catrachos*.[11]

IF I COULD CALL MY FAMILY RIGHT NOW

It took us twenty-five days to reach Guadalajara again. We just came to the shelter this morning. I haven't seen my wife and children in two months. If I could call my family right now, I'd say I love them a lot. It's a long journey, but I know it'll make things better. I'll be working and sending them money, and they'll be waiting for it. For their studies, their outfits, everything. If they walked barefoot before, now they are going to walk comfortably, in shoes.

Some days are for crying. Other days are for laughing, for having fun, for happiness. I thank God that I'm alive, with my two hands, my knowledge, my fresh perspective to make a home, have a roof over my children's heads. It's important to me that they grow up in Honduras, but that they also have a home. Because it's terrible to live like a scrounger. You want the roof, three meals a day. Back home, I live as an unwelcome guest of my parents-in-law, and I take care of six people on top of my wife and children. My children, my wife, and I are eight. Apart from us are my mother-in-law, her husband, my wife's grandfather, her grandmother, my brother, and sister-in-law. I take care of them all with my work. And I'm tired of that because if I make one hundred lempiras in Honduras, in half an hour it's down to eighty, and eggs cost three fifty, and I don't have enough for everyone. So I need to have my house. The reality is that I don't have a house because there are so many people there who aren't my children. If it were just me and my wife and my six children, it would all last me. Say I make one thousand pesos in a week—it's like forty dollars a week. Forty dollars isn't good. It doesn't last one week. If I work in the United States, live economically, and pay for my expenses, I can send

---

11. Slang for "Hondurans." See glossary.

my family about three or four hundred dollars a month. A hundred or two hundred for their roof, and two hundred more so that they can eat. In Honduras, I don't have a bed, I don't have an oven, I don't have a roof: I don't have anything because I began at the bottom. I sleep on bed mats. I just sleep with a blanket and a sweater. I don't have my own room much less my own house. I'm tired of sleeping on mats on the floor. My kids come up and say, "Why don't we have a house?" And I feel like a coward. I have to give them a house, a roof.

I have to find a friend or someone who will look out for me. I have an older brother in the United States who's thirty-six years old. He moves around between Atlanta, Miami, and New York for work. He remodels houses. I want to be like him, to find work.

I carry a picture of my son in his blue school uniform and scholar's cap in my passport. His name is Anselmo. He's about to turn ten and he's in the fifth grade. He's the only man of the house now, the head of the household, the one running the show. I tell him he has to study though. I have many dreams for my wife and children. I want to have a house for them, or if it's possible, two houses. Actually, since there are four women and two men, if God allows it, my goal is to have three houses around a courtyard: one for my daughters, one for my sons, and one for me with my wife. I want my children to study, so that they don't end up like me. The education they get depends on me as a father. When they're adults, I want for them to be hard workers because if you're not, you don't eat.

I give myself ten years to work in the United States. After ten years, if I've got anything left, I'll return to Honduras and buy a truck, a big truck. With a truck of my own, I won't need to go back to the United States. The only advice I could give to my fellow immigrants is to not just stay on the path committing wrongdoings. Take care of yourself. Take care of others. Don't get stuck halfway and decide, "I'm part of the Zetas now; I'm part of the Gulf Cartel."[12]

---

12. A Mexican crime syndicate based across the border from Brownsville, Texas.

That doesn't work for anyone. So my advice, at the very least, is if you head toward the United States, go all the way to the United States.

This is my last journey. I've suffered too much. It began as an adventure, a dream, but there are many thieves and dangers along the way. I've seen many people return with nothing and others who have died. This is my last journey. I don't want my children to be migrants. I don't want them to go through what I suffered. I'm going to give them a better future.

JULIO ZAVALA

AGE AT CROSSING: 14
BORN IN: San Pedro Sula, Honduras
INTERVIEWED IN: Washington, DC

We first speak with Julio at the office of a legal organization headquartered in Washington, DC. Julio is slouching in a chair beside his lawyers' desk and does not rise to shake hands. His face is locked in a scowl. As soon as we begin to talk though, he becomes animated. In recounting the journey of his life, he speaks with great emotion, sometimes sobbing while pounding his fists on the arms of the chair and sometimes standing up and yelling at the ceiling with clenched fists in the air. Neglected and abused by his family, Julio turned to the streets at age six, and became a child marero in order to seek protection from his family.[1] Trained to be

---

1. A marero is a member of a mara, or gang.

a fearless fighter, he struggled early on to contain his violent outbursts, which continued when he was in immigrant detention, where he was transferred into the criminal justice system for fighting. While his involvement in the gangs makes his case for legal status tenuous, he believes he will be killed if he is deported to Honduras. Julio's story presents the challenging question of what to do with young migrants who have been forced into gangs, suffer trauma, need therapy, and end up behind bars. After a few hours talking together, we go out for sandwiches, which we eat on a bench next to the reflecting pool at the National Mall. Colorful flags flap loudly in the wind. In the late afternoon sunlight, Julio sits in a cathartic calm, smiling serenely.

THE BIG STAIN ON MY LIFE

I was raised in a very ugly way. My parents split up when I was two. I don't know why they separated. This small tragedy was the big stain on my life. My parents made me feel like they had separated because of me. I was five, about to turn six, when I realized that.

My mother started to abuse me. It seemed she loved my brother more than me. She paid attention to him. He was the youngest, and she took better care of him. I received blows and insults. All this was because one day I asked her who my dad was. I wanted to know him, know who he was.

One day, when I was five years old, a man came walking down the street. My mother pointed at him as he was approaching and told me, "That's your dad." I just looked at him. I was surprised. He passed me by, and I didn't say hi to him. Maybe he didn't see me. I looked at him and thought, *He's my dad!* He looked strong. He was light-skinned and curly-haired. So that experience startled me, and I thought, *Wow, that is my father.*

Some months later, he appeared in front of my house, waiting for the bus. I saw him and ran out of the house like a crazy person without asking for permission from my mom, from anyone. I approached him and I said, "Dad, how are you?" He was happy. I never would have thought he would be. I still remember his face. He started telling me things. He told me he had to go to work, and that we could talk another day.

When he left it was horrible. My mom started beating me more and more, because I had talked to him. It was the worst punishment of my life. He had stayed in the same neighborhood after they split up. She punished me, asking me, "What are you looking for?" I'd tell her, "I want to know my dad." She'd reply, "No, what are you looking for?" She started insulting him. I told her, "Please don't call him a dog because he is not a dog," and then *bam!* She slapped me. Because of that word. From then on I was afraid of my mother. One of my uncles on my mother's side also started abusing me. He and his children were living in the same house as us. My uncle and mother stopped giving me food, started treating me badly, seeing me as less than them. I had just turned six. My uncle starved me and beat me. Even my own cousins were not saying a word to me.

At six years old, I went to the streets, looking for food, looking for something to do. The first thing I did was pick up trash, at house after house. There are a lot of things to collect. It's not like here, where everybody has their own trash service. Over there, there is a single trashcan on the street and the garbage truck comes to pick it up on certain days. I'd ask residents, "Do you have food to throw away? May I do you the favor of throwing it away?" I didn't say that I was going to charge them. And they'd say, "Yes, I have garbage to take out." They'd usually give me a scrap of food too. There were days though when I couldn't find anyone. I would go home and scrounge for food, but there was no food for me.

And one day my own uncle tried to kill me, when I was six. I remember that day he took me with him to look for wood. There was a pool in the river. I was there gathering wood next to the river when suddenly he came and pushed me in the water where it was deepest. I shouted and started going under. I didn't know how to swim at all. I can't erase that from my memory. I still have dreams about it sometimes. The last thing I remember is standing there, looking at the sunlight. The next thing I remember I woke up in the hospital. And that nasty man left me there.

I went back to my house from the hospital. I told my family, and they didn't believe me. They hit me. They said that I was lying, that I shouldn't say such things. Nobody believed me, not my mom, no one. So I told her, "I'm going to leave." I only told her that to see how she would react, to see if they would treat me better, because I was just six years old. "I'm a child! I can't live through this!" I told her as I clung to her. They were all eating. The only one who turned around to look at me was my mom. And she said, "It would be better if you left. The door is wide open." My own mother. I felt a big lump in my throat going up and down. I left. I started living on the streets. I was eating shit. I was eating food from the trash. Sometimes I wouldn't even eat. I wasn't wearing shoes. I was living on the worst way. And one day I thought to myself, *If this is going to be my life, I don't want to continue this way. I need to make more effort.* I said to myself, *I'm going up the mountain.* I started walking, looking for work. I started working, doing all kinds of jobs, whatever anyone would give me. What I wanted was money. I even started going to school. I was studying in the morning and working in the afternoon. When I had a job I would rent a room. I had my clothes, my room.

Living like that was difficult. When I started living on the streets, I looked for my father, because there was nothing standing in the way. I wanted to know him. I found out where he was working—he works at the lake as a security guard—and we started to hang out together. He showed me how to repair boats, canoes, a lot of things. He taught me how to fish. He taught me how to fire guns, how to fix them. I already knew how to use a gun because guys in

a gang had taught me. But my dad thought I was a child and that I
didn't know anything. I didn't live with him because he's married to
a woman I don't get along with.

Ever since I was very little, I had been hanging around gang
members and other people who weren't so bad. After I met my dad, I
joined a wilderness survival group of only older people. My dad was
in that group. They would hunt animals. In order to be in that group,
I had to pass a test: go alone to the mountains and face whatever was
there. You had to go to the top of the mountain and come down.
They left me only a radio and a machete. And they said when you get
lost, remember what to do. That's when I started to feel everything.
That's when I said, *I'm going to defeat my fear.* I even ran down the
cliffs. I can run any place, whatever the situation is. They taught me
how to face my fear. They showed me how to clean and gut animals,
how to prepare them. I was eating all kinds of animals in the mountains. I skinned snakes, deer, and ate everything raw!

There were times when I wouldn't go, but it became addictive.
From the moment they accepted me it became a vice, every Sunday.
When I didn't go I'd feel empty, tired, bored. But when I was in the
mountains, everything changed for me. The jungle was something
completely different. There were fallen trees, and I'd jump over them.
I'd climb the mountain, and sometimes I'd climb a tree and jump to
another tree. I felt free. I felt such strength. I was never tired.

Sometime after my uncle tried to drown me, and I was left traumatized, I went to the river by myself to learn how to swim. I remember that at first I was paddling like a puppy with my hands stretched
out. I was scared! I spent a week doing it every day until I learned.

In my country there is a river that we call Río Grande. The ponds
are beautiful: green, crystalline water. There is a place to dive from
extreme heights. That was my goal. *I'm going to overcome my fear of
the water and everything here.* There were other people there who were
saying, "That child, what is he doing, going up on the cliff? Hey, you're

going to kill yourself!" I took a moment to overcome my fear. Adrenaline, that's another kind of fear. I was shaking, laughing. When I looked down, I could feel my heart pound: *boom, boom!* The people below looked so small. I prepared myself, stepped back, and *foom!* I felt the air in my face, and was thinking to myself, *I'm not landing! What's going on?* I went up again. I dove four times into the water. I'd climb up and dive again. The exhilaration I felt was so strong!

After that my dad asked me, "Have you learned how to swim yet?" We were at a lake, a big one outside of San Pedro. "I'm going to show you," I told him. I dove into the water and started to swim. "Hey, where are you going?" he asked. I didn't respond. When I reached the other side, he looked very small. He was just a silhouette.

A PERSON WITHOUT FEELINGS

One day I was fishing at the lake and all of a sudden a guy came, fully armed, a gang member. He was running away from the police. He asked me, with his gun out, very scared, "Hey, hey! Where can I hide?" And I told him, "I'll take you somewhere." My dad had shown me some caves. I took the man to the caves since I didn't know what else to do. And I explained to him, "You can reach the lake that way," and so on. A few days later, I ran into him, and he was with a lot of gang members. He said, "This guy over there respects me. He helped me, so nobody is going to do anything to him."

That was the protection I was looking for. He was about thirty. I looked up to the gang members. At the age of six, I started smoking weed. I smoked tobacco as well but mostly weed. I'd found two kilos of weed, thrown away in the trash. I decided to try it, to see what it was like. I liked it. I grabbed a piece of paper and I threw the weed in, rolled it into a joint, and I smoked it the best I could! There was a drug dealer in the area and it was his weed. He'd dropped it, and since I was going through the trash, I found it. He told me, "Look,

I lost the drugs." "Oh, it's yours?" I asked. "Yes, thank you, you just saved my life," he replied. The gang was going to kill him for losing that weed. And he couldn't remember where he'd put it. I saved his life. His nickname was Crack. I started hanging out with him, and he told me, "Hey! You smell like marijuana." He couldn't believe I was so young and had smoked it. Then I suddenly became *El Fumador*.[2] I became known by that nickname. People would say, "Respect him. If you help him, he will help you, and if you don't, he will still help you."

At about the same time, the issues with my uncle started. He started to look for me. I'd see him on the street, but I'd always move out of his way. But after a while it started to become more intense. He was trying to hurt me. I couldn't see a path forward, a solution. I was like a little worm facing this huge giant. He wanted to kill me, finish me off. I felt a lot of pressure. I didn't have anywhere to go. I made the decision to turn to the gang members for protection. I didn't have anyone else. There were three other youngsters, two boys and one girl. We'd all grown up on the streets, taking care of each other.

The gang leaders trained me when I was very little. They said they wanted us for a special operation. We kids were perfect for this kind of training. We were their goldmine. That's what they used to say. Over the next few years, hanging out with the gang, it turned me into a person without feelings.

When I was fourteen, I had something with a girl. I found out she was pregnant, that she'd had the baby boy. But I didn't know him. Her family didn't like me because I was a kid from the streets. Her mother even tried to kill me. She threw hot water at me and came after me with a machete, saying, "You're not good enough for my daughter! You're not worth anything!"

Not long after this, the leaders gave me a mission, to kill someone. I failed the first time. They caught me and gave me another mission. They rarely do that. It depends on the case. It has to be

---

2. *El Fumador* means "The Smoker."

special, and since I was one of these four kids, they gave me another opportunity. They told me I had to kill my relatives. I had to kill my family—my mom, my uncle, and the other people in their household—to be liberated from the past, to become their homie completely. So I said yes. I accepted the mission to kill my family. The leaders of the gang gave me guns.

I went to my mom's house. The family was all gathered there. When I came in, the first person I saw was my uncle. When I was about to point my gun at him, a little girl approached me and said, "Hello! How are you? Who are you?" My uncle told her, "He is your cousin." I felt stupid. I didn't know my uncle had a daughter. I stood there in shock. The girl's mother came in, pregnant. I asked my uncle, "Who is she?" He told me, "She's my wife. She's expecting." I thought, *I can't take this little girl's life. I can't.* When she turned to me, the look she gave me changed me instantly. I felt something was connecting us. I thought to myself, *Look at this little girl. Look at this baby who is about to be born, who is in her mother's belly.* I turned around and left. This was the biggest mistake I ever made, because I should have killed my family. I am condemned. If the gang members in Honduras ever find me, I'm done with because I am marked.

I didn't have a solution. I felt a huge pressure, you know. I went to my dad's house. I wanted to hide over there. I couldn't sleep. I had no appetite. I was smoking drugs, and it had no effect on me. I had to do something. I left the guns behind and I left for the United States. But before I left town, I went to find my son. I looked at him. I held him for a while. In a way, the only one who supported me was my ex-girlfriend. She was the only one who understood me. She would tell me, "I see everything you've done." She knew almost everything about my life. She lived in the same neighborhood. She had accepted me even though she knew I was in the gang.

WHEN YOU REACH THE MIDDLE,
THE CURRENT CARRIES YOU

My trek started spontaneously after I had visited my son. I was fourteen. The trip was very long, and I did it all alone, without knowing
anything. Some days I would walk along the railway tracks, day and
night. I had a lot of bad luck when I entered Mexico. I had to walk
through the mountains to avoid getting caught. I crossed the border
from El Ceibo into Tabasco. I walked into the wilderness of Tenosique at five in the morning, and I arrived at 11:30 at night.[3] I had
nothing. When I arrived in Tenosique, I sat down next to the other
migrants, I took off my shoes, and my feet had huge blisters and
wounds. I couldn't stop walking because I had heard many stories.
I've seen rape. I've seen death.

I witnessed a scene with a young woman. We were about to
enter Veracruz. I was sleeping when she arrived on the train. Then
other people who were looking to rape her followed. I heard cries.
I wondered what to do. I had a huge fury inside of me. Why didn't
I do anything? I felt like pulling them aside, throwing them off the
train. But I stayed still, with this great weight. They were armed. I
couldn't do anything. They were on top of her, one at a time.

All the people who ride the train at night are armed because the
bandits come up and start beating people up, throwing them off the
train, assaulting them. I was by myself, and I grabbed a small stick
and a rock. I met seven people from different countries and the seven
of us agreed that we had to protect ourselves. When someone came
aboard at night, we started making noise, banging the sticks and
rocks on the metal sides of the train. It lets the thieves know that if
they come up onto the train, it's not going to go well for them, that
we will fight.

---

3. El Ceibo is a town on the Guatemalan side of the border with the Mexican state
of Tabasco. Tenosique, Tabasco, is a dangerous sixty-two-kilometer trek through
the jungle from El Ceibo, where many are assaulted by robbers and police officers.

When we arrived at Córdoba, Mexico, I lost them all. There is a big train station, and when we got off the train, there were tons of people and Mexican immigration police asking for documents. Everybody got restless. I started to run as well, with a group of people. I got on another train. The immigration officers were busy with all these people. I took the opportunity to get on that train, and it started going.

When we arrived at Veracruz, the train stopped. It was very weird. There is a stretch where it only goes through mountains. You don't see anything, only mountains, monkeys. All I thought was, *Well, it's going to stay here.* I stayed there down on the floor of the train. I was half asleep, half awake, and shortly after I heard noise in the mountains. My heart started to pound. Could it be an animal that is going to eat me? I don't know. I saw people who were well armed, some thieves, gangsters, coming onto the train, baring their tattoos so nobody would mess with them. They were MS-13—in Veracruz, they are in control. When I saw them, I thought, *They are going to kill me.* I didn't feel anything. I felt something blank, white. I was sweating, and when I looked at them, everything left me. I went numb. When they saw me, they said, "Look, there is nothing. Leave this shit!" After half an hour the train left. Soon after we heard gunshots. When the train was leaving, they started to attack. They got the group of migrants who were in front and threw them off the train.

When one comes up from Veracruz to the north, there is a place where the Zetas stop the train in clear daylight. They are armed to the teeth. They wear normal clothes. One look at the weapons and you say, "No thank you. I don't have any problem!" There are so many of them. When they go to stop the train, they drive their trucks right up to the side of it, looking up onto the train. Some are on top, and others are in front. When the train stops, they say, "Hey, we are from such-and-such organization, so cooperate. We are looking for someone." Or, "We're just stopping to see what's happening." Sometimes they demand money.

Heading north toward the border, I thought about suicide. I've almost committed suicide many times in my life. You can't imagine that huge thing that you feel when you tell yourself, *You're not worth anything.* I've been there. This is what I tell myself when I am on the edge: *You're being weak.* I start to see myself as I did before, as a bad person. In Monterrey, it hit me very hard. One day I wrapped a rope around my neck. I let myself fall, and then caught myself right away.

I came to the border between Mexico and the United States in Nuevo Laredo at exactly eleven in the morning. The first thing I did was to check out the scene. I started to see people, hear conversations, find out about what time it was possible to cross and when it wasn't. I investigated all day long until I decided to cross at nine in the evening. When I was about to cross, another person appeared. He was older, from Monterrey. He found where I was hiding! His name was Juan. He asked me, "What are you going to do?" I replied, "I am about to cross." He asked, "Who are you with? Are you with a *coyote*?" I answered, "No, I don't have a *coyote*. I'm by myself." And we crossed. It was very dark and the river looked dangerous. The water was high and swirling. The river sounded so stormy, so strong. My heart was beating as if it was going to burst. From nine at night, when we crossed, we only had about thirty minutes because the border patrol would likely arrive. This is the time they usually have a shift change. They leave the patrol cars with the lights on and they go.

We had to cross, get dry, change clothes, and go. I told Juan we were going to dive into the water upstream to end up across from where we were. When you dive into the water, you start to push with all your strength. When you reach the middle, the current carries you. You don't touch the rocks. I took off all my clothes, and put them in a bag. I tied it to myself like a backpack. The truth is, I'd never swum that way, never felt such strength. I don't know if it was the fear or the motivation. Juan had brown skin, but he looked white, because he was so nervous. It is called the Río Bravo, the *fierce river*, and that night it was fierce![4]

When we crossed, the border police were there. As soon as we got out of the water, we started to run and threw ourselves into the mountains. Then we dried ourselves and put our clothes back on. There was a dam where the immigration patrol car was parked, and we started to crawl, hiding, without seeing anything, tapping the ground with sticks to feel where we were going. When we saw that there was no one in the car, we said, "Let's go!" and started to run up the hill. They spotted us. We managed to cross, and as soon as they saw us the patrol chased us, and we kept running, but we'd already entered Laredo, Texas. We were already running through the city. Then suddenly we entered an alley, and the officers came to the other entrance. One was over here, one over there, with the dogs. We stayed there with our hands up, and they started yelling at us with the megaphone. I stood there thinking, *If only we had stayed longer at the river, we could have pulled it off.*

MY COUNSELORS TOLD ME, "YOU'RE CHANGING"

The border patrol locked me up in San Antonio, Texas. When I entered this country, I had thousands of problems, thousands of secrets that I haven't told anyone. My whole life, I have never had the opportunity to talk to someone. I met a woman who became my counselor. Her name was Rosa. She told me, "I know you think of yourself as someone who has a lot of issues." She saw me. She told me, "Don't worry. If you share your story, it will stay between us." It was my mistake to tell her. I usually keep things to myself, but that day I saw her as a very sincere person. I thought, *I'm going to trust you.* I had

---

4. In Mexico, the Rio Grande is called Río Bravo.

doubts, and I said, *Ojalá, ojalá.*[5] I told her everything. A few days later the border patrol sent me to jail. I felt betrayed. They told me, "We're sending you to a place with homies. They're going to treat you like a homie." I was sent to a prison in Shenandoah, Virginia.[6] I got there and there were four walls and plenty of ex–gang members.

I had problems in Virginia. I assaulted an officer in the prison. I am a quiet person, but I always have this badly formed side. When someone does something to me, I let him. If he does it again, I let it be. One day, a guy came and took me away from my cellblock. He insulted me in the worst ways. I didn't want to fight with him, because as soon as I left my country I thought, *I'm not a bad person. I am a new person. I'm going to change. If someone is looking for problems, I'll withdraw. It's better.* That's what I said, and that's how it was. Until one day someone started insulting me, and I laid him out. I fought with that man. After fighting with him, I fought with other people: with officers, with everybody. I lost control. My other self came out. I'm someone who has self-control, but when I lose it, nobody can control me. At first I could control myself, but in the days that followed, there was always this inner voice that said, *Enough, enough!* Then, there was a big incident with a guard. I started to fight however I could. And I hit him in the teeth and whenever he asked me for it, I gave it to him. That was the problem, and I really lost control.

Sometimes they had me in solitary, *solito.* They had my hands cuffed behind my back. I couldn't move. I had to eat without my hands. I was a threat for the people there. When I slept, there were cameras on four sides. The room was dark. But darkness doesn't scare me. I got used to it. I feel safe, good, when I'm in the dark. Every morning I would wake up and I was in my cell. I didn't have my clothes.

---

5. *Ojalá* is an expression meaning "I really hope."

6. He was most likely sent to the Shenandoah Valley Juvenile Center, as part of the detention process for unaccompanied minors.

From maximum security, they sent me to even higher security. You feel very pressured. I asked the guard who took me there, "You're sending me to another jail? Tell me the truth. Don't play me." And he just cuffed me, just like that. *Click, click, click.* They sent me to Trenton, New Jersey. All the gangs from New Jersey and New York are there, not a lot of Central Americans. I had injured my hand, and people asked me, "What happened to you?"

I had an anxiety crisis. The prison guards paid attention to me, sent me to a counselor. I told him I needed to find a way to change. He told me, "We're going to do it if you really want to change, and I see you. I can see you want to change for real, but you're fighting with yourself, your inner self." I started therapy. I started looking for ways to control my anxiety, my anger, to not lose myself, and if I did lose myself, to regain control. I started to attend meetings, do a lot of exercises. I stayed four or five months, there, in this calm mind-set. My counselors told me, "You're changing." Everyone started to notice. The counselor said, "We're going to give Julio another opportunity. He's not going to be in maximum security anymore. He's going to go to limited security in New York." The prison counselor told me, "We're giving you another opportunity because we see you are doing well."

I'd made a promise, and I was keeping it. I started off at Children's Village in Dobbs Ferry, New York, saying, "My name is Julio. This is my goal: to change, to move forward, have a new life." All the people there were fine with me. In detention, the inmates used to look at me with fear, because they saw me as a gang member. Here in the shelter I gained the respect of the whole campus. Even though I was still a teenager, I became a sort of inspiring figure for the boys. The pills I was taking to calm myself down helped a lot, too. I was able to sleep.

In New York, the other boys came to me for advice. They'd say, "I want to be like you." And one day I wondered, *How can you want to be like me since I'm a bad person? I've suffered so much. I've done things.* One boy told me, "I want to be like you because you help everybody. You have a good heart." He started telling me things that made me think, *That's who I am now.* All my life, since I was a child, I'd always heard, "You're trash, you're useless."

When I was in New York, I called my dad in Honduras. I said, "Hi! This is Julio." He replied, "Oh, you're alive? I thought you were dead. Where are you?" When I told him where I was, he got scared. He said, "You've gone so far!" Then I called my mother in Honduras. "Look, Mother," I said. "You don't greet me, don't say a word to me. Nobody's perfect in this world. It is what it is. You're my mother, so I forgive you. Don't treat me like your son. Treat me like any person, but treat me well." That's how we started to talk again. In another conversation, I told her, "I'm your child whether you wanted it or not. You said you wanted to have an abortion, but you didn't. You had me! You have me!" We'd never spoken about these things before. She said, "I've had a change of conscience. I thought you were dead."

Later, I called to wish my mom a happy Mother's Day. My aunt picked up. She told me my mother was dead. She had been killed by gang members. And then she said, "It's your fault." So I wondered, *How many other people have to die until they find me?* Someone from the prison was listening in and writing down what we talked about. He broke into the conversation and said to my aunt, "Look, we're going to cut the call because you can't talk to him this way. You don't know how he is doing!" "Yes, I do!" she said. My family has always blamed me for everything. They curse at me, yelling, "Look, your days are numbered because we're going to kill you."

At that point I couldn't feel anything for anyone, not even for my mom. *She died.* All day long, I was left with this. I didn't cry. Since childhood I've swallowed my tears. But I had to cry. I told the other inmates, "They are burying my mother, and I can't stand the pressure." It all came pouring out.

I CALL IT MY OTHER SELF

I've learned how to cry, for real. Now, when I feel something, I cry. Back in prison people would tell me, "You're an incredible person." Everybody would ask me, "How can you bear so much?" I can bear a lot. I've borne so much. But that day I couldn't anymore because of my mom's death. *It doesn't matter if she's been the worst shit. She is your mom.* That's what made me break down. I made a promise of one day of silence. I told everyone in the therapy group, "Today, I'm not going to talk because I forgive her with all my heart, so that she can rest in peace." The next day they buried her. I spent the whole day without talking, from six in the morning to six in the evening. I fasted on my day of silence. And that's how I finally forgave my mother.

After completing the program in New York, Julio was placed in a house in Washington, DC, in 2015, where he was working with his lawyer to attain legal residence through asylum and Special Immigrant Juvenile Status.[7]

I had an experience here in DC about two weeks ago, before my birthday. My bike got stolen. It was during the day. I'd left it outside, and I felt bad because that was my transportation to go to work. I walked and got attacked by some people. They told me they were gang members. I was walking with my phone, and there were a few people in front of me. I went to the other side of the street to avoid them. I heard them start threatening me. And I saw a knife coming in my direction.

When I turned around and saw the person coming toward me, the knife coming toward me, I grabbed it from him. We started to fight. He was a bit taller than me. When I took the knife from him,

---

7. Special Immigrant Juvenile Status is a provision under the Immigration Act of 1990 that allows immigrants to apply for residency if they entered the United States as minors and were neglected, abandoned, or abused.

another person came and took the knife from me. At that moment, I really felt like making him disappear. I had the opportunity to kill him and either return to my country or move to another place permanently. I had a thousand ways to turn him into a corpse that day. But in that moment I also started to control myself. I started to breathe, to calm myself down, to control myself, and my other self appeared. The bad one came back. *Go on. Come back. Kill him. Make him disappear. You are El Fumador!* The first thing I did was walk away, pull out my phone, and call my lawyer. If I hadn't taken the moment to call her, I would've done something terrible. But in that moment I started to respect myself because I overcame my other self. From early childhood I've felt something within me. I call it my other self. It's almost impossible to describe. When something is about to happen to me, I sense it. When someone is about to do something to me, even in my dreams, my heart warns me. I'm a quiet person, but I can also be very dangerous. You can't imagine. To see a person almost kill you and maintain your composure! I kept myself together. The change I made in Trenton, in jail, was real.

I am renting a room in a house in DC where there are only people from Central America. It's a big house, with three stories, and we share the rent. There are people of all ages: youngsters, children. The neighborhood has Brazilians, Boricuas, a few Salvadorans, Guatemalans, and also quite a lot of Ecuadorians.[8]

There was a time when I abused drugs. Now that I've overcome that, I feel proud. I had all kinds of vices, and one day I said, *Just one vice, marijuana.* I stopped drinking alcohol. I used to drink seven beers a day, seven Imperiales, big 40-ounce beers. *This is the last one I'll have,* I told myself. Cigarettes as well—I bought one and thought, *This is the last time I smoke.* I smoked cocaine too. Everything. Sometimes I can't sleep. I dream about people, a lot of things.

---

8. *Boricua* is a slang word for a Puerto Rican, especially one who lives in the United States.

I have bags under my eyes all the time. Marijuana helped me to relieve 100 percent of my stress, to sleep. It helped me to accomplish a lot of things. There were moments when I didn't want anything in my life. I was very depressed, and I'd roll a joint and smoke it. It would calm me down.

I have a tattoo now. It's a rosary. This rosary means a lot to me. I used to be Catholic. It represents my ex-Christianity, the fact that I was a Christian in my heart. I also use it to pray. In my country the rosary also means the gang, the 18. With an image like this, you have to be careful. Most Central Americans don't have tattoos. In our countries a simple tattoo is death. In our country, the rosary is a very strong symbol. You can only get the rosary or the "18" when you've gone past the rank of *clika,* the trainee.

I've been in the United States for about four years. I started to go to school when I entered this country. I also exercise a lot. I have a routine: two hours on the bike nonstop. After the two hours, the timer rings, and I stop. I lock it up and go swimming, to cross to the other side of the reservoir. After swimming, even though I feel tired, I start running.

I remember the gang leaders telling me, "If you are a beast, control your beast. You know what you're capable of. Don't tell anyone, and if they say you can't, don't say anything. Just laugh, because you know what you're capable of." It was very hard, but I see life in a different way now.

In May 2018, Julio's lawyer tells us that while his asylum case was still pending, he "took a turn for the worse." Partially due to his frequent hospitalizations for physical and psychiatric issues stemming from trauma, which made it difficult to maintain steady work, he developed an opioid addiction and became homeless. He fatally overdosed in April 2018.

ISMAEL XOL

AGE AT CROSSING: 15
BORN IN: Xolcuay, El Quiché, Guatemala
INTERVIEWED IN: San Francisco, California

Ismael is studying English and political science at the City College of San Francisco. We meet on campus on a cloudy Friday evening in February 2016; most students have left for the weekend. Dressed in a crisp button-down shirt, necktie, and trench coat, Ismael speaks slowly and deliberately about his experiences. Although he is only in his twenties, he has the composure of an older man, and takes on a fatherly tone when speaking of his eleven siblings. Burdened by having to support such a large family in a depressed rural economy, his father moved to the United States when Ismael was young. At age fifteen, Ismael left the highland village of Xolcuay, Guatemala, to join his father in Florida to help support his family back home. His brother Maynor accompanied

223

him through Mexico to the US border and then left him with smugglers who took him into the United States. When Ismael arrived, he only spoke K'iche'. After joining his father in Florida, where he worked in construction, he set off on his own in order to pursue higher education. He is a sponsor for his younger brother Geovanni, who won his own asylum case and lives with Ismael. While Ismael's DACA status allows him to live and work legally in the United States for now, President Trump's decision to end the program has filled him with uncertainty about whether he will be able to fulfill his dreams.[1]

THEY CREATED THIS COMMUNITY
NEAR THE HIGHWAY

My hometown is named Xolcuay. It's in north-central Guatemala, and it's at a very high altitude. Now, it has about five thousand people. The men wear typical Western clothing while the women wear traditional long dresses, all handwoven. K'iche' is the native language of the community, but more people have started to speak Spanish. Even my dad speaks a little Spanish. Before the civil war, our village was deep in the mountains and then, during the civil war, the houses were all spread out since the army killed the people who lived farther up in the mountains.[2] Since there wasn't a road to get in, it would take about half an hour to walk there. Sometime after the civil war slowed down a little bit and the people gathered again, they created this community near the highway.

My mom had a previous husband, but he was killed during the war. He was the father of my older sister. During the war, my mother

---

1. DACA (Deferred Action for Childhood Arrivals) is an immigration policy signed into law by President Obama that allows some immigrants brought as children to apply for renewable two-year deferred action from deportation.

2. The Guatemalan Civil War lasted from 1960 to 1996 and some of the most intense fighting took place in the 1980s. See "Historical Timeline."

went to work on a coffee plantation in the mountains, and that's where she met my dad. They got married and then came back to the town she used to live in. My dad is from another town about five hours away by car. It's in another state, Huehuetenango, even higher in the mountains.

We are a family of eleven kids. I was born in 1988. Of my two older brothers, Hilmar lives in Monterrey, Mexico, and one of my sisters, Yoselin, is married and lives in the same town as him. I think it's a big city. The rest of my siblings live in Xolcuay, except two brothers who just moved here. In the United States, I have two other brothers. Miguel lives in Georgia and Esteban lives in Pittsburgh. Miguel and Esteban are in their twenties. I also have an older brother in Mexico, Maynor, and an older sister in Guatemala. Whenever one of my brothers tells me he is thinking about coming to the United States, I tell him that I will send him to school. And since they don't want to go to school, they purposely live far away from me! We actually don't talk to each other that much. Even though they are my family and we have nothing against each other, we sort of have our own lives.

In Guatemala, if you speak a language other than Spanish, you are basically discriminated against. The sad story is that now, even though we understand that the Maya culture has been here forever, there are still those who don't care about it or treat it as something that doesn't have value. It's our culture, something that we have to value or respect. In Guatemala those same people at some point moved from small towns, where they didn't speak Spanish, to the bigger town, and then started speaking Spanish! And when they come back to their hometowns, they discriminate against people who don't speak Spanish, against their own people. This idea has taken root for generations. It's a shame that during my childhood everyone was trying to speak Spanish and leave the original language behind. They are trying to escape from something that they're told is bad.

I WASN'T A VERY GOOD STUDENT

I went to school, but unfortunately I wasn't a very good student. I tried my best, but it just didn't work out. I only spoke a bit of Spanish and since the classes were in Spanish, it was difficult. I quit in the first grade. There's no family support. In Guatemala in the countryside, families don't see education as a necessity. If you go, if you don't go, it's the same.

My dad had a bakery and I'd just help out with his business. He'd make *pan dulce*, sweet breads. I have lots of brothers, siblings. They'd wake up very early, but it wasn't necessary for me to wake up early because I was a kid. I could wake up at any time and help out. It wasn't an obligation. Sometimes I'd just go out and play, like a regular kid. We sold the bread in different towns in a car. And people would come to my dad to make a big order, for example, a thousand quetzales' worth. Then he'd work during the weekdays and on the weekend take it to the people. This was his routine. It's funny. It probably sounds like we had a shop, but we didn't. People just knew. It was just a house, and people knew that it was the bakery. I think my dad got tired of working from home and decided to end the bakery business. One of the major reasons was that the oven requires a lot of wood to heat. Logs were becoming expensive, and it took a lot of effort to obtain wood. He moved to the United States in 2001 and worked on construction sites in Florida. My mom was a housewife and in a typical Maya family the woman is the one who takes care of the kids. And since we're eleven siblings, joining my dad in the United States would have involved bringing all the kids, and I believe it wouldn't have been easy.

The houses were very close to each other, so we had a garden outside of town where we grew food. We also bought food at a market once a week or so: beans, meat, or just about anything that's not available in the town. We had to go to the mountains to gather logs for the fire sometimes. We would carry them on our backs and sometimes rent horses. At one point, we had chickens, pigs, horses, and cows. We kept them on my dad's property.

I used to like soccer. But my mom didn't want me to play outside. Whenever I did go out to play soccer with the kids in the streets my mom would ask me, "What are you doing playing outside?" And she used to hit me, saying, "Why don't you understand? You have to stay inside!" I think it was her maternal instinct. Our village was a very peaceful place. It's much safer in the small villages than in the city. In the community, everyone looks out for each other. But the fact that she had survived the war probably added to her overprotectiveness.

We had a K'iche' Bible, but we weren't taught the Maya culture. Our town was more Christianized and many other churches would come out to try to convert us. These days, there are more and more Jehovah's Witnesses. They're on every corner in my town. They go to every house and try to convince you to convert. In the same small town there are probably five different churches. I just don't have any religion. I was raised Catholic. My mother was a very religious person. She was active in the church and a member of every organization in the church. I feel like it helped me to become who I am, but at the same time I got to understand Catholicism. It's not what we knew. It didn't come to save all the people or to help all the people but to convert people, make these people slaves, and to take all the gold and resources of these new places that they discovered. I study religion and find it very interesting because in all religions, the main idea is to live peacefully, to love your neighbor. Although their books say this, nobody does it. Nobody lives in peace with their neighbors.

I FELT THIS EMOTIONAL TRANSFER

Rigoberta Menchú is from the same region, where people were most affected by the war. We were literally on the other side of the mountain that she's from. She's a really interesting person too.[3] I have only seen a documentary about her during the war, when she was telling her story to the world. And that was it. She was probably the same age as my mom. I saw the film when they were condemning Ríos Montt, the military leader during this war who was ordering the killings. He was the president, a military general. He wasn't elected president; he took over in a coup d'etát.[4]

I remember my mom was talking to me about the war. A group of people had gathered together and fled to a safe place. She was telling us kids that the adults and older kids carried all the stuff. The little kids just walked out without anything. She said they even went for days with no food. They survived, and I can't imagine how much they really suffered. She told me about it with such deep emotion, a very deep sadness. She cried all the time and remembered what the family went through. I felt this emotional transfer to all of my siblings, even me, because I'm very sensitive to things.

"NO, NOT YOU"

When I was just a kid in Guatemala, I thought, *Why not go to the United States? I could go live with my dad and help support our family.* In Guatemala or Latin America, we see the United States as a country where you can just go and grab the money. We know this idea is just in our heads, but everyone who comes here thinks that. And when I asked my dad if I could come, he said, "No, not you," because I was the third child, the second-to-the-eldest brother. My sister had gotten married, and my older brother had just moved out.

---

3. Rigoberta Menchú is a K'iche' survivor of the war who was the narrator of a testimonial oral history book. She is a political and human rights activist who won the Nobel Peace Prize in 1992 and ran for president of Guatemala in 2007.

4. Ríos Montt was a military leader and dictator who was convicted of genocide in 2013.

I was the one who was supposed to look after the family.

I was fifteen years old when I came to the United States, in 2003. I planned to come and work a little bit and then go back to Guatemala. My father didn't want me to come. He said, "No, I need you to be there because of your mom. You have to take care of your mom." I said, "No, I want to go." Finally, I convinced him and then took this trip from Guatemala to the United States by bus.

I COULD ONLY TRUST MY BROTHER

I came with my brother Maynor, who was around twenty years old at that time. He brought me into Mexico, and we traveled by bus across Mexico. It wasn't that hard for me to cross Mexico because of my brother. He helped me, guided me. Most who cross Mexico come on this dangerous train. We walked across the border, through a forest. We crossed from one town into another. I think we crossed at Tecún Umán with a large group of migrants.[5] We crossed and then went somewhere near the highway where there's the best chance of crossing. We stopped the bus, jumped on, and rode to Tuxtla Gutiérrez.[6] That's where we stayed overnight. After that we traveled from there to Mexico City, which is the capital, the biggest city. We stayed one night and then from there we transferred onto another bus, to Santa Ana, I think, but I'm not quite sure.

We got to Sonora and that's the transfer point where we would cross the border and enter the United States. From the city of Altar, Sonora, we jumped into a van that brought us into the desert. It looks like a road, but it's made by the trucks that have driven there so many times. We got there in about three hours, and then from that

---

5. Tecún Umán is a city of eleven thousand people across the Mexican border and the Suchiate River from Ciudad Hidalgo. It is named after one of the last K'iche' rulers.

6. Tuxtla Gutiérrez is the capital in the Mexican state of Chiapas.

point, we were left to walk across the border. At that point I was very naïve. I could only trust my brother. He said he knew those people who were crossing with us, but I think he lied to me to make me feel safe with strangers. Maynor took me to the US border just to help me feel comfortable. Then he dropped me off with those people and went back to Guatemala.

So we started to walk and at some point, when the sun came out, we stopped near a highway. The leaders said some people were going to pick us up in a car. I could have never imagined that car ride. And when they said, "Oh, the car's here, we have to jump in," it was just like a dream. You have no time to think twice or ask, "Where am I going to sit?" I was still asking myself, *How did that happen?* They just said we had to go and then everybody went. I just ran to the car. There were many people, and some even got into the trunk. They actually packed people in the trunk. It was terrible. We were in Arizona, in the desert. I think the people in charge were *coyotes*, but my brother didn't tell me all this. I got into the front seat of the car. I was squished between people and I just wanted it to end because the ride took about five hours. It was so hot and cramped.

THAT'S WHY I HATE PAN BIMBO!

When we got to our destination, we didn't even have the chance to look around outside. We got to this building and tumbled out of the car. I was so weak. Everyone was angry. Whatever you did, these Mexican smugglers would punch you. They weren't acting like friends who would help you cross.

These smugglers are doing it for business, but because what they do is illegal, they have to make sure that everything they do stays in the dark and doesn't come out, into the light. I was so weak, so tired. It was just like a nightmare. I was sitting against the wall, and there were so many people in that room—even people jammed in the closet—and somebody said something. Then three people came through the door. They started punching the *coyote*. I could hear them kicking him like *pum, pum, pum!* Nobody cared. There were lots of people. They didn't let us go. They asked for money. It's terrible because I stayed there for a week I think. They transferred me to somebody's house and put me in this room with a guy who fought with his wife all the time. I could hear him hitting her. I thought that he would punch me too. *If he killed me, who would know?*

My dad was supposed to pay for my ride, from there to Florida. He sent my bus ticket, but no money for food and water. I didn't have any money. The *coyotes* at the safe house gave me my ticket and dropped me off at the bus.

It was very scary. They fed me the same thing, Bimbo bread with a piece of ham and cheese, every day. That's why I hate Pan Bimbo![7] Every day, I heard this ringtone, "*tere-re-ren-ten-teen-teen-teeen!*" For six months I couldn't stand to hear that song or that ringtone. It would remind me of being trapped in that room.

I DIDN'T EAT FOR TWO WEEKS

So on my trip from Arizona, I had no money, just a ticket. I was naïve and I didn't know how the system worked here. The guy who dropped me off said, "Here's two dollars." And I thought, *Two dollars? It has to be a lot of money!* When I got to the bus, he said, "You're going to transfer at this point and then from there you're going to transfer to Fort Myers." There were three transfer points. I didn't speak Spanish or English. I thought, *How am I going to do this?*

I got onto this bus, and after what seemed like a couple of weeks, I arrived somewhere in Michigan. I hadn't eaten for two weeks. You know that you're there, but you don't feel all there. The driver waved his hands like he was saying, "You have to leave, get out!" I didn't

---

7. Pan Bimbo is a processed white bread, the Mexican version of Wonder Bread.

understand his gestures, so I took out my ticket to show him. He seemed to say, "Okay, come back later on when we leave." I just sat on the bench right in front of the bus because I was afraid that it would leave without me.

I only had two dollars. I went to a small store and showed the cashier a dollar, but I couldn't explain what I wanted. I think he asked, "What do you want?" I just grabbed some chips and showed him a dollar. He motioned, "No." And then he came from behind the counter and grabbed a Snickers bar and said, "This, this." I said, "Yeah," and he gave me back ten cents. That's the only time I had something to eat.

I got to Chicago and the bus station was near some huge buildings. I saw this guy with a turban who I thought was a terrorist from the Middle East. I was thinking, *Oh my god! He can blow us up!* This guy was probably just a businessman.

And from there we went down south to Fort Myers. My dad finally met me, and I was so glad. It had been two years since I'd seen him. And when I saw my dad, I thought, *I'm safe. I'm safe.*

"SCHOOL IS FOR LAZY PEOPLE"

I was working construction with my dad. At that point, I was the head of one of the groups of workers. I was still only fifteen when I started working as a foreman. For the first two years that I worked for the company that my dad works for, I was following the manager around and I started to read the blueprints. I wanted to understand how everything worked. One Saturday, everyone who was working gathered around me, and I led the group! I felt confident, and since the only thing I really wanted was a raise, I asked my boss for one. He asked me, "What do you know?" and I told him about the skills I had. The following Monday we had our safety meeting, and he announced that he'd hired two more people. He said, "We have a new

group and Ismael will be the lead." I was shocked! My English was
very limited. But almost all the workers were Latino. My Spanish
was okay at that point, and since everybody spoke Spanish, that's
how I communicated with them.

At that point I was still just a kid. But my dad told me clearly,
"You have to work because there is no other option." I started work.
My dad went to church every Sunday and he took me with him. At
church I used to see all these kids running around, playing soccer
outside. All these kids were having fun. I'd just sit on the stairs,
watching them, and I thought, *I want to play.* But since I didn't
know how to socialize, and I didn't speak the language or know
how to communicate, I'd just stay put. At the same time, I thought,
I am a grown man. I'm not that kid anymore who just wants to play.
I have responsibilities. And this gave me the idea to learn English.
I said to my dad, "You know what? I want to go to school." And
he said, "No way. What do you want to go to school for? School
doesn't pay you. School doesn't feed you. School is for lazy people."
I said, "Well, I'll do my best. I don't know how I'm going to do it,
but I'm going do it." And he said, "You can do whatever you want,
but just remember, you have to take care of yourself. Then it's not
a problem for me."

The boss also encouraged me to learn English, because I couldn't
communicate with some of the other people who ran the company.
My dad was in the group that I would supervise. I asked my boss if
he would let me work over the weekends because I wanted to learn
English, to go to school during the week. And he said, "Great! I want
you to go to school, and if you want to work weekends, you have the
job." I went to school and worked weekends for a year. I was still the
foreman. I was young, so skinny, and so short. But my boss saw me
as a potential leader who could do the job. He got me a big truck, so
big that when I drove it, I couldn't see over the dashboard. I could
just see through a hole in the steering wheel. I'd never driven before.

After nearly ten years in Florida, working, saving money, and learning some basic English, I moved to San Francisco in 2012. I've been here for four years, and I love it. I work for an organization here that provides services for Guatemalan immigrants. I work full time, forty hours a week. Every now and then the job asks me to work overtime. I don't like it, but I don't say no. Nobody wants to lag behind. Whatever comes in the future, I'm just open to it. My boss, who is Guatemalan, understands that I am a student. For example, she asked me last week if I could stay one more hour after work, and I said, "Yeah, I'll do my best." I'm going to school, so I need to leave early some days. And she said, "No problem. I understand that." She's a little bit flexible when it comes to school.

A year after I moved to San Francisco, I found out about AB 540 status for students and that's when I started studying at City College.[8] I graduated with an associate degree in December, but I am still studying and hope to transfer to a four-year university. I only have temporary residency in the United States and a temporary authorization to work through DACA, which was set up by the Obama administration. I have to renew my status every two years and pay a fee. In the 2016 presidential election, I'm rooting for Senator Sanders, but who knows if he's going to win. The other day I was watching a video about how delegates have been established and how they elect the president. It's not about the popular vote. And Trump is saying, "Even if I shoot somebody, I won't lose any voters." That's terrible. I'm worried that if he's elected, my DACA status could be in jeopardy.

Because of my job I have to travel to Oregon, Washington, and Alaska. We assist Guatemalans who live in the United States but don't have the proper documents. The only document they might have is a valid Guatemalan passport. They can't travel because they're afraid something might happen.

---

8. AB 540 is a law that allows undocumented students in California who meet certain criteria to pay in-state tuition rates at state universities and community colleges.

I visited New York last December. That was my first time there and it was fun. My friend is a chiropractor and has an office two blocks from Central Park. He took me around sightseeing. We went to the West Village. It wasn't too cold when I was there. I was just there for one day because there was a layover on our way to Puerto Rico. It was a long weekend with friends. It's very Latin American. It was an escape to see something else.

I'd like to continue work to help my community. I'd like to major in political science, though I still have mixed feelings about that. I'm fond of it as a theory, but I need to involve myself more and do something. I've never thought about teaching but am considering working for the government to help the community, to make a change.

Now, my hometown is totally different. I've seen pictures. There are new things that I never got to see. When I came here I remembered houses made out of wood, and now everybody has new houses made out of brick and concrete. They aren't preserving their Maya heritage. They're all learning Spanish at school.

We speak on the phone with Ismael on a Sunday afternoon, almost six weeks after President Trump announces in September 2017 that he is ending the DACA program, and that Congress will have six months to work to pass a new law to protect DREAMers.[9] Ismael's voice is subdued and his answers are shorter than usual. He is at home doing his homework and helping his younger brother with his.

My youngest brother, Geovanni, arrived since the last time we spoke. I wasn't expecting him to make the trip. I was against it. Even my other brothers who live here now, I would have never advised them to come. But I don't have control over what they decide. My other brother, Esteban, who made the journey, told me about it when he was already on his way. I couldn't tell them, "Don't do it." They were

---

9. See "DREAMers" in glossary.

already here. I have a brother in Idaho, Miguel, and Geovanni here with me. He made it, but got caught crossing the border. He's sixteen. One Saturday, I was just lying in bed since it was the weekend and I wasn't working, and I got this call early in the morning, around 9 a.m. Someone says, "Hello, may I speak to Ismael?" I replied, "Yes, who's speaking?" and the voice said, "I am a social worker from a shelter. Do you know anybody who has been traveling lately?" I asked, "Traveling where? What are you talking about?" He said, "Yeah, we just want to see if you know someone who is trying to cross the border. There's somebody who said that he's your relative, and we just want to see if you know him." He identified him, and I said, "Yeah, Geovanni's my brother. Where is he?" He responded, "He's been captured crossing the border and he's going to be here in Arizona." Then this whole process started. I have to be his sponsor, and it has been a lot of work. My older brothers in Idaho and Pennsylvania couldn't help him because they're very new to the system here as well.

Geovanni has been living with me for a year and six months. He likes drawing, and two of his drawings that he did through a program that he attended this summer were selected to be part of an art exhibit. He's a very good kid. His plan wasn't to live with me at first. When he was still living in Guatemala, I told him that if he lived with me, I would send him to school. He said, "No, I don't want to do that." His plan was to live with one of my other brothers, who wouldn't have made him study. But I was the one the immigration services called and after that his only option was to come with me. He has decided that he likes school! He hadn't attended school for four years when he arrived.

MAYBE I'LL BE DEPORTED

I'm sad to know the president has made this decision about DACA. It is unbelievable that this administration's agenda is clearly to go backward instead of forward. It's no surprise to me though. This was going to happen; we just didn't know when. But it's hard for me right now to digest this news.

I quit the other organization after three years; it was time to make more money. I got a new full-time job. I'm processing visa applications for business executives. It's not very meaningful.

I'm the only one of my siblings here who is on DACA. Geovanni is doing well in school. Last week, I had a meeting with his teacher. All the teachers were saying that he is a good guy. He works hard. He's still having trouble conversing in English but he understands what people say. He can read and write, but he can't speak the language. I'm taking an English class and a history class. If everything works out as planned, I'm hoping to transfer to a university soon. But I think that DACA is over. Once my few years of work authorization are over next year, I guess I'll leave this company as well. I don't think I'll be able to get my work authorization back. My DACA would have expired in 2019, but now I guess it'll become invalid in March 2018. The expectation that in six months Congress will be able to create a replacement law and pass it is very unrealistic. Now they have all of this damage from the hurricanes that have been happening, which is important to take care of as well, of course. With all of that going on, I don't see how they can reform immigration law as well.

I have to live day to day not knowing if I'll be able to keep working here, even living here. Maybe I'll transfer to the university next year as planned, or maybe I'll be deported back to Guatemala.

ITZEL TZAB

AGE AT CROSSING: 18
AGES OF CHILDREN: 4, 5
BORN IN: La Libertad, Petén, Guatemala
INTERVIEWED IN: Berkeley, California

We meet Itzel at the East Bay Sanctuary Covenant, an organization that was founded in the 1980s to offer safe haven to refugees fleeing the civil wars in Central America. The organization has provided legal, social, and educational services to thousands of clients for more than three decades. Its humble office consists of a low-ceilinged basement space across Bancroft Way from the University of California, Berkeley. Itzel enters the lunch-room, waves from the doorway, and joins us for burritos and corn chips. She carries a small backpack and is poised and confident. We make our way down a hallway to a vacant cubicle, where we sit across from each other at a small desk. Itzel grew up in rural poverty in Guatemala, where her

239

family experienced deadly assaults by violent neighbors. With two young daughters, she traveled north after the family of her ex-boyfriend, Osmin, started to harass and threaten her. Her story sheds light on the challenges facing women and girls who have fled abusive partners and are trying to establish a new life in the United States. Although she speaks with reserve, her face brightens when she describes her days at Oakland International High School and her dreams of pursuing a law degree.[1]

THEY KILLED MY PAPÁ

All in all, we are eleven siblings. Two sisters and four brothers are in Oakland, and four sisters are in Guatemala. My brothers came to Oakland before me, to help my mom financially because she's a single mother in Guatemala. My mom's name is Maria. She has land. She can survive. There you have a lot of space. You can plant fruit, vegetables, and all that. For example, back in my former house with my mom, we had oranges, mangos, tangerines, grapefruits, avocados, cilantro, mint—a lot of food. I had my own horse named Jalisco. I took care of the horses. Since I was a child I've always liked horses a lot. I love to ride them and go to the fields to see the cattle, go up into the mountains. This is what I miss the most. But when I came here they sold the horses.

When I was about five, my father had a friend who worked raising livestock and cultivating the soil. His friend had a lot of kids, and no money, so my dad helped him a lot. He gave him money and a piece of land so the guy could work. He sent food for his kids, everything. My dad had a lot of land, many fields. My dad told his friend to work the land so that he could provide for his kids, but the guy didn't want to work. He never used the land. My dad even

---

1. Oakland International High School is a public school located in Oakland, California. Its stated mission is "to provide a quality alternative education for recently arrived immigrant students."

put the piece of land in his name, but he never worked. My dad was working all the time and when he told his friend he couldn't help him anymore because he had given him land, and he didn't work—and my dad had kids to support too—the man got angry and killed one of my brothers. But my dad was like, *No, I'm not going to do anything. We leave these things to God.*

Then the man killed another guy, a neighbor we knew, in front of my dad's house. The man went to the father of the dead guy and told him that my dad had killed him. From there, the problems only got worse. The father of the dead guy said he was going to kill my father and came to look for him at our house two nights in a row. My dad left us, and they searched for him. On February 7, a Monday, he left for work and when the man who he had given land to saw him on his horses with my other brother, he went out with seven men and they killed him. They killed my Papá. They hit my brother, but they didn't shoot him. He fell to the ground but recovered.

My mother had spoken with the authorities in the village after my brother was killed, but they didn't pay any attention to her. The man had even said in front of the authorities that he was going to kill my dad, and they never did anything! After my dad was killed, the police found the attackers' identification cards and passports in their backpacks, which they left behind when they fled. Maybe they were planning to leave the country before they were caught. The police just let them off! The man who actually killed my brother and father now lives next door to my mom, and he sometimes comes by and threatens to kill her.

SHE WOULD DEFEND ME AT ALL COSTS

I was assaulted twice when I was a little girl in Guatemala. The first time, I was about nine. I had to cross a small mountain to go to school. It was about a twenty-minute walk. After crossing over the small mountain, the school was right there. The two friends I usually walked with didn't go to school that day, so I was by myself. As I was walking I heard, "*Tsssss*." I didn't pay attention, but it repeated a second time, and then the third time I heard, "Stop right there!" I turned and saw a man with his face covered. He had a gun in his hand that he was pointing at me. He said, "I'm going to rape you right now, so shut up and don't scream or I'll kill you." When I heard he was going to kill me I dropped my backpack and ran screaming. He didn't shoot, because I was on the little hill, and I ran screaming below where there were houses. A woman came out and said to me, "What's the matter, little girl? What's happening?" I said, "A man wanted to kill me and said he was going to rape me!" All the neighbors came out and hugged me, saying, "Don't be afraid. It's okay. You're here." One of them went to get my backpack, and a teacher came by and took me to the school. They called the police. This was at seven in the morning, and the police didn't show up until noon. In Guatemala, the police do almost nothing.

About a year after the first incident, a man came and said he wanted to rent some land from my mom in her pasture for his horse, and my mom said it was okay. He was there for fifteen days and after that he said he was going to take his horse and not pay anything. My mom told him that it was okay not to pay. She told him to take the horse and made it clear that she didn't want problems. After a bit he came back to the house. He began to pull my hair and hit me, and he told my mom he was going to rape me. My mother screamed no at him, saying that she would defend me at all costs. He began to hit my mother and didn't let me leave the room.

When my nephew came in and saw what was going on, he called for my brother, and when my brother came the man took out a machete and tried to attack him. My mom grabbed the machete and took it away from the man. They were fighting and he couldn't do anything. After a bit he left.

THEY GAVE ME MY GIRLS BACK

I have two daughters. One, Jazmin, is four, and the other, Laura, is about to turn three in October. When I started dating Osmin, the father of my children, I was about to turn twelve. I started living with him in a house close to my mom's. When I was pregnant that year with Jazmin, he began to hit me. He said that I was his wife, and he had the right to hit me whenever he wanted.

I stopped going to school then. I worked for a time, but after that it was difficult because I had my girls. Osmin drank. He left the house and came back when he wanted. When I was one or two months pregnant with the youngest girl, he told me that he was going to go to the United States because he wanted to help the girls. The two girls needed milk, and in our country it's difficult because everything, including milk, is expensive, and after he'd arrived in the US, he only sent a hundred dollars a month. There were times that the girls didn't have anything to eat. They cried, and I became very weary.

My mom provided for us. She fed us and clothed my two daughters for a year. After a year, she was no longer able to, so my daughters and I suffered a little because we had nothing. Then I got sick, and my boyfriend called me and told me that I should bring my daughters to one of his cousins to take care of them. This cousin was like a distant aunt to my daughters. She was older than me. I started leaving my daughters with her to take care of them.

When I went to get them on the third day, his cousin said that she couldn't let me leave with my girls because a judge had given them to her. I went to the family court and asked them why they'd given them to her when I'd just left them for three days while I was recovering. They told me that the woman had told them that she'd taken care of them for much longer, and that I'd abandoned the girls without her knowing anything about me, that I hadn't called or anything. Because of this, she wanted custody of the girls. The judge, without investigating the case, gave her custody of my daughters. I told the judge that I wanted custody, and she said they were going to hold a new hearing. She said it was going to be difficult to give me the girls because of the things the woman had testified to.

One of my sisters, who was in Oakland, sent money and we paid for a lawyer to represent me in court. By the time the court date came up, my daughters had been with the cousin for seven months. After a lengthy trial, the judge finally said that the girls were mine and that I was free to take them back. The cousin said that we'd have to pay her to get the girls back. I wasn't going to give money to her—she had taken them because she wanted to. So that day they gave me my girls back. The cousin hadn't taken good care of them. One had severe pneumonia and a skin infection, and they were both suffering from malnutrition. I had to take them to the pediatrician.

After they gave me my girls back, Osmin's family started to call me and said they were going to kill my girls and me. They called me a lot. I called my sister in Oakland and told her what was happening, and she said, "Okay, I'm going to send you money to arrange a trip here with your daughters." We made the trip.

TREATED US LIKE CRIMINALS

I came with my two daughters at the end of 2015 with a *coyote*. We went in a bus from my hometown until the US border at Piedras Negras, Coahuila, directly across from Rosita, Texas, over two hundred kilometers from San Antonio. The *coyote* who brought us took us to another point on the border. He told me that he was going to take us across a bridge, that we weren't going to have to walk, that we weren't going to have to go into the river. He left us, and then another man took us. He took us for just five or ten minutes into the mountains, and then he stole some valuable gold that I'd brought with me. My sister had already paid him, but he demanded more.

He then turned us over to a gang member who brought us into the hills, and there he left us alone, lost. There were a lot of gang members drinking, smoking drugs. We were still in Mexico, close to the US border.

Three of the gang members wanted to hurt me and took us to the river. They left me there in the middle of the river with my daughters. I gathered the girls, Laura on my front and Jazmin on my back. At one point, I thought we'd gotten out of the river. I yelled, "We made it!" But we still had to cross further. There was mud that pulls you under, quicksand. I started to sink. Thank God, my daughters got out. There were a lot of vines, and they threw me some so I was able to get out. We finally crossed the river. When we got out, we were very thirsty. I felt like I was going to pass out because the sun was really hot. At this point, we were in the United States, in Texas.

We'd just crossed the river and next to it there was a really tall fence. It was made of black metal poles that are curved at the top and probably six meters tall. We had to climb over it. We didn't have shoes and the sand was so hot, scorching our feet. The girls were crying. We felt hopeless. And then we saw La Migra coming. Two or three officers approached us on foot and said, "Where are you coming from?" I said, "Guatemala." And then they said, "We're going to take you to a station and you're going to be okay."

The migration station was like a jail. It had really cold air. They treated us like criminals. It was one room with a lot of people, and there were no beds or chairs. We sat on the floor and at first no one gave us water or food. There were bathrooms, but they were very dirty. The water they finally gave us had a lot of chlorine in it. It gave me a stomachache. After a while they brought us some food. It was like a bean burrito, but it was really gross. They said they were going to keep us there until they found a house to send us to. I was sixteen.

We were there for about six days, and then one day, at close to midnight, they told me to sign some papers because they were going to send us to a house in Arizona. They said that after a couple hours they'd bring us, but they didn't take us that day. The next day they woke me up and said, "Get ready because we're going to bring you to an airport so you can go to Arizona." I got up with the girls, and we were in a car almost all day. From there we went to the airport in Texas. After that another man showed up, a counselor with La Migra, who told us that at most we were going to be in the United States for six months, and then they were going to send us back. He said that those who came to the United States were not welcome, that it's not our country.

"FIRST YOU'RE GOING TO EAT"

We went up in the airplane and got to the airport in Arizona. From there they picked us up and took us to a house in Youngtown, near Phoenix. There were about 150 people there. It wasn't a jail. It was a house called Hacienda del Sol. After we arrived, a man who worked there came out and told me, "My dear, come. First you're going to eat, and then I'll take you to the house store so you can get clothing for your kids. After that I'll take you to your room so you can lay down and rest." He gave us food and then explained to me that I was going to have a social worker to reunite us with my sister, and a counselor I could speak to if I felt bad.

After we ate, they gave us clothes, everything that we needed. They'd already given me a room, which was fairly large. I couldn't close the door or touch the window because it had an alarm, but everything was clean. There was a bathroom with a door. I had a bed for me, one for Jazmin, and a crib for Laura.

The next day, they called my sister in Oakland. They asked her for digital copies of her fingerprints and her papers, and she sent everything. The rest of the time they tried to keep us occupied so we weren't feeling hopeless. At six they woke us up because at seven we went downstairs for breakfast. After breakfast we went to some classrooms, and they taught classes in English. At noon, we ate lunch. Later we went back to the classroom to do projects like planting flowers and art. They gave us materials we could use to make drawings and paintings. They took care of the kids in a daycare where they had a lot of toys. It was great. We had three meals daily and three snacks. We were there for about fifteen days.

When all of my paperwork was gathered, my caseworker came in and said to me, "Okay, tomorrow you will leave. All we need is to take a photo of your kids, and you'll all go on a plane." The next day, a caseworker took me to Oakland. My sister came to pick us up. We got here on June 24. I had been in Arizona for fifteen days, and in Texas for seven days, so we had only been in the United States for less than a month.

As soon as we arrived in Oakland, my sister and I started looking for a lawyer. We went to two places in San Francisco, but they didn't want to help me. I think the first place was in the Mission. At the second place, they told us to go to a third place, the East Bay Sanctuary. Once we got there, I described what my life was like with the kids' father, a little about the poverty and the rapes. I worked with two students from the Sanctuary, one of whom spoke Spanish.

I went to the Ninth Circuit Court on Montgomery Street in San Francisco and then waited for five months for a hearing. A few weeks after the hearing, I found out that my appointment was at 1 p.m. the following day. My case had been accepted! I was really happy. I could file my application for permanent residence the next year. Meanwhile, I could work while my asylum case was processing. They gave me an employment authorization card. After five years, I could apply for citizenship and a passport. I'll be able to travel anywhere except Guatemala.[2]

---

2. Asylees are generally not permitted to return to the homelands from which they fled.

THE DOORS HAVE OPENED FOR ME

Well, I feel good here, *gracias a Dios*. I have help, and I'm better than when I was in my country. Back there I couldn't go to school because I was taking my daughters to school. I would've liked to graduate from high school and go to school to study to become a lawyer.

I've been in the United States for a year now. Here I have two sisters and four brothers. We're seven altogether. My twenty-three-year-old sister had already lived here for about seven years when I came. She works at a restaurant. I live in Oakland with my sister, near Highland Hospital. It's not dangerous in this area. It's mostly Chinese. I'm starting to figure out how to get around on public transportation. I've gone to San Francisco. I like it. I understand a little English, but I'm afraid to speak. My teacher told me, "Don't be afraid to speak. Nobody is born with a language already known. Everything is learned."

Right now I'm going to Oakland International High School, but during my vacations I work. The school is really good. They teach us a lot and help a lot if we have problems. There are many Hondurans, Salvadorans, Guatemalans, Mexicans, Arabs, and Chinese—people from everywhere! I have a lot of friends at school and feel like I'm part of a community. I've had a lot of support from my teachers, classmates, and fellow Guatemalans. Those who know more than me always help me feel comfortable. I've never felt sad, even if I don't know what the teacher is saying, and I didn't understand anything at first because it was all in English. Sometimes I even slept at my desk because I didn't understand anything, but now, after six months, I have a little more confidence. The more time I spend in school, the better I get and the more I learn. I plan to go to college if God wills it. I'm about to enter the tenth grade, so I have two more years to finish high school.

In Guatemala, things are more difficult, and I felt for a time that the doors had been closed. Coming here, I feel that the doors have opened for me to move forward with my dreams. The counselors at school told me where I could apply for welfare at a local social service office. I didn't want to go, but I went. And I got a bit of money to pay my rent and all. I'm trying to do what my teachers advise, like I need to get a laptop computer because I have a Rosetta Stone account and I can improve my English at home. With this program, I practice pronunciation, and I write and talk. We're reading books in English.

My kids aren't afraid anymore. They're calm. Jazmin goes to school from 9 a.m. to 2:45 p.m., and after that she's at home with me. We pay for someone to take care of Laura. I'd like to graduate from college here and for my children to graduate as well. Then maybe we could go back to Guatemala. My daughters say, "We're going to be doctors to take care of the many people who are sick. We're going to take care of the children so they don't get sick." They really like the doctor who takes care of them because when she gives them their vaccines, she says, "These vaccines are made so that children don't get sick, so this disease doesn't appear." The doctor chats with them. She says, "After the vaccine, I'm going to give you a sticker." They say, "When we're older, we're going to vaccinate children and give them stickers!"

We reconnect with Itzel a year and a half after our first interview at the East Bay Sanctuary. When we speak on the phone, she's excited to talk and tells us that shortly after our interview, she had a problem and had to drop out of Oakland International High School. She'd tell us more when we met. We pick her up in front of her apartment. The Bay Area is experiencing a record-breaking heat wave and the thermometer in our car reads 112 degrees. We drive to a nearby Boston Market restaurant with air conditioning, to catch up over ice water and lemonade. Itzel speaks slowly and deliberately and her large eyes are radiant. She's wearing a sparkling engagement ring. When she begins to speak of her fiancé, her serious demeanor becomes punctuated by giggles.

I FOUND MYSELF IN A SITUATION

I had to leave school shortly after I first shared my story with you because I was in debt to my sister's husband, my brother-in-law. He told me that I had to start paying him $1,000 a month. I owed him money I'd borrowed to pay for my daughters' babysitter. When I went to school five days a week, I had to pay a babysitter to look after my daughters every day. I took them to the babysitter's house nearby very early in the morning before school. After school, I'd pick them up. She charged me $50 a day, one thousand per month, for the two. I had to pay for the babysitter and I couldn't work. I found myself in a situation. Only by leaving my studies could I work to pay him back. I left school even though I really didn't want to.

I worked in San Bruno, in a sandwich production kitchen. It was far from here. I had a friend from here who would take me there. We had to leave at four in the morning to cross the Bay Bridge and the city every day. The work wasn't hard. It was kind of a line of people and on one end you start with bread, and each person puts one thing on it. After I had paid back my brother-in-law, I wanted to reenroll in school, but I was told that I couldn't because I was eighteen. It had only been about five months since I left, but they wouldn't let me come back.

I was looking around for programs to start school again earlier this year. I spoke with the director of the school where I'd been studying, but she said that the easiest way forward for me would be to sign up for another program. She wasn't really offering to help me find a program.

"DO YOU WANT TO MARRY ME?"

I met my boyfriend Pablo about two and a half years ago. There was an older man I knew in my neighborhood named Hugo. I was walking by his house one day after school, on the way to pick up my daughters. It was in the afternoon and Hugo was on the street, working on a car. He greeted me, "How are you, Itzel?" I told him, "Good." Then he said, "I want to introduce you to my friend, Pablo." Pablo was helping Hugo fix his car. He was wearing a T-shirt and workpants and his hands were all greasy. He has a medium build and is thin and handsome! He's from a village called San Vicente in El Salvador.

After we'd known each other for a year, we started talking and talking more and more. He told me that he wanted me to be his girlfriend. And I told him yes! A little while later, we were in the living room of my house, and he said, "I brought you a gift. Open it." He gave me this ring! He asked me, "Do you want to marry me?" And I told him, "Yes." I also told him that we had to think things out well if we were going to get married. I was so happy. We're planning to get married, but we're not sure when.

I'm nineteen. Pablo is twenty-eight. He's been here for about eight years. In April of this year, his application for a U visa was approved.[3] He works every day in construction, seven days a week. The girls like Pablo a lot and call him Papá. He always takes care of them. He doesn't have children. Pablo hasn't gone to school in the United States, but he speaks English. He learned in the streets and at work. His bosses only speak English. He sometimes talks about wanting to go to school, but he works a lot and really doesn't have time.

I live with Pablo now. I didn't have a place to live and couldn't afford rent. Apartments are very expensive these days and there aren't many vacancies. He said, "If you want, come live with me." We've been living together for one year. We live in a tiny studio apartment on the second floor. My younger sister, who is sixteen, came to live with my older sister in her little apartment and there wasn't space for all of us. She is younger, so I thought it would be better for me to leave. She came here from Guatemala and I think she has a

---

3. The U visa is a nonimmigrant visa given to people who are victims of crimes.

case open for a T visa.[4] I'm actually not sure if she's in school. My younger sister is rebellious. We all get along well, though. My brothers and sisters all get together often.

These days I wake up at 4:40 in the morning. Pablo leaves for work at five. It's still totally dark when we wake up. Sometimes Pablo and I drink coffee and my older daughter drinks milk and asks, "When am I going to be old enough to drink coffee?" I prepare a sandwich for him and after he leaves, I get breakfast ready for the girls. Pablo grabs his backpack and leaves. He works in San Francisco, on a building project for a hospital, and there's a lot of traffic in the morning. He's a union worker so he gets paid well, about $1,500 a month. They take like five hundred for taxes, so a thousand is what's left over. The company gives us medical insurance.

Morning is a calm time of day, a special time for our family. The girls like sandwiches, eggs. They are a bit picky. My daughters usually bring food from home to school and only sometimes buy food there. Sometimes I ask my little one what she ate at school, and she says, "I didn't eat anything. They were making bean sandwiches, and I don't like beans!" She's in T-K right now.[5] They get up to get ready for school at six. It takes them a long time to get ready. One puts on one shoe and then fifteen minutes later puts on the other. It takes my younger daughter like forty minutes to eat!

I like where we are living. Behind us are more apartments so there isn't a backyard, but there's a yard in front of the house. The girls sometimes play in the front yard. It's gated off so I don't have to worry about them going in the street. It's a calm neighborhood, more or less, and we know most of our neighbors. At the same time there are a lot of drugs in this area. People sell in the streets and

---

4. The nonimmigrant status T visa is given to people who have been victims of human trafficking.

5. "T-K" is transitional kindergarten, a public school program that admits children one year before kindergarten.

sometimes people have parties in the street, drinking, smoking. Sometimes they make a lot of noise at night having their parties, playing loud music from their cars. They are loud, but they don't really bother anyone. Since we know everyone on this block, they don't bother us at all. Sometimes I get scared because they have their enemies as well. Sometimes people fight outside and yell. When I'm busy, I don't just let the girls play outside alone. If I have time, I go outside with them and play for a little while.

After I get the girls ready, I drive them to school. It only takes three minutes. The school is very diverse, with white students, Asians, Latinos, everyone. It's a great school and it's bilingual. The girls are learning English quickly and at the same time they're not forgetting their Spanish. At home, though, they want to speak English now. My younger daughter's preschool was all in English. She talks to me in English, and I talk to her in Spanish. We tell her, "We speak Spanish at home." Now that she's in the bilingual school, the same school as her sister, she's speaking Spanish again. They both love school. The first time I dropped them off at school, they both cried, but not now.

I'm not working now, so when I drop them off, I return home to clean. It's a little lonely. One gets out at 2:45 and the other at six. If I found the right program, I'd love to study in the mornings when my daughters are at school. Pablo always says, "Go to school and study! Don't miss this chance like so many young people do!" I read about some eighty-year-old woman who finally graduated from college, and I think I'm in a good position to go to school now and I should take advantage of it. To be a lawyer, I need to study English, complete a GED program, enter community college, transfer to a university, and then complete law school. I know it's a long road, but I want to do it.

I'm in contact with my daughters' father. He moved near Washington, DC, before I left and he's still there. He only knows that I live in California. I don't like to speak to him, but the girls want to talk to their daddy. The little one says, "I want to talk to Papá! Let me talk to him!" He's their father. I can't not let them talk to him. He doesn't try to talk to me that much. He's pretty calm. Sometimes he says, "I want to talk to you," but I say, "No, I don't want to talk." He called today and said that he wanted to send a message to the girls, so I gave them the phone.

Sometimes my younger daughter tells me that she misses my mother. She hardly remembers Guatemala, but she remembers her grandmother. My mother is sick and just had an operation. She's getting better, but she lives alone in Guatemala. For the moment, she's not in danger. I miss Guatemala a lot sometimes. I want to be there to take care of my mom. Sometimes she says that she's too hungry to get out of bed. "What do I do?" she asks. "I have no one." Pretty much our whole family is here now. My mother tried to apply for a visa but hasn't been given one, and the trip through Mexico is so dangerous. And now with the new president, Trump, I hear that they aren't letting people into the United States even if they have a legitimate asylum request. He's even threatening to end the DACA program.[6]

Pablo comes home from work at seven in the evening. I always have dinner ready when he gets back. Tonight I'm going to prepare some pork ribs in salsa. I cook tamales, *guisados* with chicken, with beef.[7] It has a lot of spices and ingredients like *pepita de ayote*.[8] You mix all of them together and make a red sauce. I can find most of the ingredients that I cooked with in Guatemala here in Oakland. Sometimes I make *tamales de chipilín*.[9] Some people call them *bol-*

---

6. DACA is the Deferred Action for Childhood Arrivals program.

7. Guisados are stews.

8. Pepita de ayote are squash seeds.

9. Chipilín (*Crotalaria longirostrata*) is a leguminous plant originally from Central America and southern Mexico.

litos. Some have chipilín and others are made with beans. There's a store nearby that makes them fresh on Wednesdays. We eat empanadas in Guatemala as well. Every afternoon, people take their carts out in the streets and sell empanadas. They sell them all over the place. The señoras come to the schools and sell them at lunch.

THE ROOSTERS ARE SINGING

Where I'm from, after three in the afternoon, everyone is out walking in the streets. There are little carts and stands for selling empanadas, tacos. There aren't any plazas there. The only place to gather besides the street is the soccer field, where people play on Sundays. The street is filled with the smells of food and the sounds of people. Everyone greets one another. People are selling things, calling out: "Empanadas, empanadas!" Some people sit around in chairs. Some even bring televisions outside to watch the telenovelas. Here we really don't see that. I don't like to go to the parks around here because everyone is smoking pot and later I get a huge headache. Sometimes I go to San Leandro, near Hayward. There's a pretty park there.

Pablo wants me to go to El Salvador to meet his family. He says, "I'll buy the tickets and we can go." He has to wait until he has permanent residence status, but I can travel anywhere except Guatemala with my Guatemalan passport. When I apply for US citizenship, I think I have to give up my Guatemalan passport. My older sister, who I was living with here, visited Guatemala last year. She says that she could hardly stand the three days that she was there. She said she felt like crying and wanted to return. In Guatemala, only the main roads where the cars pass are paved. Everything else is dirt. When it rains, it gets muddy. She told me, "There are a ton of dogs everywhere, peeing all over the place! But the roosters are singing good morning."

TEN THINGS YOU CAN DO

1. Volunteer to use your special skills. Can you design a flyer, write an article, analyze a legal brief? These and many other skills can be invaluable to underfunded and understaffed nonprofits working to support immigrants and refugees in your community.

2. Use the power of your voice and vote. Learn about US policies in Central America and voice your opinions. Let your local, state, and federal representatives know that caring for young migrants and DACA students are priorities for you. Write an email that clearly states your views and forward it to your friends and acquaintances to circulate.

3. Be generous. Make monetary donations to the general operating funds of nonprofit organizations such as Kids in Need of Defense and the National Immigrant Justice Center. Consider sponsoring REDODEM, the network of casas de migrantes in Mexico.[1] Support local organizations in Central America that are working to combat violence and protect human rights. For example, the Council of Popular and Indigenous Organizations of Honduras (Consejo Cívico de Organizaciones Populares e Indígenas de Honduras, COPINH), founded by Berta Cáceres, works to protect

---

1. The Red de Documentación de las Organizaciones Defensoras de Migrantes (REDODEM, Documentation Network of Migrant Defense Organizations) is the largest network of migrant shelters in Mexico.

the rights of Indigenous Lenca people. The Black Fraternal Organization of Honduras (Organización Fraternal Negra Hondureña, OFRANEH) works to protect Garifuna rights.

4. Look for migrant service agencies in your area that assist youth refugees from Central America. See if you can work with small groups of refugees or one-on-one to help them transition to their new home.

5. Support initiatives to keep families together and reunite children with relatives. When kids are separated from their families, they can fall prey to gangs, drug abuse, and exploitation.

6. If you are an educator or parent, petition local school officials to provide academic and social programs to help migrants and their families. Learn about and support schools like Oakland International High School.

7. Consider being a foster parent, legal guardian, or sponsor for a child awaiting immigration proceedings. Contact local organizations that help refugees find temporary homes.

8. Promote initiatives that combat rape, child abuse, domestic violence, and sex trafficking in Central America, Mexico, and the United States. Consider supporting organizations such as the International Women's Health Coalition that are seeking to reduce teenage pregnancy and promote healthy choices for women in Central America.

9. Share this book's narratives with people to stimulate discussions. Organize a group of friends to read and discuss the book and suggest it to your local librarian.

10. Put an "Immigrants and Refugees Welcome Here" sign in your window at home or at work to publicly show your support. Download a poster for free at www .newamericanstoryproject.org.

HISTORICAL TIMELINE

1,000 BCE to 900 CE: The Petén jungle, encompassing Guatemala, Honduras, and southern Mexico, is home to a vast Maya civilization. Ten to fifteen million Maya live in villages clustered around elaborate ceremonial centers featuring one-hundred-foot pyramids. The city of Tikal rivals cities in ancient Rome and China. Around 900 CE, the Maya civilization sharply declines, due to drought, disease, and warfare. The city centers collapse and survivors disperse, five hundred years before Christopher Columbus's arrival.

1492: Columbus begins to explore and colonize the islands along the Caribbean coast.

1500s: The majority of Latin America becomes dominated by Spanish and Portuguese forces in the form of military takeover, administration of governmental offices, Christian conversion, forced labor, and taxation. Nine out of ten Indigenous people are killed or die of diseases, with an estimated two million Indigenous people remaining at the end of the century. The African slave trade begins. An average of over one million natives die annually over the century, in what has been called "the greatest genocide in human history."[1]

1523: The Indigenous Maya are defeated by Spain, and Guatemala becomes a colony of Spain. Pedro de Alvarado initiates the conquest

---

1. Juan Gonzalez, *Harvest of Empire: A History of Latinos in America*, rev. ed. (New York: Penguin, 2011).

of Central America.

1821: Guatemala wins its independence from Spain.

1823: The Congress of Central America declares independence from Spain and Mexico.

1838: The Central American Federation splits into Guatemala, El Salvador, Honduras, Nicaragua, and Costa Rica.

1898: The so-called Banana Wars begin, in which the United States intervenes in various Central American countries, suppresses workers' rights movements, and pursues its economic and military interests. They last until 1934.

1906: The US Naturalization Act is passed, standardizing the naturalization process and requiring some knowledge of English as a prerequisite to citizenship.

1917: The United States enacts the Immigration Act of 1917, or the Literacy Act, the first major restrictive immigration act that marks a turn toward nativism.

1924: The United States passes the Johnson-Reed Act, setting the first restrictive quotas on immigration and bringing in a national-origin quota system.

1927–33: Augusto Nicolás Sandino, also known as Augusto César Sandino, leads a rebellion against the occupying forces of the United States in Nicaragua.

1931: Guatemalan president Jorge Ubico is elected in a one-candidate campaign. Considered Central America's Napoleon, Ubico rules an authoritarian regime until 1944, giving immense dispensations to the United Fruit Company. His removal in 1944 by pro-democracy rebellion leads to the Guatemalan Revolution, which lasts until President Jacobo Árbenz Guzmán is ousted in a coup d'état organized by the United States in 1954.

1932: The Salvadoran peasant massacre takes place on January 22, when the Salvadoran army, under General Hernández Martínez, fights back against the peasant forces of Augustín Farabundo Martí, a Marxist-Leninist activist. Known as La Matanza (the Killing), around thirty thousand Pipil Indians are killed.

1937: General Anastasio Somoza García is elected as president of Nicaragua.

1952: The US Immigration and Nationality Act of 1952 grants refugee status only to people escaping Communist regimes.

1954: A CIA-sponsored coup overthrows democratically elected President Árbenz of Guatemala, after the United Fruit Company and the US State Department demand $16 million from him for nationalizing land. When Árbenz refuses, US secretary of state John Foster Dulles and CIA director Allen Dulles, both former partners of the United Fruit Company's main law firm in Washington, advise President Eisenhower to authorize the CIA's "Operation PBSUCCESS," a plan to overthrow Árbenz.[2] After he is overthrown in 1954, Guatemala is ruled for decades by a series of authoritarian regimes that commit human rights violations against Indigenous peoples.

1961: On July 19, the Sandinista National Liberation Front (Frente Sandinista de Liberación Nacional, FSLN), named after Augusto Sandino, is established in Nicaragua.

1965: The United States passes the Immigration and Nationality

---

2. Gonzalez, *Harvest of Empire*, 137.

Act, also known as the Hart-Celler Act, abolishing the old quota system based on national origin and establishing a new policy based on reuniting families and attracting labor.

1965: Nicaragua's General Somoza is assassinated by the poet Rigoberto López Pérez. He is succeeded by his younger brother, Luis Anastasio Somoza Debayle.

1967: On October 4, the United Nations adopts the Protocol Relating to the Status of Refugees. A total of 146 countries, including the United States, are parties to the protocol. It ensures that people have the right under international law to seek asylum in the closest safe nation.

1972: An earthquake destroys much of Managua, Nicaragua, and kills between five thousand and eleven thousand people. The Nicaraguan people's tolerance for their government decreases in response to the Somoza administration's theft of millions of dollars of aid money and its failure to rebuild Managua.[3]

1979–82: After a successful coup by the Salvadoran army, the Revolutionary Government Junta of El Salvador, a military dictatorship, rules for three years.

1980: The US Congress passes Public Law 96-212, the 1980 Refugee Act, which allows refugees to apply for political asylum because of a "well-founded fear of persecution based on race, religion, nationality, membership in a particular social group, or political opinion."[4]

- In El Salvador, five opposition guerrilla groups in the countryside join together to form the Farabundo Martí National Liberation Front (FMLN). A right-wing death squad assassinates

---

3. Gonzalez, *Harvest of Empire*, 132.

4. "Refugee Act of 1980," National Archives Foundation, https://www.archives-foundation.org/documents/refugee-act-1980/.

Archbishop Óscar Romero, a critic of the Salvadoran junta.[5]

- On December 2, four US Catholic missionaries are raped and killed by five soldiers in the El Salvador National Guard.

1981: On December 11, the worst recorded massacre in Latin American history takes place in the village of El Mozote in El Salvador. At a time when the United States is funding the Salvadoran army with a million dollars a day, the army kills more than eight hundred civilians in a single scorched-earth-style operation.[6]

1982: In Guatemala, General Efraín Ríos Montt seizes power in a military coup on March 23. During his one year of rule, he is responsible for widespread human rights abuses and counterinsurgency terror. The Reagan administration backs Montt because he is an evangelical Christian. The United States also sponsors attacks on the Nicaraguan army by Nicaraguan Contras in Honduras.

1984: Half a million Salvadorans fleeing violence have entered the United States. Many settle in sanctuary cities such as Los Angeles and San Francisco, California.[7] Many refugees are not granted legal status.[8] Salvadoran teens land in barrios already dominated by gangs such as the Mexican Mafia. Over the next decade, Salvadorans will create their own gangs, MS-13 and Barrio 18.[9]

5. Gonzalez, *Harvest of Empire*, 134.

6. Sarah Esther Maslin, "Remembering El Mozote, the Worst Massacre in Modern Latin American History," *Nation*, December 13, 2016.

7. Gonzalez, *Harvest of Empire*, 138.

8. Susan Gzesh, "Central Americans and Asylum Policy in the Reagan Era," Migration Policy Institute, April 1, 2006.

9. Ioan Grillo, *Gangster Warlords: Drug Dollars, Killing Fields, and the New Politics of Latin America* (New York: Bloomsbury Press, 2016), 200–202.

1986: The US Immigration Reform and Control Act (IRCA) of 1986 is signed by President Reagan. It is aimed at prohibiting employers from hiring undocumented immigrants and offering a path to citizenship to undocumented immigrants in the United States who can prove that they have resided in the country since January 1, 1982, and have also maintained a clean criminal record during that period.[10] The law legalizes 2.7 million previously undocumented immigrants.[11]

1987: The Esquipulas II Accord is signed by five Central American presidents on August 7 in Guatemala City to promote national reconciliation in their respective countries.[12]

1989: Fatalities of the wars in Guatemala, El Salvador, and Nicaragua have passed a quarter-million, five times the US death toll in Vietnam. More than 140,000 have died in Guatemala, 70,000 in El Salvador, and 60,000 in Nicaragua.[13]

1990: The US Census estimates that the number of Salvadorans in the United States has increased from 94,000 in 1980 to 701,000. The Guatemalan population in the United States has increased from 71,642 to 226,000, and the Nicaraguan population has increased from 25,000 to 125,000.[14]

1992: After ten years of war, almost one-fifth of the Salvadoran population has been displaced. In January, a truce is successfully negotiated at Chapultepec Castle in Mexico, ending the war. A civilian police

---

10. Robert Pear, "President Signs Landmark Bill on Immigration," *New York Times*, November 7, 1989.

11. Brad Plumer, "Congress Tried to Fix Immigration Back in 1986. Why Did It Fail?" *Washington Post*, January 30, 2013.

12. Johanna Oliver, "The Esquipulas Process: A Central American Paradigm for Resolving Regional Conflict," *Ethnic Studies Report* 17, no. 2 (July 1999): 153.

13. Gonzalez, *Harvest of Empire*, 130.

14. Gonzalez, *Harvest of Empire*, 129.

force is established, and the FMLN becomes a political party.[15]

1993: The Truth Commission organized to investigate violence and death in El Salvador's civil war finds that the US-backed death squads who operated in the war are still a "potential menace" in the country. The commission's members hear testimony from eight hundred victims.[16]

1993–2005: In these twelve years, US immigration authorities deport more than fifty thousand Central America immigrants with criminal records. Instead of breaking up gangs in Los Angeles, this effort spreads the gangs throughout the Northern Triangle (the region consisting of Guatemala, Honduras, and El Salvador). With an estimated one hundred thousand or more members in El Salvador alone, the members of MS-13 and Barrio 18 work internationally with various local gangs in major US cities, engaging in extortion, immigrant smuggling, and racketeering.[17]

1994: The North American Free Trade Agreement (NAFTA) goes into effect. Assuring economic success to the treaty's southern participants, NAFTA lifts tariffs protecting Mexican corn, making it nearly impossible for Mexican corn farmers to survive in the wake of the flood of American corn.

- The US Border Patrol Strategic Plan is initiated. A precursor to Prevention Through Deterrence, the Strategic Plan develops the US government's organized plot to funnel migrants through the border-crossing routes with the highest risk of death.

---

15. Terry Lynn Karl, "El Salvador's Negotiated Revolution," *Foreign Affairs*, Spring 1992.

16. "Summary of 1993 UN Truth Commission Report of El Salvador," School of the Americas Watch, March 17, 1993.

17. Luis J. Rodriguez, "A Gang of Our Own Making," *New York Times*, March 25, 2005.

1996: A peace accord is administered in December in Guatemala by President Álvaro Arzú Irigoyen and Guatemalan National Revolutionary Unity (URNG), a political party that started as a guerrilla organization and then laid down its arms, ending thirty-six years of armed conflict.[18]

1997: On January 28, both parties in the US government sign the *Flores v. Reno* Settlement Agreement, which seeks to keep children in the "least restrictive environment possible" and release them from detention "without unnecessary delay." The settlement was a result of the case of Jenny Flores, a fifteen-year-old unaccompanied migrant from El Salvador, who was held in adult detention along with men and women.[19]

1998: Hurricane Mitch kills thousands in Central America and leaves hundreds of thousands homeless in Honduras and Nicaragua.

- On April 20, a new penal code is enacted in El Salvador, removing any and all exceptions to its law prohibiting abortions.

2000–2013: Over these thirteen years, an estimated 11.7 million people are apprehended while trying to cross the border between Mexico and the United States.[20]

2004: The Dominican Republic–Central American Free Trade Agreement (CAFTA-DR) is signed into law in 2004 by President George W. Bush to gradually remove most trade barriers on products

---

18. Larry Rohter, "Final Peace Near, Guatemala Braces for Complications," *New York Times*, December 19, 1996.

19. Rebeca M. López, "Codifying the *Flores* Settlement Agreement: Seeking to Protect Immigrant Children in U.S. Custody," *Marquette Law Review* 95, no. 2 (Summer 2012): 1651.

20. Jason De León, *The Land of Open Graves: Living and Dying on the Migrant Trail* (Berkeley: University of California, 2015), 6.

passing between Costa Rica, the Dominican Republic, El Salvador, Guatemala, Honduras, and Nicaragua, and the United States. Small farmers in Central America struggle to stay in business as cheap corn and rice from the United States flood the markets.[21]

- The Intelligence Reform and Terrorism Prevention Act directs the Department of Homeland Security (DHS) to increase immigration detention capacity by eight thousand beds a year between 2006 and 2010.[22] See appendix essay on "Arrests and Detention in the United States."

2006: The UN-backed International Commission against Impunity in Guatemala (Comisión Internacional contra la Impunidad en Guatemala, CICIG) starts its work to root out corruption in Guatemala's government.

- On December 10, the newly inaugurated president of Mexico, Felipe Calderón, declares a war on drug traffickers and sends 6,500 troops into his home state of Michoacán. Over the next ten years, the violence escalates, with almost two hundred thousand people murdered and more than twenty-eight thousand disappeared.[23]

2009: In the midst of a constitutional crisis, the Honduran military follows orders by the Honduran Supreme Court to oust democratically elected president Manuel Zelaya on June 28. After the military flies Zelaya to Costa Rica in the middle of the night, the Honduran

---

21. "A Raw Deal for Rice under DR-CAFTA: How the Free Trade Agreement Threatens the Livelihoods of Central American Farmers," Briefing Paper 68, Oxfam, November 2004.

22. "Immigration Detention Bed Quota Timeline," National Immigrant Justice Center, April 2014, 1.

23. Nina Lakhani, "Mexico's War on Drugs: What Has It Achieved and How Is the US Involved?," *Guardian*, December 8, 2016.

Congress appoints Speaker of Congress Roberto Micheletti as his successor. The US-backed coup government gives coup loyalists positions of power.[24] In 2011, Secretary of State Hillary Clinton admits to using her power to keep Zelaya from returning to office.

2009–16: The Obama administration deports 2.7 million people through immigration orders, more than any administration in US history. The DHS notes that immigration over the southern border has changed significantly, with the majority of the migrants coming from Central America instead of Mexico.[25]

2010: Seventy-two migrants, mostly from Central America, are massacred by the Los Zetas drug cartel in the Mexican village of El Huizachal in the municipality of San Fernando, Tamaulipas. The fifty-eight men and fourteen women are shot in the backs and their bodies are piled together.[26]

- In December, President Obama submits the bipartisan federal DREAM Act to protect children of undocumented immigrants from being deported from the United States. The bill fails to get the necessary votes in the Senate.

2011: According to the United Nations, Honduras reaches its peak of per capita murders at 91.4 murders per 100,000 people.[27]

- In May, the Obama administration releases the "Blueprint for

---

24. Elisabeth Malkin, "Honduran President Is Ousted in Coup," *New York Times*, June 28, 2009.

25. "President Obama's Legacy on Immigration," Immigration Impact, American Immigration Council, January 20, 2017.

26. "Massacre in Tamaulipas," editorial, *New York Times*, August 29, 2010.

27. "UNODC Homicide Statistics 2013," United Nations Office of Drugs and Crime, www.unodc.org/gsh/en/data.html.

Building a 21st Century Immigration System," a revised version of the DREAM Act.

2012: In March, a truce is negotiated in El Salvador between the imprisoned gang leaders of MS-13 and Barrio 18. José Miguel Insulza, the secretary general of the Organization of American States, facilitates the truce, while about two hundred soldiers stand by in case it breaks down and violence erupts within the prisons.[28] Following the truce, the country's murder rate drops by more than 50 percent and for two years remains at that level.[29]

- In June, President Obama orders ICE to defer from deporting child migrants in a policy change known as Deferred Action for Childhood Arrivals (DACA).

2013: Salvadoran president Salvador Sánchez Cerén calls off the truce in favor of a *mano duro*, or "iron fist," approach, which intensifies militarized offensives against the gangs. This approach backfires and violence begins to increase.

- Bipartisan immigration reform offering a path to citizenship for DACA recipients is proposed by eight US senators. The US House of Representatives does not act on the bill and allows it to expire.

- Following the investigations of two truth commissions and the publication of a report by the Roman Catholic Church and another by the United Nations, the Guatemalan court convicts Efraín Ríos Montt, former general and president, of genocide

---

28. Randal Archibold, "Gangs' Truce Buys El Salvador a Tenuous Peace," *New York Times*, August 27, 2012.

29. Alberto Arce, "El Salvador Throws Out Gang Truce and Officials Who Put It in Place," *New York Times*, May 20, 2016. See also appendix essay on "The Rise of the *Maras*."

and crimes against humanity.[30]

2014: In the spring and summer, tens of thousands of women and unaccompanied children from the Northern Triangle arrive at the US border, seeking safety and asylum. President Obama declares a humanitarian crisis. Obama and the DHS implement an "aggressive deterrence strategy." A media campaign is launched, highlighting the risks involved with making the trip through Mexico. The DHS also sharply increases the detention of women and children awaiting asylum hearings.

- On June 20, the Obama administration reacts to the increase of unaccompanied youth migrants from Central America crossing the US border. A fact sheet describes the problem from the White House's point of view, outlining steps Obama has proposed to respond.[31]

- In July, Mexico launches its Southern Border Plan to serve as a deterrent against Central American migrants and to send a message that the journey to the United States is not worth the risk.[32] With broad public support, the US government publicly endorses the plan. See appendix essay on "Arrests and Detention in Mexico."

- The Obama administration signs into law the Central American Minors (CAM) program, which allows parents of Central

---

30. "Guatemala: Ríos Montt Convicted of Genocide," Human Rights Watch, May 10, 2013.

31. "Fact Sheet 1: Unaccompanied Children from Central America," The White House: President Barack Obama, http://obamawhitehouse.archives.gov/the-press-office/2014/06/20/fact-sheet-unaccompanied-children-central-america.

32. Jonathan T. Hiskey et al., "Understanding the Central American Refugee Crisis," American Immigration Council, February 1, 2016, www.americanimmigrationcouncil.org/research/understanding-central-american-refugee-crisis.

American minor refugees to request refugee or parole status for their children fleeing Central America.

- President Obama ends the six-year-old Secure Communities Program, which had mandated that local police share fingerprints and personal information of people booked in local jails with federal authorities so they can target undocumented immigrants.

2015: The murder rate in El Salvador climbs to 105 per 100,000 inhabitants, the highest in the world.[33]

2016: Data from the Institute of Legal Medicine in El Salvador places San Salvador as the world's most murderous city.[34]

- In a March 3 home invasion, armed gunmen murder Honduran Indigenous leader and environmental activist Berta Cáceres and wound Mexican environmental activist Gustavo Castro Soto. Despite the fact that the Inter-American Commission on Human Rights had charged the Honduran government with protecting Cáceres, no protection is given on the day she is murdered.[35]

- In April, the leaders of MS-13 and Barrio 18 offer to stop the violence in exchange for concessions from the Salvadoran government, but the authorities under the Cerén administration refuse to negotiate. See appendix essay on "The Rise of the *Maras*."

- In October, the *Wall Street Journal* reports that more than forty

---

33. Douglass Farah, "Central American Gangs Are All Grown Up," *Foreign Policy*, January 19, 2016.

34. Robert Muggah, "It's Official: San Salvador Is the Murder Capital of the World," *Los Angeles Times*, March 2, 2016.

35. Elisabeth Malkin and Alberto Arce, "Berta Cáceres, Indigenous Activist, Is Killed in Honduras," *New York Times*, March 3, 2016.

thousand people are detained by ICE, marking a historic high.[36]

- In December, Donald Trump is elected president on an anti-immigrant platform. At the start of his campaign in June 2015, Trump promises to build "a great wall" and to "make Mexico pay" for it.[37]

2017: In January, newly inaugurated President Trump signs an executive order banning refugees from Iraq, Syria, Iran, Libya, Somalia, Sudan, and Yemen. After mass protests and chaos at several airports and other venues across the country, a federal judge in New York blocks the travel ban.

- President Trump signs an executive action that removes protections for DACA recipients, giving Congress a six-month window to pass legislation to protect DREAMers.

- In May, Médecins Sans Frontières/Doctors Without Borders reports that since 2013, roughly two-thirds of Central American migrants it treated have reported being victims of violence, and one third of women have reported being sexually abused,[38] while more recent reports claim that up to 80 percent of women have faced sexual abuse.[39]

---

36. Jennifer Chan, "Immigration Detention Bed Quota Timeline," National Immigrant Justice Center, January 13, 2017.

37. Aaron Rupar, "Trump's Border Wall Is Looking More Like a Fence That the American Taxpayers Will Pay For," ThinkProgress, January 26, 2017.

38. Doctors Without Borders, *Forced to Flee Central America's Northern Triangle: A Neglected Human Rights Crisis*, May 2017, www.msf.org.br/publicacoes/report-forced-to-flee.pdf.

39. While a previous report by Amnesty International had estimated the number at close to 60 percent, a 2014 interview with migrant shelter directors by Fusion put the number at closer to 80 percent. See Deborah Bonello and Erin Siegal McIntyre, "Is Rape the Price to Pay for Migrant Women Chasing the American Dream?," *Splinter*, September 10, 2014.

- Rights groups, including Amnesty International and Human Rights First, sue US Customs and Border Protection (CBP), alleging that it is turning asylum applicants away at the border, using tactics including "misrepresentations, threats and intimidation, verbal abuse and physical force."[40]

- In June, Mexican authorities announce a 50 percent decrease in total migrant apprehensions since November 2015. The CBP reports a 75 percent drop in apprehensions at the US border. This decrease is attributed to the "Trump Effect," a broad term that refers to the president's hostile rhetoric and his promises of increasingly tough immigration law including barring all entry at the border and separating parents from children.[41]

- In August, President Trump announces his Reforming American Immigration for Strong Employment (RAISE) Act, which sets out to slash legal immigration into the United States. The RAISE Act reduces the number of green cards issued to low-skilled immigrants by 50 percent and introduces a merit-based system that would assess potential immigration cases based on education, fluency in English, age, and job offers.[42]

- On August 16, the Department of Homeland Security (DHS), under Acting Secretary of Homeland Security Elaine Duke, ends the CAM parole program, which President Obama created to deter minors fleeing Central America from attempting to enter the United States without documentation. This process was set into

---

40. Tal Kopan, "Does Border Drop Mean Trump's Tough Talk Is Working?," CNN, March 9, 2017.

41. Stephanie Leutert, "An Increasingly Difficult Immigration Climate," *Lawfare*, June 6, 2017.

42. Alice Stewart, "Trump Proposal a Good Start on Immigration," CNN, August 5, 2017.

motion when President Trump signed an executive order titled Border Security and Immigration Enforcement Improvements in January 2017, requiring parole cases to be handled on a case-by-case basis. While roughly three thousand individuals were able to travel to the United States and reunite with families through the program, their conditional approval is now rescinded.

- On August 25, Guatemalan president Jimmy Morales announces his decision to expel the head of CICIG, the UN-backed International Commission against Impunity.

- On September 10, California passes Senate Bill 54, variously referred to as the California Values Act or the "sanctuary state" bill, to prohibit state and local law enforcement from holding or questioning people on their immigration status.

- On October 8, President Trump tells Congress that he will consider protecting eight hundred thousand DREAMers only if Congress approves building a wall along the US-Mexico border, hiring ten thousand more immigration officers, denying federal grants to "sanctuary cities," making asylum laws tougher, and making it harder for Central Americans to seek refuge in the United States.[43]

2018: On January 8, the DHS announces the end of TPS for nearly two hundred thousand Salvadorans who have lived, worked, and started families in the United States since the 2001 earthquakes in El Salvador. This announcement comes weeks after the Trump administration announces the end of TPS for forty-five thousand Haitians and a year after he ends the protection for twenty-five hundred Nicaraguans.[44]

---

43. Jeff Mason, "Exclusive: Trump Seeks Border Wall, Crackdown on Unaccompanied Minors for 'Dreamer' Deal," *Business Insider*, October 18, 2017.

44. Miriam Jordan, "Trump Administration Says That Nearly 200,000 Salvadorans Must Leave," *New York Times*, January 8, 2018.

- Between January 19 and 22, the US government shuts down after failing to vote on a budget. The Democrats demand the legal protection of two to three million DREAMers, and the Republicans demand funding of the border wall.

- In late January, Honduran president Juan Orlando Hernández is sworn in for a second term as widespread allegations of election fraud lead to violent protests across the nation, in which dozens of protesters are killed.[45]

- In January and February, ICE responds to the passage of the California Values Act by raiding 222 businesses in Southern California and 77 in Northern California.

- On March 7, Attorney General Jeff Sessions, challenging sections of the California Values Act and three other "sanctuary state" laws, sues California for allegedly violating federal immigration laws by refusing to cooperate with federal immigration authorities.[46] California countersues the federal government.

- In the final weeks of March, more than a thousand migrants, mostly from Honduras, assemble and begin a northward trek from Tapachula, Chiapas. The caravan, organized by Pueblo Sin Fronteras, passes through immigration checkpoints without being stopped.[47] After tweeting that the caravan is coming to receive US social services and therefore DACA should not be reinstated, President Trump announces in the first week of

---

45. Gustavo Palencia, "Honduran President Sworn in amid Protest after Election Chaos," Reuters, January 27, 2018.

46. Adam Liptak, "Sessions Targets California Immigrants Using a Ruling That Protected Them," New York Times, March 7, 2018.

47. Adolfo Flores, "A Huge Caravan of Central Americans Is Headed for the U.S. and No One in Mexico Dares to Stop Them," BuzzFeed, March 30, 2018.

April that he will deploy the military to help control the border. Texas sends 250 National Guard troops within seventy-two hours, and Arizona announces that it will follow suit with 150.[48] Defense Secretary James Mattis authorizes funding for 4,000 troops.[49]

- Data gathered by the Office of Refugee Resettlement confirm about seven hundred refugee children from Central America, including about a hundred under the age of four, have been illegally separated from their parents as they arrive at the US border seeking protection.[50]

- At the end of April, 345 members of the Central American migrant caravan reach the border at Tijuana and apply for asylum. The Department of Justice and DHS both call for more prosecutors and judges at the border to expedite the processing of their asylum claims.[51]

- As the CBP begins separating child migrants from their parents at military bases, reports released by the US Department of Health and Human Services say that the federal government lost track of almost fifteen hundred children who had been placed with adult sponsors.[52]

---

48. Dave Montgomery and Manny Fernandez, "Texas Begins Sending National Guard Troops to Mexican Border," *New York Times*, April 6, 2018.

49. Montgomery and Fernandez, "Texas Begins Sending National Guard Troops."

50. Caitlin Dickerson, "Hundreds of Immigrant Children Have Been Taken from Parents at U.S. Border," *New York Times*, April 20, 2018.

51. Kate Morrissey, "Migrants from Central American Caravan Face a Long Road to Asylum," *Los Angeles Times*, April 29, 2018.

52. Ron Nixon, "Federal Agencies Lost Track of Nearly 1,500 Migrant Children Placed with Sponsors," *New York Times*, April 26, 2018.

- On May 4, amid escalating political violence in Honduras, President Trump announces that he will end TPS for more than fifty thousand Hondurans who have lived, worked, and raised families in the United States for over two decades.[53]

- An ACLU report released in May uncovers widespread abuse of child migrants by the CBP, including violence, sexual abuse, and verbal abuse.[54] This comes just after a CNN investigation finds 564 deaths of people crossing the border that the CBP have failed to account for over the last sixteen years, over half of which have occurred in the last four years.[55]

- On May 7, Attorney General Jeff Sessions enacts a "zero-tolerance" policy on the US-Mexico border, vowing to prosecute any adult crossing the border and to separate any children from their parents or caretakers.[56] In the next six weeks, more than two thousand children are forcibly separated from their parents, prompting the UN to condemn the actions as illegal and request that the Trump administration immediately cease the inhumane practice.[57] A former Walmart Superstore in southern Texas operated by Southwest Key becomes the largest licensed shelter for migrant children,

---

53. Elizabeth Oglesby, "Trump's TPS Decision Undercuts US Goals in Honduras, *The Hill*, May 11, 2018.

54. Avery Anapol, "ACLU: Border Agents Physically Abused Migrant Children," *The Hill*, May 25, 2018.

55. Bob Ortega, "Border Patrol Failed to Count Hundreds of Migrant Deaths on US Soil," CNN, May 15, 2018.

56. Richard Gonzales, "Sessions Says 'Zero Tolerance' for Illegal Border Crossers, Vows to Divide Families," NPR, May 7, 2018.

57. "U.S. Child Migrants: 2,000 Separated from Families in Six Weeks," BBC, June 15, 2018; Nick Cumming-Bruce, "Taking Migrant Children from Parents Is Illegal, U.N. Tells U.S.," *New York Times*, June 5, 2018.

holding some fifteen hundred children.[58] Visitors and workers at various detention youth centers report that the facilities are understaffed and children are not allowed to touch other children or staff. One worker reports that children at the Estrella del Norte shelter in Tucson, Arizona, were attempting suicide.[59] Doctors who visit the shelters say that family separation creates toxic stress and can lead to permanent psychological trauma.[60]

- In spite of the Trump administration's hopes that separating families at the border will deter refugees from fleeing Central America, May marks the third consecutive month in which the number of people arriving at the border has increased. Nearly fifty thousand are arrested at the border that month.[61]

- At the end of May, a UN report shows that the United States has been funding paramilitary officers known as the Special Reaction Forces in El Salvador that have been illegally executing suspected gang members.[62]

- Jeff Sessions announces on June 11 that victims of domestic violence as well as gang violence will no longer be eligible for asylum.[63]

---

58. Manny Fernandez, "Inside the Former Walmart That Is Now a Shelter for Almost 1,500 Migrant Children," *New York Times*, June 14, 2018.

59. Molly Hennessy-Fiske, "'Prison-Like' Migrant Youth Shelter Is Understaffed, Unequipped for Trump's 'Zero Tolerance' Policy, Insider Says," *Los Angeles Times*, June 14, 2018.

60. Kristine Phillips, "'America Is Better Than This': What a Doctor Saw in the Texas Shelter for Migrant Children," *Washington Post*, June 16, 2018.

61. Simon Romero and Miriam Jordan, "On the Border, a Discouraging New Message for Asylum Seekers: Wait," *New York Times*, June 12, 2018.

62. Nick Paton Walsh, Barbara Arvanitidis, and Bryan Avelar, "US-Funded Police Linked to Illegal Executions in El Salvador," CNN, May 23, 2018.

63. Maya Rhodan, "The Trump Administration Dropped Asylum Protection for Survivors of Domestic Violence," *Time*, June 11, 2018.

- On June 19, as a group of protesters including Democratic and moderate Republican politicians gathers at the border, Zeid Ra'ad al-Hussein, the UN High Commissioner for Human Rights, calls for an immediate halt to separating families at the border and condemns the action as child abuse.

- On June 20, amid public outcry, President Trump signs an executive order ending his administration's policy of separating children from their parents who are detained after crossing the border without documentation. The plan seeks to keep families together in detention until proceedings for crossing the border are complete, challenging the 1997 *Flores* Settlement, which restricts the government's power to keep children in detention.[64]

- The US Supreme Court upholds President Trump's so-called Muslim Ban.

- On June 27, the House vote against (301 to 121) a "compromise" immigration bill that would have provided a path to citizenship for DREAMers, created a "path to citizenship based on merit," shrunk legal immigration, allowed migrant families to be "detained indefinitely," made the rules for asylum more strict, and allocated $25 billion for work on a border wall and other security measures.[65]

- On November 8, the Ninth Circuit Court upholds a preliminary injunction that the Trump administration cannot end DACA. On December 21, Trump announces that the government will shut down unless it funds his $5.7 billion border wall proposal.

---

64. John Wagner, Nick Miroff, and Mike DeBonis, "Trump Reverses Course, Signs Order Ending His Policy of Separating Families at Border," *Washington Post*, June 20, 2018.

65. Mike DeBonis and John Wagner, "House Rejects Immigration Bill Pushed by Trump in Last-Minute Tweet," *Washington Post*, June 27, 2018.

2019: On January 8, Trump defends his argument that a wall is needed in a televised address. Four days later the government shutdown enters its twenty-second day and thus becomes the longest in US history. At this writing, the shutdown, which has left eight hundred thousand federal employees without pay, remains unresolved as Republicans and Democrats trade offers and counteroffers on the wall proposal, as well as the future of DACA and TPS.

GLOSSARY

AB 540—A California law that allows eligible undocumented college students to qualify for in-state tuition. *See also* DREAM Act (California).

asylum—In the United States, the right to asylum is stipulated by federal and international law. As a member of the United Nations, the United States is obliged to recognize the 1951 Convention Relating to the Status of Refugees and its 1967 Protocol. The US Refugee Act of 1980, which was established to bring US law into compliance with the 1967 Protocol, defines a refugee eligible for asylum as follows: "any person who is outside of his country of nationality (or in the case of a person having no nationality, is outside any country in which he last habitually resided), and who is unable or unwilling to return to such country because of persecution or a well-founded fear of persecution based on race, religion, nationality, political opinion, or membership in a particular social group."

Barrio 18—Also referred to as the "18th Street Gang," "Mara 18," "Calle 18," or simply the "18." Barrio 18 is a multiethnic transnational gang that formed in Los Angeles in the 1980s. It is considered to be the largest transnational gang, with tens of thousands of members in Los Angeles alone. After some of its leaders were deported to war-torn Central America, Barrio 18 grew throughout Central America. Its rival gang is known as MS-13. See appendix essay on "The Rise of the *Maras*."

La Bestia—Spanish for "the Beast." A colloquial term referring to the cargo trains in Mexico on which migrants travel to the United States. See appendix essay on "La Bestia."

cartel—A criminal organization that is involved in drug trafficking. In 2012, Mexican cartels—also known as "La Mafia," "La Maña," "*narcotraficantes*," or "*narcos*"—were said to make an estimated $19–$29 billion a year from the drug trade. Approximately 93 percent of the cocaine that crosses into the United States comes through Mexico. Mexican cartels have been responsible for over fifty-five thousand deaths since 2006, when the Mexican Drug War began.[1] See appendix essay on "Mexican Drug Trafficking Organizations (DTOs)."

casa de migrante(s)—Also *casa del migrante*. Spanish for "migrant house," this term refers to the migrant shelters throughout Mexico that provide services including food, temporary boarding, and clothing. See appendix essay on "Casas de Migrantes."

catracho—A colloquial term for a person from Honduras.

CBP—Customs and Border Protection is the US federal agency that manages the country's borders. Part of the Department of Homeland Security, it has more than sixty thousand employees and is one of the largest anti-terrorism organizations in the world.

chapín—A colloquial term for a person from Guatemala.

Chuj—Also spelled "Chuh." A Mayan language spoken by an estimated forty thousand people in Guatemala and ten thousand in Mexico. It is a member of the Q'anjob'alan subgroup of the Western

---

1. Michael B. Kelley, "By the Numbers: Why the Mexican Drug War Should Keep You Awake at Night," *Business Insider*, June 2012.

branch of the Mayan family. Most Chuj speakers live in San Mateo Ixtatán, San Sebastián Coatán, and Nentón in the department of Huehuetenango, Guatemala.

Contras—Refers to multiple US-backed right-wing rebel groups deployed between 1979 and 1991 to fight against the left-wing democratic socialist Sandinista Junta of the National Reconstruction government of Nicaragua. *See also* Sandinistas.

coyote—A smuggler who is hired to help migrants cross the US border. Current prices range between $6,000 and $10,000 per person. In the past few years, it has become nearly impossible to cross the border without a *coyote* since Los Zetas, a Mexican drug smuggling organization, requires payments to pass and will only accept them from the *coyotes*. Estimates say that *coyotes* transport as many as one million migrants per year, with annual revenues of as much as $7 billion a year. In the narratives, *coyote* is always in italics to avoid confusion with the animal.

DACA—Deferred Action for Childhood Arrivals. In 2012, the Obama administration stopped deporting undocumented students who met the eligibility requirements of the DREAM Act. During Obama's second term, eight hundred thousand people who were brought to the United States as children without documents earned temporary legal status.

DHS—The Department of Homeland Security is a cabinet department of the US federal government that is in charge of public safety. It was created by the George W. Bush administration in response to the 9/11 attacks in the United States, and it brought together the Animal and Plant Inspection Service, the Internal Naturalization Service, the US Border Patrol, and the US Customs Services into one agency. It has over 240,000 employees and was allocated annual budgets of $40.6 billion in 2016, $42.4 billion in 2017, and $44.1 billion in 2018.

DREAM Act (federal)—The Development, Relief, and Education for Alien Minors Act is an American legislative proposal that would grant conditional residency for qualifying undocumented minors pursuing education and the possibility of earning permanent residency. The bill was first introduced to the Senate in 2001 and since then has been reintroduced several times without success.

DREAM ACT (California)—Not to be confused with the federal DREAM Act, the California DREAM Act was divided into two bills, AB 130 and AB 131, which were both signed into law by Governor Brown in 2011. AB 130 allows students who meet AB 540 criteria to apply for non-state-funded scholarships for colleges and universities, while AB 131 allows these students to apply for in-state tuition (*see also* AB 540). Similar laws have since been passed in Illinois, Kansas, Massachusetts, Maryland, Minnesota, Nebraska, New Jersey, New Mexico, New York, Oregon, Texas, Utah, Washington, and Wisconsin.

DREAMers—The term used for people who would qualify for protections under the federal DREAM Act.

green card—A US Permanent Resident Card. Permanent residence is granted to nonresidents for two- or ten-year periods and can often be renewed. Permanent residents can apply for naturalization after a determined period of time, often five years, in order to become US citizens.

Gulf Cartel—One of the oldest and most dominant contemporary crime groups in Mexico. Its origins can be traced back to 1984. Its power and territory has lessened in recent years as Los Zetas have gained more control.[2]

hielera—Spanish for "icebox" or "freezer," this term is used colloquially by Spanish-speaking CBP detainees to refer to the frigid detention facilities. Many migrants have reported the extraordinarily cold temperatures and the lack of bedding or chairs. Many also tell of being fed frozen ham sandwiches once a day. Many migrants, and especially minors, have reported multiple abuses at the hands of CBP agents, including sexual and physical assaults as well as inhumane living conditions. *See perrera* and appendix essay on "Arrests and Detention in the United States."

ICE—Immigration and Customs Enforcement, the enforcement branch of the DHS, responsible for Homeland Security Investigations and Enforcement and Removal Operations. In the first weeks of the Trump presidency, arrests of immigrants increased by over 30 percent. While the Obama administration directed ICE to arrest only immigrants with criminal records, arrests of immigrants with no criminal records have more than doubled since Trump's election.[3]

INS—The Immigration and Naturalization Service was a US Department of Labor agency from 1933 to 1940, then a US Department of Justice agency from 1940 to 2003, when most of its functions were transferred to the DHS. Before 1933, immigration and naturalization were handled by two separate agencies.

IRCA—The Immigration Reform and Control Act of 1986 set out to reform the status of undocumented immigrants as established by the

2. "Gulf Cartel," Insight Crime, March 2017, www.insightcrime.org/mexico -organized-crime-news/gulf-cartel-profile.

3. Maria Sacchetti, "ICE Immigration Arrests of Noncriminals Double under Trump," *Washington Post*, April 16, 2017.

Immigration and Nationality Act of 1965. IRCA gave eligible undocumented immigrants the ability to apply for legal residency. Applicants had to prove that they had maintained an unbroken residence in the United States since January 1, 1982, had no criminal record, and had registered with the Selective Service. IRCA allowed 1.6 million of the approximately 3.6 million undocumented immigrants in the country to obtain legal status, and an additional 1.1 million to obtain legal status through provisions for special agricultural workers, known as SAWs. See "Historical Timeline," 1986.

K'iche'—Also spelled Kiché or Quiché, K'iche' is referred to as *Qatzijob'al* by its speakers, which translates as "our language." It is a Mayan language primarily spoken in the central highlands of Guatemala. The more than one million speakers of K'iche' make up over 7 percent of the Guatemalan population, representing the second most commonly spoken language in Guatemala after Spanish. The *Popol Vuh*, a Maya creation myth and a central text of the Maya, was written in classical K'iche'.

Ladino—This term is commonly used to refer to non-Indigenous Guatemalans, mestizos, and Westernized Indigenous people. While it has been thought to derive from a mix of *ladrón*, the Spanish word for "thief," and *Latino*, Ladino doesn't always hold a negative connotation.

Mam—A Mayan language with over a half million speakers in the Guatemalan departments of Quetzaltenango, Huehuetenango, San Marcos, and Retalhuleu, and over ten thousand in the Mexican state of Chiapas. There are also thousands of Mam speakers in Oakland, California, and Washington, DC. Mam is part of the Quichéan-Mamean branch of the Mayan language.

maras—A term referring to large gangs, primarily the MS-13 and the Barrio 18. Also called *marabuntas*, the word *mara* means "gang," or "street posse," in Central American Spanish. See appendix essay on "The Rise of the *Maras*."

mareros—Members of a mara.

Maya, Mayan—*Mayan* generally refers to the languages of the Maya culture, while *Maya* generally refers to all other non-linguistic aspects of the people, culture, and civilization.

La Migra—A Spanish slang term for a migration agent, officer, or agency.

MS-13—Also known as "Mara Salvatrucha," "MS," or "Mara," MS-13 is a transnational gang that started in Los Angeles in the 1980s. Most members are Salvadoran, and its main rival gang is Barrio 18. *See also* Barrio 18 and appendix essay on "The Rise of the *Maras*."

mojados—Deriving from *mojado*, "wet" in Spanish, the pejorative slang term is sometimes used by Spanish speakers to refer to undocumented immigrants, whose backs become wet while swimming or wading across the Rio Grande to reach the United States. The term may have evolved as a response to the racist term *wetback*.

Norteño—Spanish for "northerner," this term refers to a member of the Norteños, a loosely connected group of gangs in Northern California, the majority of whom are Mexican Americans. Their rivals are the Sureños, a group of gangs roughly south of Bakersfield. *See also* Sureños.

narcos—Spanish term for narcotic traffickers and their armed gangs.

pandilla—Spanish for "gang."

pandillero—Spanish for "gangster."

perrera—Spanish for "dog catcher" or "dog kennel," this term is used colloquially by Spanish-speaking detainees of the CBP to describe the trucks and vans that the CBP uses to transport detained migrants. *See also hielera* and appendix essay on "Arrests and Detention in the United States."

Programa Frontera Sur (Southern Border Plan, SBP)—On July 7, 2014, Mexican president Enrique Peña Nieto, in partnership with Guatemala's Otto Peréz Molina, launched this plan to work together as neighboring countries to make the border area safer and prevent human rights abuses. See appendix essay on "Arrests and Detention in Mexico."

Prevention Through Deterrence—A CBP policy developed in the 1990s that aims to reduce border crossings by undocumented migrants by funneling them through the most hazardous and life-threatening sections of the border, thereby deterring future crossing attempts. See appendix essay on "Arrests and Detention in the United States."

Q'eqchi'—Also spelled Kekchi, K'ekchi', and kekchí, Q'eqchi' is a Mayan language spoken primarily in northern Guatemala and southern Belize.

renta—Spanish for "rent." Protection money extorted by a gang.

Río Bravo—Name for the Rio Grande in Mexico, a river that flows from Southern Colorado to the Gulf of Mexico. It forms part of the border between Mexico and Texas. Major international border crossings bridging the river are located in Ciudad Juárez, Laredo, McAllen, and Reynosa.

sanctuary cities—This term is used to describe US cities whose local governments and police forces refuse to share people's immigration status with the federal government. By federal law, this information-sharing policy is legally required by the DHS, although many feel that the law violates the Tenth Amendment. Since taking office in January 2017, President Trump has threatened to cut federal funding to these cities, and the US Department of Justice has sued the state of California to revoke its sanctuary provisions.

Sandinista—A member of the Frente Sandinista de Liberación Nacional (FSLN)—in English, Sandinista Liberation Front—a rebel group that overthrew Nicaraguan president Anastasio Somoza Debayle in 1979, bringing an end to forty-six years of rule by the Somoza family. The group was named after Augusto César Sandino, who led the resistance against US occupying forces in Nicaragua in the 1930s. The Sandinistas governed Nicaragua from 1979 to 1990. Nicaragua's current leader, Daniel Ortega, served as a Sandinista president from 1985 to 1990 and was elected president again in 2007.

Sureño—Spanish for "southerner," this term refers to a member of the Sureños, a loosely connected group of gangs in Southern California, mostly made up of Mexicans and Mexican Americans. Their rivals are the Norteños, a group of gangs north of Bakersfield.

TPS—Temporary Protected Status. Part of the US Immigration Act of 1990, Congress created this status to provide temporary protection to people who could not immediately return to their home countries. TPS was granted to Salvadorans, Guatemalans, Hondurans, and Nicaraguans following Hurricane Mitch in 1998. It was extended in September 2008, at which point 229,000 Salvadorans became eligible. Although recipients of TPS are able to apply for work authorization, there is no path toward permanent residence. Trump announced an end to the TPS program in November 2017. See "Historical Timeline."

Zetas—Los Zetas is a Mexican criminal organization led by ex-members of the Mexican Army who, before breaking off on their own, served as the security branch of the Gulf Cartel. They are responsible for attacks on migrants near the southern and northern borders of Mexico. Because migrants are often forced to travel across the borders along the same clandestine routes as drug smugglers, they are easy prey to assault and extortion by this organization. For undocumented migrants, it is almost impossible to cross the Mexico-US border without paying off Los Zetas.

APPENDIXES

1. Risk Factors for Children

In El Salvador, 40 percent of children under five are chronically malnourished, and 17 percent of Salvadoran kids go hungry. Nine percent of Salvadoran babies are born with low birth weight.[1] Child abuse is rampant; 42 percent of Salvadoran women and 52 percent of men report having suffered physical violence as children before the age of fifteen.[2]

In Guatemala, child abandonment is widespread in villages and cities, hidden from the view of tourists. According to a report by the Joint Council on International Children's Services, a Guatemalan child is abandoned every four days; in three-quarters of cases, they are newborn babies. Impoverishment, unstable unions of underage parents, physical abuse, alcoholism, and inability to find work close to home are factors in why parents abandon children. Children who are physically disabled or have learning difficulties are more likely

---

1. "10 Facts about Hunger in El Salvador," World Food Programme, 2018, www.wfp.org/stories/10-facts-about-hunger-el-salvador.

2. "Violence against Children," Pan American Health Organization, Regional Office for the Americas of the World Health Organization, January 30, 2018, www.paho .org/hq/index.php?option=com_content&view=article&id=11122%3Aviolence -against-children&catid=1505%3Aintra-family-violence&Itemid=41533&lang=en.

to be abandoned. Adolescents forced onto the streets are often re-cruited by gangs who treat them "like family" in return for selling drugs or committing robberies, stabbings, and gun homicide.[3]

In Honduras, 60 percent of the population lives in poverty. Chil-dren constitute 36 percent of the population. Fifty-two percent live in single-parent families—most led by women struggling to raise large families. Crime rates are high, and where women are the of-fenders, Honduran policy requires that babies up to two years old be imprisoned with their mothers. Some children are born behind bars.[4]

From 2012 to 2015, the United Nations High Commissioner for Human Rights worked with the Committee on the Rights of a Child in Honduras to investigate reports of child slavery, prosti-tution, and pornography. In 2015, they concluded: "The Commit-tee noted the absence of a strategy to prevent the sale of children, child prostitution and child pornography, including addressing root causes of poverty and stigmatization of segments of the population. Experts raised concern about the very high number of trafficked children in Honduras, noting that *up to 500 child victims of traffick-ing returned by land routes from Mexico every week*."[5]

The cycle of children having children is a root cause of infant mortality, childhood ill health, family insecurity, poverty, and hun-ger, thus propelling children to flee and seek better lives in El Norte. A 2007 UNICEF report states, "Persistently high levels of adolescent fertility . . . are closely linked to conditions of increased poverty and

---

3. "Abandoned in Guatemala," Casa de Sion / Safe Homes for Children, 2016, http://casadesion.org/wp/abandoned-in-guatemala/.

4. "Why Honduras?," Friends of Honduran Children, 2018, http://honduranchildren.com/why-honduras/.

5. "Committee on the Rights of the Child Reviews the Reports of Honduras," United Nations Human Rights Office of the High Commissioner, May 21, 2015, www.ohchr.org/EN/NewsEvents/Pages/DisplayNews.aspx?NewsID=15994 &LangID=E (italics ours).

vulnerability and lead to difficult situations for the young mother, her family and her offspring."[6] In rural communities, the rate of infant mortality persuades parents to have multiple children in order to till the fields and survive. But having too many mouths to feed keeps families on the edge of hunger and forces children to quit primary school and work in the fields. Yet high birth rates are falling significantly. Between 2016 and 2017, the birth rate in Guatemala fell from 35.05 to 24.1. In Honduras, it fell from 32.65 to 22.4. In El Salvador, it fell from 29.02 to 16.2.[7] Family planning efforts by nongovernmental organizations and charities seem to be having a positive effect.

While birth rates are falling, homicide rates for children are rising. In Central America, children ages zero to nineteen face the highest homicide rates in the world, according to InSight Crime, an organization dedicated to the study of organized crime in Latin America.[8] Adolescents ages twelve to nineteen account for 95 percent of child slayings. In Honduras, 30 out of 100,000 children under nineteen were murdered in 2017, while in El Salvador the figure was just over 20, and in Guatemala the figure was just over 10.[9] Police in El Salvador attribute the high murder rate to gangs targeting children for recruitment.[10]

---

6. Jorge Rodriguez and Martin Hopenhayn, "Teenage Motherhood in Latin America and the Caribbean," *Challenges*, no. 4 (January 2007): 5.

7. Birth rate is measured by births per 1,000 people. See "Central America and the Caribbean," Index Mundi, March 2, 2018, www.indexmundi.com/central _america_and_the_caribbean.html.

8. Tristan Clavel, "540 Children Were Murdered Last Year in El Salvador: Report," InSight Crime, January 31, 2017, www.insightcrime.org/news/brief/540 -children-murdered-last-year-el-salvador-report/.

9. Parker Asmann, "Ten Countries with Highest Child Homicide Rates All in Lat. Am: Report," InSight Crime, June 6, 2017, www.insightcrime.org/news /brief/ten-countries-highest-child-homicide-rates-all-latam-report/.

10. "Contraceptive Prevalence, Any Methods (% of Women Ages 15–49)," World Bank Group, http://data.worldbank.org/indicator/SP.DYN.CONU.ZS?locations =SV-GT-HN-US-ZJ&name_desc=true&view=chart.

2. *The Rise of the* Maras

In the 1980s, the wars in El Salvador, Guatemala, and Nicaragua led to thousands of deaths, while hundreds of thousands of survivors fled for the United States. According to US Census estimates, the number of Salvadorans in the United States increased from 94,000 in 1980 to 701,000 a decade later. The Guatemalan population in the United States increased from 71,642 to 226,000, and the Nicaraguan population increased from 25,000 to 125,000.[11] The war in El Salvador in particular gained international attention due to the number of human rights abuses against civilians at the hands of US-backed death squads. During the wars, Central America became "a global ideological battleground where Cold War powers engaged in proxy battles for control and influence."[12] Despite human rights organizations' assertions that human rights abuses by the Salvadoran military were widespread, the Reagan administration sent billions of dollars of support and aid to El Salvador's government and military in these years.

As a result of the Cold War US refugee policy, which primarily awarded asylum to refugees fleeing what the government considered Communist or socialist regimes, many refugees from El Salvador were left undocumented in the United States. What grew into the maras originally formed as street gangs in Los Angeles in the 1970s and '80s, as Salvadoran youth pursued protection from local street gangs. In 1996, changes in US immigration law greatly increased the deportations of Salvadorans, both undocumented and legal resi-

---

11. Juan Gonzalez, *Harvest of Empire: A History of Latinos in the United States* (New York: Penguin Books, 2001), 129.

12. Laura Pedraza Fariña, Spring Miller, and James Cavallaro, *No Place to Hide: Gang, State, and Clandestine Violence in El Salvador* (Cambridge, MA: Human Rights Program, Harvard Law School, 2010), 13.

dents, who had criminal records. The deportees included gang members and leaders who joined with the existing gangs in El Salvador and began to form what have grown into international criminal organizations. In particular, two rival gangs—Mara Salvatrucha (MS-13) and Mara 18—have engaged in vicious clashes for the control of neighborhoods. MS-13 also goes by the names MS and Mara, while Mara 18 is also known as the 18th Street Gang, Calle 18, Barrio 18, and La 18. The US Southern Command estimates that there are around seventy thousand gang members in Central America's Northern Triangle, which encompasses El Salvador, Guatemala, and Honduras. Their principal activities include "extortion, kidnapping, and controlling the neighborhood illegal drug market."[13]

In early 2012, the Roman Catholic Church, social workers, and gang members facilitated a truce between the imprisoned leaders of the rival gangs. While at first the administration of Salvadoran president Mauricio Funes denied involvement in the truce, it was later revealed that it had actively supported it. The truce was controversial among the Salvadoran public, with some angered by the concessions that the imprisoned gang leaders were awarded, and others hopeful for the effects it might have. In the first half of 2012 following the truce, homicides in El Salvador dropped by 32 percent, kidnappings by 50 percent, and extortion by 10 percent.[14] In early 2015, in the midst of continued controversy surrounding the truce, Salvadoran president Salvador Sánchez Cerén called off the truce in favor of a "*mano duro*," or "iron fist," approach, which intensified militarized offensives against the gangs. This approach backfired and violence began to increase. In April 2016, the leaders of the rival maras offered to stop the violence in exchange for concessions from the government, but the authorities under the Cerén administration refused

---

13. "MS13," InSight Crime, March 9, 2017, www.insightcrime.org/el-salvador-organized-crime-news/mara-salvatrucha-ms-13-profile/.

14. Randal C. Archibold, "Gangs' Truce Buys El Salvador a Tenuous Peace," *New York Times*, August 27, 2012.

to negotiate. Since then, President Trump has used MS-13 violence in the United States as a central piece of his proposals for hardline immigration reform and increased deportation.[15]

3. Violence against Women

The Human Rights Watch World Report of 2010 indicates that, of the 722 women murdered in Guatemala in 2008, 27 percent of them were raped or tortured.[16] From 2010 to 2018, in the US legal system Guatemalan women between the ages of fourteen and forty were considered part of a "protected social group" because of the high rates of violence against them. In 2009, the United States granted asylum status to Rodi Alvarado, who had spent fourteen years in court seeking asylum as a victim of spousal abuse in the mid-1980s. The fact that women in Guatemala were considered to have membership in a "social group" had profound implications on the future interpretation of asylum law.[17] This classification was codified in the US Board of Immigration Appeals ruling on Lesly Yajayra Perdomo in 2010.[18] From that point on, Guatemalan victims of domestic violence were considered for asylum. A Board of Immigration ruling in 2014 further

15. Óscar Martínez, "Trump Is Making MS-13 Stronger," editorial, *New York Times*, February 17, 2018.

16. Human Rights Watch, *World Report 2010*, www.hrw.org/world-report-2010.

17. Diana Haynes, "Misogyny and Racism in Sessions' Unraveling of Asylum Law," *Gender Policy Report*, June 18, 2018.

18. Amy Lieberman, "Appeals Case Gives Hope to Guatemalan Refugees," *Women's E-News*, October 1, 2010.

codified this ruling.[19] However, in June 2018, the Trump administration ruled that victims of domestic violence, as well as gang violence, are no longer eligible for asylum.[20] In doing so, the executive branch singlehandedly ruled against years of established judicial precedent.

A 2011 study by the Geneva Declaration on Armed Violence and Development found that El Salvador had the highest rate of femicide in the world, while Guatemala had the third highest and Honduras had the sixth.[21] Between 2000 and 2011, the number of annual cases of femicide in El Salvador rose from around two hundred to six hundred, while the number of reported cases of domestic violence increased from around fifteen hundred to six thousand.[22] Guatemala and Honduras experienced comparable increases. A 2015 study by the Geneva Declaration found that El Salvador and Honduras led the world in femicide rates. El Salvador's rate was 14.4 homicides out of 100,000 women, and Honduras's rate was 10.9 homicides out of 100,000 women.[23] Between 2011 and 2015, Honduras experienced the largest increase of femicide in the world. While some of the femicides occurred inside the home, the study found that "intimate partner femicide was

19. "Matter of A-R-C-G- et al., Respondents," 26I&N Dec. 388 (BIA 2014), https://www.justice.gov/sites/default/files/eoir/legacy/2014/08/26/3811.pdf.

20. Tal Kopan, "Trump Admin Drops Asylum Protections for Domestic Violence Victims," CNN, June 11, 2018.

21. "When the Victim Is a Woman," in *Global Burden of Armed Violence 2011*, Geneva Declaration on Armed Violence and Development, www.genevadeclaration.org/measurability/global-burden-of-armed-violence/global-burden-of-armed-violence-2011.html.

22. "Central America: Femicide and Gender-Based Violence," Center for Gender and Refugee Studies, Hastings College of the Law, University of California, http://cgrs.uchastings.edu/our-work/central-america-femicides-and-gender-based-violence.

23. "Lethal Violence against Women and Girls," in *Global Burden of Armed Violence 2015*, Geneva Declaration on Armed Violence and Development, www.genevadeclaration.org/measurability/global-burden-of-armed-violence/global-burden-of-armed-violence-2015.html.

responsible for only a fraction of all victims of female homicide."

While many Central American women and girls are fleeing violence and sexual abuse in their home countries, an estimated 80 percent face rape during their journeys through Mexico toward the United States.[24] Many have come to see rape as a terrible rite of passage on the journey. A 2010 Amnesty International report states, "Women and girl migrants, especially those without legal status traveling in remote areas or on trains, are at heightened risk of sexual violence at the hands of criminal gangs, people traffickers, other migrants or corrupt officials. . . . Many criminal gangs appear to use sexual violence as part of the 'price' demanded of migrants. According to some experts, the prevalence of rape is such that people smugglers may require women to have a contraceptive injection prior to the journey as a precaution."[25]

For many women and girls who survive this abuse in their home countries and on the migrant trail in Mexico, the abuse does not end when they arrive in the United States. The American Civil Liberties Union (ACLU) website displays an interactive map tallying the number of allegations of sexual violence in US detention centers.[26] As of 2018, data collected by the ACLU show almost two hundred allegations of sexual abuse in immigration detention facilities since 2007, with the highest numbers reported in Texas, Arizona, and California.

---

24. While a previous report by Amnesty International had estimated the number at closer to 60 percent, migrant shelter directors stated that number was closer to 80 percent when they were interviewed in 2014 by the news website Fusion. See Deborah Bonello and Erin Siegal McIntyre, "Is Rape the Price to Pay for Migrant Women Chasing the American Dream?" *Splinter*, September 10, 2014.

25. Amnesty International, *Invisible Victims: Migrants on the Move in Mexico*, 2010, www.amnestyusa.org/wp-content/uploads/2017/04/amr410142010eng.pdf.

26. "Sexual Abuse in Immigration Detention," American Civil Liberties Union, www.aclu.org/issues/immigrants-rights/immigrants-rights-and-detention/sexual -abuse-immigration-detention-0. The details about the allegations were drawn from Freedom of Information Act documents obtained by the ACLU.

4. Arrests and Detention in Mexico

For the past few decades, Mexico's southern border with Guatemala has for the most part been a semi-permeable membrane, with Central Americans crossing into Mexico and vice versa, many settling across the border and starting families. On July 7, 2014, Mexican president Enrique Peña Nieto, along with Guatemala's Otto Peréz Molina, launched the Programa Frontera Sur (Southern Border Plan, SBP), promising that as neighboring countries they would work together to make the border area safer and prevent the human rights abuses faced by Central Americans throughout Mexico. Mexico's implementation of the SBP proposed to ensure the border's safety, inclusiveness, and efficiency through five lines of action: (1) formal and orderly transit, (2) border management and more security for migrants, (3) protection and social action for migrants, (4) regional co-responsibility, and (5) interinstitutional coordination.

President Obama strongly praised the plan, which led to the deportation of 107,814 Central American migrants from Mexico in 2014, a 35 percent increase over the 80,079 deported in 2013.[27] This increase has disproportionately affected children: the 18,169 children deported in 2014 represents a 117 percent increase over the 8,350 deported for 2013. After the implementation of Programa Frontera Sur, the number of "unaccompanied alien children" apprehended at the southwest border of the United States dropped from 10,631 in June 2013 to 2,234 in September of the same year.[28] The

27. Unidad de Política Migratoria, "Boletín Mensual de Estadísticas Migratorias 2014," www.wola.org/sites/default/files/Boletin2014_.pdf.

28. "Southwestern Border Unaccompanied Alien Children FY 2014," US Customs and Border Protection, November 24, 2015, www.cbp.gov/newsroom/stats/southwest-border-unaccompanied-children/fy-2014.

Obama administration used this drop to argue that the crisis had improved, as fewer migrants were making the treacherous journey. Whereas in 2014 and 2015, the United States announced that it would contribute $90 million a year to help Mexico secure its southern border, only a fraction of the promised amount was paid. According to the Congressional Research Service, as of January 2017, only $24 million had been delivered by the State Department.[29]

The bilateral effort to control Mexico's southern border began before the SBP. The Mérida Initiative was signed into law in 2008, and one of its pillars focuses precisely on "creating a 21st century border." In 2011, Obama's commissioner of US Customs and Border Protection, Alan Bersin, who earned the nickname "Border Czar" under President Clinton, said that "the Guatemalan border with Chiapas is now our southern border," after the United States launched a "Mexico-Guatemala-Belize Border Region Program," providing $50 million for immigration officers' training and equipment.[30]

While the plan's stated objectives include protecting the human rights of migrants and especially youth, it has amplified the human rights crisis in Mexico for Central American migrants. According to a June 2014 report published by the Washington Office on Latin America (WOLA), although violence in Central America has not diminished, fewer migrants from Central America are arriving at the US border.[31] Between October 2014 and April 2015, Mexico apprehended 92,889 Central American migrants, almost double the

29. Adam Isacson, Maureen Meyer, and Hannah Smith, *Mexico's Southern Border: Security, Central American Migration, and U.S. Policy*, WOLA, June 29, 2017.

30. Adam Isaacson, Maureen Meyer, and Gabriela Morales, *Mexico's Other Border: Security, Migration, and the Humanitarian Crisis at the Line with Central America*, Washington Office on Latin America, June 2014, www.wola.org/sites /default/files/Mexico%27s%20Other%20Border%20PDF.pdf.

31. Isaacson, Meyer, and Morales, *Mexico's Other Border*.

number of the previous year.[32] The WOLA report shows that the rise of controls, detentions, and deportations primarily has had two troubling consequences, namely (1) a sharp increase in human rights violations against migrants, and (2) an overall increased exposure to danger during the journey.

Although the Trump administration, and even some journalists, have cited the reduced numbers of Central Americans arriving at the US border as a positive sign that fewer people are venturing on this treacherous trip, there are still comparably high numbers of migrants leaving Central America, only to be turned away from the US border and remain under threat in Mexico.

5. La Bestia

Migrants call cargo trains in Mexico *La Bestia* (the Beast) or *El Tren de la Muerte* (the Death Train), in reference to the high risk of death they face riding on the trains, both in the physical dangers of riding and the threats posed by gangs, cartels, and police. Mexico's National Migration Service, El Instituto Nacional de Migración, reports that of the 64,061 foreign nationals who were detained in the year 2009, 60,383 were from the Northern Triangle of Central America. Furthermore, according to the consul of El Salvador, Vilma Mendoza, "around 30 percent of those who ride the trains are 'cyclical migrants,' men and women who attempt to return to the

---

32. Alice Miranda Ollstein and Esther Yu Hsi Lee, "The 'Caravan of the Mutilated' Shows What People Risk When They Come to America," ThinkProgress, June 19, 2015, https://thinkprogress.org/the-caravan-of-the-mutilated-shows -what-people-risk-when-they-come-to-america-af863b966ac3/.

United States after deportation, or after a failed attempt."[33] Óscar Martínez, Salvadoran journalist and author of *The Beast: Riding the Rails and Dodging Narcos on the Migrant Trail*, claims that more than 250,000 people attempt the trip yearly and an estimated 20,000 are kidnapped.[34] Although migrants are able to use the trains to bypass Mexico's many police checkpoints and forty-eight detention centers, La Bestia has left many migrants dead or severely injured.

A 2010 report by the Comisión Nacional de los Derechos Humanos (National Human Rights Commission) confirms, "Mexico [is] experiencing a hidden epidemic of kidnappings, with the majority of the most severe abuses occurring in the states crossed by the freight trains on the principal routes used by migrants, such as Chiapas, Oaxaca, Tabasco, Veracruz and Tamaulipas."[35] In 2014, President Obama declared the riding of cargo trains by minors a humanitarian crisis.[36] As of May 9, 2014, train operators have prohibited passengers from traveling on the trains as part of the Mexican government's Programa Frontera Sur. The government has been criticized for its negligence in the countless violations of human rights among the Central American migrant population and for the fact that, while policies are said to be in place to increase the safety of the migrant, they have had largely the opposite effect.

33. Karl Penhaul, "La odisea hacia el sueno americano en el 'Tren de la muerte,'" *Expansión*, June 24, 2010.

34. "No Beast So Fierce: Óscar Martínez and Pedro Ultreras in Conversation," Verso Books blog, October 12, 2013, www.versobooks.com/events/739-no-beast-so-fierce-oscar-martinez-and-pedro-ultreras-in-conversation.

35. Amnesty International, *Invisible Victims*.

36. "No Country for Lost Kids," *PBS News Hour*, June 20, 2014.

6. Casas de Migrantes

Red de Documentación de las Organizaciones Defensoras de Migrantes (REDODEM, Network of Documentation of Migrant Defense Organizations) is the largest of a number of networks of migrant shelters known as *albergues*, or *casas de migrantes*, and humanitarian organizations across Mexico that serve the needs of migrants. Inside the shelters, migrants are safe from the fear of deportation and can receive services that can include showers, lodging, food, clothing, medical treatment, and legal services. The shelters collect demographic information and publish their findings in annual reports. Out of the 30,321 migrants who registered with REDODEM in 2015, 51.93 percent were from Honduras, 23.22 percent were from El Salvador, and 14.82 percent were from Guatemala. Of those, 89.14 percent were male and almost 10 percent were under the age of eighteen. In 2015, REDODEM registered 1,768 victims of human rights violations within Mexico and has recorded the testimony of hundreds of victims: 45.72 percent suffered abuses at the hands of criminal organizations, and 41.51 percent were abused by Mexican authorities.[37]

Since Mexico first implemented the SBP, Mexican authorities have been focused on increasing the deportation of Central American migrants from the country. Despite this, the shelters are considered a protected space where migrants can rest knowing that within their walls they are safe from deportation. However, while we were visiting La 72 in July 2016, Mexican authorities positioned directly outside the shelter detained two migrants upon their return from looking for work.

---

37. Red de Documentación de las Organizaciones Defensoras de Migrantes, *Migración en tránsito por México: rostro de una crisis humanitaria internacional*, 2016, www.enterculturas.org/sites/default/files/informe_redodem.pdf.

The shelters rely primarily on community and international donations for their survival. Norma Romero is one of the founders of Las Patronas, a group of women in Veracruz, Mexico, that began to throw bags of food and water up to the migrants on the cargo trains in 1995. In her words, "We don't receive aid from the government."[38]

At every shelter we visited for the purpose of this book, the staff spoke of receiving multiple death threats and have solicited governmental bodies for protection. Many, such as La 72 in Tenosique, told us that they had received no responses to their pleas for protection. Martín Martínez, a cofounder of Estancia del Migrante González y Martínez in Tequisquiapan, received a pager device from the local police that he could use to contact the police should he encounter danger. Guadalupe Serrano Medina, one of the managers of Casa de la Caridad Cristiana in San Luis Potosí, told us about a fake migrant shelter that a crime organization had started on the other side of the train tracks from their shelter to lure migrants away from safety and into the hands of kidnappers. Many legitimate shelters have to move after they receive death threats. In the face of these threats, and surviving without true governmental support, the casas de migrantes continue to support migrants and are often the only source of aid for them.

---

38. Sergio Adrián Castro Bibriesca, "La Patrona, un oasis en el camino de los migrantes," *Des Informémonos*, September 2011.

7. Mexican Drug Trafficking Organizations (DTOs)

The war on drugs in Mexico has caused ever-increasing violence throughout the country. The corrupting influence of crime organizations dominate the nation's political debates and continue to increase in power through the use of terror to seize territory and grow economically. Since 2006, when Mexican president Felipe Calderón initiated a greatly expanded counter-narcotics campaign, drug cartels in Mexico have contributed to the deaths of over one hundred thousand people, including politicians, students and journalists. In the last decade, the United States has contributed over $2 billion dollars to this campaign.[39]

The warring cartels are in a constant state of transformation, splintering and renaming themselves. According to a 2016 report by the US Drug Enforcement Agency, the top cartels are as follows: Sinaloa, Jalisco New Generation, Juárez, Gulf, Los Zetas, and Beltran-Leyva Organization. During the seventy-one-year rule of the Institutional Revolutionary Party, the cartels created a "system-wide network of corruption that ensured distribution rights, market access, and even official government protection."[40]

The Gulf Cartel, one of Mexico's largest cartels in terms of profits and power, experienced its peak of power in the early 2000s before its enforcement wing, Los Zetas, made up of dissenters of the Mexican military, split off to form its own DTO. The Sinaloa Cartel is more decentralized, and therefore more adaptive in the face of efforts by

---

39. Brianna Lee and Danielle Renwick, "Mexico's Drug War," Council on Foreign Relations, May 25, 2017.

40. David Shirk, *The Drug War in Mexico: Confronting a Shared Threat*, Council on Foreign Relations, March 2011.

police, military, and rival cartels to challenge their control of territory. La Familia Michoacana, headquartered in the southwestern state of Michoacán and neighboring provinces, split apart in early 2011, giving rise to the Knights Templar.

Since its split with the Gulf Cartel in 2010, Los Zetas has "generat[ed] revenue from crimes, such as fuel theft, extortion, human smuggling and kidnapping, that are widely seen to inflict more suffering on the Mexican public than transnational drug trafficking."[41] Among the Central American migrants we spoke with, many discussed assaults by Los Zetas, particularly along Mexico's southern and northern borders. In order to cross into the United States, Los Zetas demands money from migrants and has developed a system in which the *coyotes* pay them per migrant in return for a *clave*, or password, that the group uses to pass.

Seventy-two migrants, most of whom were from Central America, were massacred in 2010 in the state of Tamaulipas, along the border with Texas. At least 193 bodies were found in forty-nine clandestine graves in San Fernando over the next year. Memos that were declassified by Mexico's attorney general's office in 2014 contain testimony by members of Los Zetas that the Mexican police had helped them by "intercepting people."[42] Since then, reports of police working with Los Zetas have increased. Many migrants we spoke with recounted times of being assaulted by plainclothes people who could have been Los Zetas or the police.

---

41. June S. Beittel, *Mexico: Organized Crime and Drug Trafficking Organizations*, Congressional Research Service, April 25, 2017, 18.

42. "Mexican Police Helped Cartel Massacre 193 Migrants, Documents Show," NPR, December 22, 2014.

8. *Arrests and Detention*
in the United States

US Customs and Border Protection (CBP) reported that in 2014 and 2016, the number of Central Americans apprehended at the US border exceeded the number of apprehended Mexicans.[43] The increases came with large spikes of unaccompanied children and "family units": In 2016, CBP reported that 46,893 unaccompanied children from the Northern Triangle of Central America had been apprehended, up from 28,387 in 2015 and slightly down from 51,705 in 2014. The number of reported apprehensions of family units from the same area was 70,407 in 2016, up from 34,363 in 2015.

Following President Trump's inauguration in 2017, increased apprehensions of Central Americans at the border, as well as messages sent to Central America that even asylum seekers were being turned away—together what many dubbed the "Trump Effect"—resulted in significantly decreased numbers of Central American migrants in detention that year. The numbers in detention have increased significantly since.

Detention Centers

The US Immigration and Customs Enforcement (ICE) agency utilizes mostly private, for-profit prisons to hold immigrants who are awaiting the outcomes of legal trials. Maintaining the largest detention system in the world, the United States holds between 380,000 and 440,000 people annually, and a congressional mandate requires

---

43. Jeh Johnson, "United States Border Patrol Southwest Family Unit Subject and Unaccompanied Alien Children Apprehensions Fiscal Year 2016," US Customs and Border Protection, October 8, 2016.

ICE to have 34,000 beds in use at all times.[44] In the 2016 fiscal year, the United States allotted a $2.3 billion annual budget to detention, which is roughly equivalent to $124 per adult detainee per day.

Multiple reports have cited poor living conditions at detention centers that violate the human rights of the detainees. As many detention centers are within federal prisons, the detained, like the prisoners, have limited mobility and privacy. Studies conducted by human rights organizations have found other widespread abuses within the facilities such as sexual assault, abuse, and harassment.[45]

The war on drugs in the 1980s brought with it a new level of detention. Legislation required that immigrants with certain types of criminal records be detained. In 1996, the Antiterrorism and Effective Death Penalty Act and the Illegal Immigrant Reform and Immigrant Responsibility Act increased mandatory detention and allowed for the detention of any noncitizen. Following this legislation, two private prison corporations, the GEO Group and the Corrections Corporation of America (now known as CoreCivic), were formed. These corporations have successfully lobbied the government for enlarged incarceration agendas and today collect taxpayer dollars for immigrant detention.[46] Former US immigration officials have become corporate board members and high-paid executives of for-profit prison corporations.

Following the September 11, 2001, terrorist attacks, the Immigration and Naturalization Service was divided into three bodies: ICE, US Citizenship and Immigration Services, and CBP. Immigration

---

44. "Immigration Detention 101," Deportation Watch Network, www.detentionwatchnetwork.org/issues/detention-101.

45. "U.S.: Immigration Detainees at Risk of Sexual Abuse," Human Rights Watch, August 25, 2011, www.hrw.org/news/2010/08/25/us-immigration-detainees -risk-sexual-abuse.

46. "Detention by the Numbers," Freedom for Immigrants, www.endisolation .org/resources/immigration-detention.

has since come under increased examination, and under the Obama administration, the detention program was expanded substantially.

In 2010, the private prison industry lobbied Congress to enforce a requirement that a minimum of thirty-four thousand beds be filled by migrants on any given day.[47] Individuals who would have previously been released are kept in the detention centers because of the industry-mandated quotas. While in detention, the detained work for a dollar a day "cooking, serving and cleaning up food, janitorial services, laundry, haircutting, painting, floor buffing and even vehicle maintenance."[48]

In 2014, the US government expanded its family detention program in an effort to prevent mothers and children from making the trip northward. Many of the mothers and children held in these facilities while seeking asylum live in substandard conditions. A 2016 ACLU report reveals that, during the Obama presidency, fifty-six deaths, including six suicides, occurred in detention facilities, most of which pointed to substandard medical care.[49] Most of these deaths have not been investigated.

On August 11, 2016, the Obama administration announced that it would begin phasing out private prisons over a few years, criticizing the deplorable conditions of the prisons.[50] However, states were still able to contract with private prisons. President Trump, whose presidential campaign was generously sponsored by the GEO Group, has expressed

---

47. Jacqueline Stevens, "When Migrants Are Treated Like Slaves," *New York Times*, April 4, 2018.

48. Stevens, "When Migrants Are Treated Like Slaves."

49. American Civil Liberties Union, *Fatal Neglect: How ICE Ignores Deaths in Detention*, February 24, 2016, www.aclu.org/report/fatal-neglect-how-ice-ignores-death-detention.

50. Mark Jacob Stern, "The Federal Government Is Finally Ending Its Use of Private Prisons. That's Not Enough," *Slate*, August 18, 2016, www.slate.com/blogs/the_slatest/2016/08/18/federal_government_disassociates_with_private_prisons.html.

his desire to expand the for-profit detention center system and to end the "catch and release" policies in which immigrants can be released from detention and assigned dates to appear in court.[51]

Between 2010 and 2017, 1,224 complaints of sexual abuse in detention centers, mostly in ICE custody, were filed, and only forty-three were investigated.[52]

In April 2018, the Trump administration began prosecuting migrants attempting to cross the US border without documentation as criminals. As this "zero-tolerance" policy applies to adults only, minors crossing with adults were separated from their caretakers at the border. Nearly two thousand children were separated in six weeks and placed in detention facilities.[53] After public outcry, President Trump signed an executive action in June ending his policy of family separation.[54]

Prevention through Deterrence

Prevention Through Deterrence is a US Border Patrol policy originating in the 1990s that aims to reduce border crossings by undocumented migrants by funneling them through the most hazardous and life-threatening sections of the border. By increasing border security in urban centers such as the San Diego–Tijuana and El Paso–Ciudad Juárez border crossings, migrants are increasingly forced to attempt to cross through unpopulated desert zones.

As noted by anthropologist Jason de León in his 2015 book *Land of Open Graves*, Prevention Through Deterrence started in El Paso, Texas,

---

51. Julia Edwards Ainsley, "Trump Administration Sends Judges to Detention Centers: Sources," Reuters, March 19, 2017.

52. Alice Speri, "Detained, Then Violated," *Intercept*, April 11, 2018, https://theintercept.com/2018/04/11/immigration-detention-sexual-abuse-ice-dhs/.

53. Salvador Rizzo, "The Facts about Trump's Policy of Separating Families at the Border," *Washington Post*, June 19, 2018.

54. Richard Gonzales, "Trump's Executive Order on Family Separation: What It Does and Doesn't Do," NPR, June 20, 2018.

in 1993, when the US Border Patrol started stationing agents in military uniforms in downtown El Paso and having them question people and warn them about attempting to stay in the United States without documentation.[55] A year later, when the 1994 North American Free Trade Agreement allowed US corn and other goods to flow tax free across the southern border, Mexican peasant farmers began to find it impossible to compete with the flood of low-cost agricultural imports such as corn and wheat. This induced a large increase of economic migrants into the United States. In response to these growing numbers of migrants, the United States initiated its Border Patrol Strategic Plan in 1994. The CBP describes the plan's ethos in a 1994 report:

> The border environment is diverse. Mountains, deserts, lakes, rivers and valleys form natural barriers to this passage. Temperatures ranging from sub-zero along the northern border to the searing heat of the southern border affect illegal traffic as well as enforcement efforts. Illegal entrants crossing through remote, uninhabited expanses of land and sea along the border can find themselves in mortal danger.[56]

The most hazardous section of the border is the Sonoran Desert, located in south-central Arizona and northern Sonora, and covered by the CBP's Tucson sector. In 2000, the number of people apprehended there was 616,346, up from 92,639 apprehensions in 1993. Considering that the total rate of apprehension at the entire border did not increase in these years, the effect of Prevention Through Deterrence policies is startlingly evident.

In a 2010 report to Congress, the US Border Patrol stated, "Prevention Through Deterrence . . . has pushed unauthorized migration away from population centers and funneled it into more remote and hazardous border regions. This policy has the unintended consequence

---

55. Jason De León, *The Land of Open Graves: Living and Dying on the Migrant Trail* (Berkeley: University of California, 2015), 30.

56. De León, *Land of Open Graves*, 32.

of increasing the number of fatalities along the border."[57] While Prevention Through Deterrence has been a deliberate strategy of the US government for decades, this marked the first time it was explicitly stated in writing that the US Border Patrol uses natural obstacles and hazards to its advantage, even if it increases the numbers of deaths.

Since the election of Trump as president in December 2016, immigration lawyers and advocates, including Amnesty International and Human Rights First, have documented hundreds of cases of migrants, mostly from Central America, being turned away at the US border. According to these allegations, CBP officials have told refugees that, "Donald Trump just signed new laws saying there is no asylum for anyone."[58]

9. Immigrant Legal Aid Organizations in the United States

More than a half million immigration cases are pending in US immigration courts and 70 percent of immigrants facing deportation in the United States do so without legal help.[59] In response to the government's failure to provide immigrants with the legal representation entitled to them by law, a number of organizations offering pro bono

---

57. Ghad Haddal, "Border Security: The Role of the U.S. Border Patrol," Congressional Research Service, August 2011.

58. Joshua Partlow, "Rights Groups Sue U.S. Government, Alleging It Is Turning Away Asylum Applicants at Mexico Border," *Washington Post*, July 12, 2017.

59. David Lash, "A Critical Need for Pro Bono Immigration Work," *Above the Law*, December 1, 2016.

services are performing this work, often on shoestring budgets. The Immigration Advocates Network has a national directory of legal resources for low-income people. Visit www.immigrationlawhelp.org for more information.

Besides legal representation, youth migrants in particular need wraparound services such as psychological support and education programs, as well as housing and employment services, to thrive in the United States. The National Immigration Justice Center has a *Procedure Manual for Asylum Representation* that delineates best practices for supporting asylum seekers, including youth.[60]

---

60. National Immigrant Justice Center, *Procedure Manual for Asylum Representation*, January 2017, www.immigrantjustice.org/resources/procedural-manual -asylum-representation.

ACKNOWLEDGMENTS

First off, we want to extend our profound gratitude to the young narrators of this collection, who had the courage to share their stories and difficult experiences. We also want to thank the dozens of migrants we spoke with along our journey.

We owe a debt of gratitude to the people who work with youth refugees and made it possible for us to listen to them: Amanda Irwin and Jackie Gonzales at Centro Legal de la Raza in Oakland, California; Caroline Kornfield Roberts and Rachel Williams of the East Bay Sanctuary Covenant in Berkeley, California; Tara Tidwell Cullen, Marie Silver, and Gianna Borroto at the National Immigrant Justice Center (NIJC) and the Heartland Alliance in Chicago; Elizabeth Badger at Kids in Need of Defense (KIND) in Boston; Christina Mansfield at Freedom for Immigrants (formerly Community Initiatives for Visiting Immigrants in Confinement, CIVIC) in San Francisco; Amy Fischer and Sara Ramey at Refugee and Immigrant Center for Education and Legal Services (RAICES); Ian Philabaum at the CARA Family Detention Pro Bono Project in Dilley, Texas; Luis Enrique Gonzáles, Heriberto Vega Villaseñor, and Rafael Alonso Hernández López at FM4 Paso Libre in Guadalajara, Mexico; Ramón Márquez and Mizar Martin at La 72 in Tenosique, Tabasco, Mexico; Guadalupe Serrano Medina at Casa de la Caridad Cristiana in San Luis Potosí; Martín Martínez at Estancia del Migrante González y Martínez in Tequisquiapan; La Casa del Migrante de Irapuato in San Juan de Dios; Grupo de Ayuda Para el

Migrante in Mexicali; Carlos Holguín with the Center for Human Rights and Constitutional Law.

We give a big thanks to Voice of Witness staff and volunteers—Mimi Lok for believing in this project, the education team for developing curriculum for the book and establishing partnerships—for challenging us to go deeper and reach higher. We are grateful for Luke Gerwe for helping us envision the early stages of the project, and for Dao Tran for holding us to account and guiding us to its completion. We'd like to thank the illustrator, Christine Shields, who was able to render the faces and scenes of this journey so beautifully throughout the book. We also thank Dr. Ariana Vigil at University of North Carolina, Chapel Hill, for her work reviewing the appendixes. Finally, we thank our families, especially our wives, Jennifer Arcuni and Isabelle Rooney, for their support and encouragement through this five-year project.

ABOUT THE EDITORS

Steven Mayers is a professor of English at the City College of San Francisco. He has been conducting oral history research with Central Americans in the San Francisco Bay Area for over a decade. His master's thesis explored ways that fiction can challenge historical accounts of the past, and his dissertation, focused on the stories of Central Americans in the Bay Area, analyzed the themes of identity, home, and forgiveness. Steven's work has appeared in journals and magazines including *Versal*, *Travesías*, *Gatopardo*, and *Powerlines*, a journal published by San Francisco State University's Department of Comparative Literature. He is also a faculty advisor for *Forum Magazine*, the literary journal of City College of San Francisco. He lives with his wife and son in the Bay Area.

Jonathan Freedman is a Pulitzer Prize–winning journalist, author, and youth mentor with more than thirty years' experience reporting from Central America, Mexico, and the US border. His six-year series of investigative editorials for the *San Diego Tribune* was influential in the passage of the landmark 1986 US immigration reforms that authorized 2.7 million undocumented immigrants to become permanent legal residents. He is the author of *From Cradle to Grave: The Human Face of Poverty in America*, *Wall of Fame: One Teacher, One Class, and the Power to Save Schools and Transform Lives*, and a novel, *The Last Brazil of Benjamin East*. Jonathan volunteers as a writing mentor for immigrants, refugees, youths in detention, and students at City College of San Francisco. He lives with his family in the Bay Area.

ABOUT VOICE OF WITNESS

Voice of Witness (VOW) is an award-winning nonprofit that advances human rights by amplifying the voices of people impacted by injustice. Cofounded by Dave Eggers, Mimi Lok, and Dr. Lola Vollen, we explore issues of criminal justice, migration, and displacement, and forge space for marginalized voices to be heard. Our book series depicts these issues through the edited oral histories of people most closely affected by them. Our education program connects educators, students, and members of justice movements with oral history tools for storytelling and social change.

EXECUTIVE DIRECTOR & EXECUTIVE EDITOR: Mimi Lok
MANAGING EDITOR: Dao X. Tran
EDUCATION PROGRAM DIRECTOR: Cliff Mayotte
EDUCATION PROGRAM ASSOCIATE: Erin Vong
CURRICULUM SPECIALIST: Anna Yeung
COMMUNICATIONS & OUTREACH MANAGER: Alexa Gelbard
DONOR RELATIONSHIP MANAGER: Elisa Perez-Selsky
COMMUNITY PARTNERSHIP COORDINATOR: Ela Banerjee

COFOUNDERS

DAVE EGGERS
Founding Editor, Voice of Witness; cofounder of 826 National; founder of McSweeney's Publishing

MIMI LOK
Cofounder, Executive Director & Executive Editor, Voice of Witness

LOLA VOLLEN
Founding Editor, Voice of Witness; Founder & Executive Director, The Life After Exoneration Program

VOICE OF WITNESS BOARD OF DIRECTORS

IPEK S. BURNETT
Author; depth psychologist

SARA FELDMAN
Ready California Project Director, Immigrant Legal Resource Center

NICOLE JANISIEWICZ
Attorney, United States Court of Appeals for the Ninth Circuit

KRISTINE LEJA
Executive Director, Summer Search, San Francisco Bay Area

MIMI LOK
Cofounder, Executive Director & Executive Editor, Voice of Witness

LUPE POBLANO
Co–Executive Director, CompassPoint

JILL STAUFFER
Associate Professor of Philosophy; Director of Peace, Justice, and Human Rights Concentration, Haverford College

TREVOR STORDAHL
Senior Counsel, VIZ Media; intellectual property attorney

THE VOICE OF WITNESS BOOK SERIES

The Voice of Witness nonprofit book series amplifies the seldom-heard voices of people affected by contemporary injustice. We also work with impacted communities to create curricular and training support for educators. Using oral history as a foundation, the series depicts human rights crises in the United States and around the world. *Solito, Solita: Crossing Borders with Youth Refugees from Central America* is the eighteenth book in the series. Other titles include:

SURVIVING JUSTICE
America's Wrongfully Convicted and Exonerated
Compiled and edited by Lola Vollen and Dave Eggers
Foreword by Scott Turow
"Real, raw, terrifying tales of 'justice.'" —*Star Tribune*

VOICES FROM THE STORM
The People of New Orleans on Hurricane Katrina and Its Aftermath
Compiled and edited by Chris Ying and Lola Vollen
"*Voices from the Storm* uses oral history to let those who survived the hurricane tell their (sometimes surprising) stories." —*Independent* UK

UNDERGROUND AMERICA
Narratives of Undocumented Lives
Compiled and edited by Peter Orner
Foreword by Luis Alberto Urrea
"No less than revelatory." —*Publishers Weekly*

OUT OF EXILE
Narratives from the Abducted and Displaced People of Sudan
Compiled and edited by Craig Walzer
Additional interviews and an introduction by Dave Eggers and Valentino Achak Deng
"Riveting." —*School Library Journal*

HOPE DEFERRED
Narratives of Zimbabwean Lives
Compiled and edited by Peter Orner and Annie Holmes
Foreword by Brian Chikwava
"*Hope Deferred* might be the most important publication to have come out of Zimbabwe in the last thirty years." —*Harper's Magazine*

NOWHERE TO BE HOME
Narratives from Survivors of Burma's Military Regime
Compiled and edited by Maggie Lemere and Zoë West
Foreword by Mary Robinson
"Extraordinary." —Asia Society

PATRIOT ACTS
Narratives of Post-9/11 Injustice
Compiled and edited by Alia Malek
Foreword by Karen Korematsu
"Important and timely." —Reza Aslan

INSIDE THIS PLACE, NOT OF IT
Narratives from Women's Prisons
Compiled and edited by Ayelet Waldman and Robin Levi
Foreword by Michelle Alexander
"Essential reading." —Piper Kerman

THROWING STONES AT THE MOON
Narratives from Colombians Displaced by Violence
Compiled and edited by Sibylla Brodzinsky and Max Schoening
Foreword by Íngrid Betancourt
"Both sad and inspiring." —*Publishers Weekly*

REFUGEE HOTEL
Photographed by Gabriele Stabile and edited by Juliet Linderman
"There is no other book like *Refugee Hotel* on your shelf." —*SF Weekly*

HIGH RISE STORIES
Voices from Chicago Public Housing
Compiled and edited by Audrey Petty
Foreword by Alex Kotlowitz
"Joyful, novelistic, and deeply moving." —George Saunders

INVISIBLE HANDS
Voices from the Global Economy
Compiled and edited by Corinne Goria
Foreword by Kalpona Akter
"Powerful and revealing testimony." —*Kirkus*

PALESTINE SPEAKS
Narratives of Life under Occupation
Compiled and edited by Cate Malek and Mateo Hoke
"Heartrending stories." —*New York Review of Books*

THE VOICE OF WITNESS READER
Ten Years of Amplifying Unheard Voices
Edited and with an introduction by Dave Eggers

THE POWER OF THE STORY
The Voice of Witness Teacher's Guide to Oral History
Compiled and edited by Cliff Mayotte
Foreword by William Ayers and Richard Ayers
"A rich source of provocations to engage with human dramas throughout the world." —*Rethinking Schools Magazine*

LAVIL
Life, Love, and Death in Port-Au-Prince
Edited by Peter Orner and Evan Lyon
Foreword by Edwidge Danticat
"*Lavil* is a powerful collection of testimonies, which include tales of violence, poverty, and instability but also joy, hustle, and the indomitable will to survive." —*Vice*

CHASING THE HARVEST
Migrant Workers in California Agriculture
Edited by Gabriel Thompson
"The voices are defiant and nuanced, aware of the human complexities that spill across bureaucratic categories and arbitrary borders." —*The Baffler*

SIX BY TEN
Stories from Solitary
Edited by Mateo Hoke and Taylor Pendergrass
"Deeply moving and profoundly unsettling." —Heather Ann Thompson

SAY IT FORWARD
A Guide to Social Justice Storytelling
Edited by Cliff Mayotte and Claire Kiefer
"A vital guide from a vital organization, and it couldn't come at a more critical time." —Lauren Markham

ABOUT HAYMARKET BOOKS

Haymarket Books is a radical, independent, nonprofit book publisher based in Chicago.

Our mission is to publish books that contribute to struggles for social and economic justice. We strive to make our books a vibrant and organic part of social movements and the education and development of a critical, engaged, international left.

We take inspiration and courage from our namesakes, the Haymarket martyrs, who gave their lives fighting for a better world. Their 1886 struggle for the eight-hour day—which gave us May Day, the international workers' holiday—reminds workers around the world that ordinary people can organize and struggle for their own liberation. These struggles continue today across the globe—struggles against oppression, exploitation, poverty, and war.

Since our founding in 2001, Haymarket Books has published more than five hundred titles. Radically independent, we seek to drive a wedge into the risk-averse world of corporate book publishing. Our authors include Noam Chomsky, Arundhati Roy, Rebecca Solnit, Angela Y. Davis, Howard Zinn, Amy Goodman, Wallace Shawn, Mike Davis, Winona LaDuke, Ilan Pappé, Richard Wolff, Dave Zirin, Keeanga-Yamahtta Taylor, Nick Turse, Dahr Jamail, David Barsamian, Elizabeth Laird, Amira Hass, Mark Steel, Avi Lewis, Naomi Klein, and Neil Davidson. We are also the trade publishers of the acclaimed Historical Materialism Book Series and of Dispatch Books.

ALSO AVAILABLE FROM HAYMARKET BOOKS

Bananeras: Women Transforming the Banana Unions of Latin America | Dana Frank

Fields of Resistance: The Struggle of Florida's Farmworkers for Justice | Silvia Giagnoni

The Long Honduran Night: Resistance, Terror, and the United States in the Aftermath of the Coup | Dana Frank

No One Is Illegal (Updated Edition): Fighting Racism and State Violence on the U.S.-Mexico Border | Justin Akers Chacón and Mike Davis

Radicals in the Barrio: Magonistas, Socialists, Wobblies, and Communists in the Mexican-American Working Class | Justin Akers Chacón

Six by Ten: Stories from Solitary
Edited by Mateo Hoke and Taylor Pendergrass

Say It Forward: A Guide to Social Justice Storytelling
Edited by Claire Keifer and Cliff Mayotte

Turning the Tide: U.S. Intervention in Central America and the Struggle for Peace | Noam Chomsky